Business Studies Skills

RICHARD BARRETT

Stanley Thornes (Publishers) Ltd

First published in 1991 by:
Stanley Thornes (Publishers) Ltd
Ellenborough House
Wellington Street
CHELTENHAM GL50 1YD
England

Reprinted 1993
Reprinted 1995

British Library Cataloguing in Publication Data

Barrett, Richard 1955–
    Business studies skills
    1. Business practices
    I. Title
    658

    ISBN 0–7487–0174–5

Design, typesetting and artwork Black Sheep Design.
Printed and bound in Great Britain at The Bath Press, Avon.

CONTENTS

To Marie, Jamie and Michelle for their
patience, and to teachers, lecturers, students
and pupils coping with re-organisation.

PREFACE

Business Studies Skills has been written to meet the requirements of students preparing for GCSE Business Studies examinations as well as those following BTEC First Business and Finance courses.

The text is based on the requirements of all the examining bodies. As well as providing the factual information required for GCSE, the book addresses the skills required by a successful candidate on a BTEC or GCSE course of study. It is for this reason that each chapter ends with short questions, stimulus response questions, case studies and an 'On Assignment' section which gives ideas for course-work which students and teachers can develop to meet course-work requirements.

The 'Learn it Yourself' section at the end of each chapter helps students to relate what they have learnt to everyday life. Throughout each chapter there are 'Check This Out' questions which give students an opportunity to consolidate what they have learnt before moving on. Opportunities for group and individual work are given in the exercises at the end of each chapter.

Many of these exercises have been used with mixed ability groups of students on BTEC and 16+ Business Studies courses. Two appendices deal with the topics of researching and interpreting data, and include guidance on questionnaire design as well as giving hints on how to conduct research and present findings. The final appendix provides samples of examination questions from the various examining bodies.

It is recommended that the reader progresses through the book in the order in which it is presented, but once Section One has been dealt with the remaining six sections can be tackled in any order.

Thanks are due to Phil McCulloch of North Manchester College for his helpful comments on the Finance section and to my colleague Marion Gow whose comments on the first draft of the book led to several improvements. My thanks also to my friend Phil White who helped with the purchasing chapter. Thanks also to the staff at Stanley Thornes for their help in bringing this project to fruition.

Richard Barrett

January 1991

ACKNOWLEDGEMENTS

The author and publishers are grateful to the following examination boards for permission to reproduce questions from examination papers:

The London and East Anglian Group

Midland Examining Group

Northern Examining Association

Southern Examining Group

Welsh Joint Education Commitee

Any answers or hints on answers are the sole responsibility of the author and have not been provided or approved by the examining bodies.

SECTION ONE

Background to Business

AN INTRODUCTION TO BUSINESS

What do Marks and Spencer, British Rail, a tattoo artist, the group U2 and Rover have in common? The answer is that they all represent some sort of business. By this we mean that they provide goods – Marks and Spencer, Austin Rover – or a service – British Rail, the tattoo artist and U2. Goods are physical objects that can be seen, used and passed on to others. A service is something for people or for businesses that is useful to them, but cannot be seen or used in the same way by others, e.g. advice or music. Goods can be divided into *capital goods* and *consumer goods*, and services into *business services* and *consumer services*:

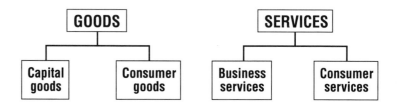

- *Capital goods* are goods used by a business to create more goods or services, e.g. lathes, computers, lorries, etc.

- *Consumer goods* are those goods used by individuals at home and in their leisure time, e.g. videos, chairs, gas cookers etc. These goods are for their own use, but not to provide other goods and services.

- *Business services* include architecture, insurance and legal advice. These help businesses to operate successfully.

- *Consumer services* include hairdressing, car repairs and service in a restaurant.

Some of the goods and services mentioned, such as insurance, computers or car repairs, can either be used by businesses or by individual consumers but clearly they will be used in different ways - either to provide other goods and services or for personal use.

The reasons for business activity vary. Marks and Spencer wish to earn money for the owners of the firm, to make a profit in other words; British Rail aim to be profitable as well as to provide a public service; religious organisations aim to satisfy spiritual needs with little thought of making a profit. We can see that any organisation, large or small, which provides goods or services is a business of some sort. Most businesses exist to make a profit but some aim to provide goods or services for religious, political or social reasons, and not for profit-making.

CHECK THIS OUT

1.1. Answer the following questions with at least a full sentence, or by writing out the missing words.

3. Give two motives for business activity.

4. What are capital goods? Give an example.

5. Most businesses exist to make a _____ .

6. Goods are _____ _____ which can be seen and handled.

1. Give an example of a business service.

2. Give an example of consumer goods.

The factors of production

Marks and Spencer and British Rail have something else in common. They use the same things to go about their business. These things are called the *factors of production*. The factors of production are LAND, LABOUR and CAPITAL.

Land

Land is not just the ground that a business stands on, but also covers the things which come from the land such as coal, wood, wheat and iron. It is easier to understand the term land if you remember that land in business studies can relate to those things which are produced through nature, as well as simply meaning the ground on which a business stands.

Labour

Labour refers to the people working in a business. Even a business run by one person uses that person's labour. Workers who are paid wages or salaries by the firm are its *employees*. Wages are usually paid weekly and salaries monthly, over the period of one year. Labour can be either:

Skilled – This refers to people who have had a good deal of training to do their job. Skilled workers will have followed some training scheme and have received recognised qualifications such as a BTEC (Business and Technical Education Council) or City and Guilds award relating to their job. Chefs, for instance, need City and Guilds qualifications.

Semi-skilled – People who do semi-skilled jobs will have received some training by their firm but it will be less than that for skilled workers. Semi-skilled workers are less likely to have recognised qualifications for their job than skilled workers. Some workers on

Skilled and semi-skilled workers

a production line will receive training from their firm only for how to do their particular job. They are therefore less skilled than those who have had a wide training in all aspects of the work.

Unskilled – Workers in this type of job will have had very little or no training. Unskilled jobs require few, if any, qualifications and tend to involve a limited range of tasks.

It should be clear that in any business a range of skills will be needed. Marks and Spencer will need skilled workers, such as accountants, as well as unskilled workers for jobs like cleaning and stacking shelves. Pop groups like U2 might use unskilled workers to carry their equipment on tour as well highly skilled sound and lighting technicians. The larger a business is the more likely it is that skilled, semi-skilled and unskilled tasks will be done by different people who are paid different wages. Who ever heard of a large firm's advertising manager having to sweep the floor? In a small business the owner might have to prepare advertisements as well as to sweep up after business hours.

Capital

Capital refers to things that the business owns and uses to create the goods or services it provides. The counters in Marks and Spencer, the guitars used by U2 and the trains owned by British Rail all represent capital. The firm's capital is of two different types:

Fixed Capital – This sort of capital is long-lasting and will not be changed very often. The premises owned by the firm, machines and equipment are examples of fixed capital.

Liquid Capital – Liquid capital is cash or things that can swiftly be changed into cash, (e.g. money in the bank). It is called liquid capital because it can easily be turned into fixed capital by the purchase of raw materials or equipment. As it flows so easily from one use to another it is called 'liquid capital'.

If a firm sells goods or a service its liquid capital will increase. If it buys a new machine it will have increased its fixed capital but reduced its liquid capital. So as firms buy and sell goods and services their different capital levels change. Firms need to make sure that they have sufficient liquid capital to meet their future debts or at least make sure that they own things (assets) which can easily be sold and turned into liquid capital. The more easily a possession – an asset – can be sold or turned into liquid capital the more *liquid* we say it is. Buildings are not sold easily or quickly and so they are the least liquid of assets; stock is quicker and easier to sell, so it is much more liquid. Chapters 8 and 9 deal more fully with this problem.

In simple terms, business is any activity which uses the factors of production to provide goods or services. Business, in other words, is based on production. As we have seen this is more complex than it first seems, but the following diagram should help to make things clear.

Fixed and liquid capital

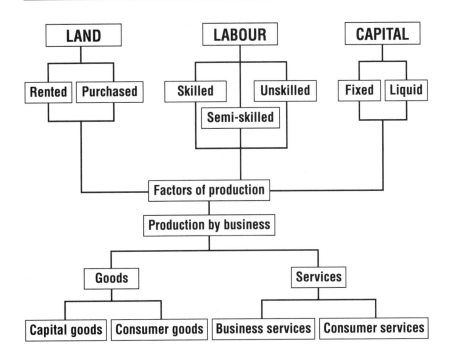

1.2. Answer the following questions with at least a full sentence, or by writing out the missing words.

5. Explain the term 'skilled labour'.

1. Name two kinds of goods businesses produce.

6. What is the difference between fixed and liquid capital?

2. What is the difference between business services and consumer services?

7. Explain, simply, what is meant by a 'business'.

3. Give three reasons why businesses exist.

8. How do wages and salaries differ?

4. Name the factors of production.

9. Land can be obtained by _____ or _____ .

Another way of analysing business activity is according to which stage of production the business activity occurs at. There are two stages of production, primary and secondary production.

Primary production

This is the first stage of production, and is concerned with obtaining food and raw materials from the earth. As it is concerned with extracting things from nature it is sometimes called the *extractive* stage of production. Jobs at this stage of production include farming, mining and fishing. All three examples involve taking things from nature for use by people. Once these natural things have been extracted they often have to be altered or treated before they can be fully used, for example fish have to be cleaned, corn has to be turned into flour, etc. This is the work of the secondary stage of production.

Secondary production

This is also known as the *manufacturing* and *construction* stage of production. Secondary production is concerned with changing the raw materials produced by the extractive industries into finished products or parts of finished products. Turning trees into planks is part of secondary production, and so is turning those planks into floorboards for a building. Products which are of little use by themselves but are used as part of a finished product are known as *semi-manufactured* goods. Engine parts in the car industry are an example of semi-manufactured goods. Occupations in secondary production include welding, joinery, baking and bricklaying.

The productive activities of primary and secondary industries draw on a range of other services which help them to work efficiently. These services are provided by another part of production called *tertiary production*.

Tertiary production

Tertiary production helps with the distribution and exchange of goods and services as well as providing a range of other services people need. There are two parts to tertiary production:

- Commerce. This includes advertising, transport, insurance and financial services. Commerce assists the distribution of goods and services. Commercial occupations include lorry driving, banking and shop managing.

- Direct Services. Services which people use to keep them happy, healthy and amused – such as those provided by doctors, dentists, footballers, hairdressers and actors – are direct services. Direct services indirectly help people to work productively.

All stages of production make use of the factors of production to provide their goods or services. As we can see even those parts of production which do not make a product can still be called *productive activity* because they support activities which do make goods or provide services.

Business in society

We have already seen that there are many different types of businesses. These businesses provide about 22 million skilled, semi-skilled and unskilled jobs, in the United Kingdom. We spend over £200 thousand million each year buying the goods and services produced by business. Our annual savings of over £26 thousand million are often invested in businesses by banks and building societies. All of this activity gives the government over £30 thousand million from income tax. This money is used to pay for schools, hospitals, the police and other public services. Business activity affects us all by giving us money to spend, paying for public services, giving us personal satisfaction (if we are lucky) or making and keeping us unemployed (if we are unlucky).

There is more to all this than luck. As we have seen, most businesses exist to make a profit, although it was shown earlier that other motives might exist. What businesses are allowed to do, what help they are given and what laws they have to obey are all determined, to some extent, by government. This includes local government, which is your town or county council, e.g. Staffordshire County Council or Harlow Town Council, and central government. Central government refers to the Houses of Parliament and the various bodies which work on its behalf (see page 222). Two important central government bodies which affect business are the Training Agency, which influences the labour supply, and the Department of Trade and Industry, whose work we will look at later.

Given the important effects local and central government can have on business, it is important that voters find out the views of potential MPs or councillors and vote for the person who they think will do the best job.

In some countries of the world business is organised in a *market* economic system. The private individuals who provide the capital for the business take all the profits after taxes and debts have been paid. In this system business activity is the responsibility of *private enterprise*. In a *planned* system the government does not allow this to happen. Business is controlled by the government and any profit or surplus is disposed of by the government, on behalf of the public. For this reason we can refer to government-controlled business activity as *public enterprise*. Most countries have a mixture of both public and private enterprise. In some places, such as the United States of America, there is very little public enterprise as the government is more committed to private enterprise. Elsewhere, in Albania for example, there is very little private enterprise as the government is more committed to public enterprise. Since 1989 many of the so-called socialist countries of Eastern Europe, such as Poland and the Soviet Union, have been trying to move from a planned state-controlled or *command* economy towards a capitalist or *market* economy. Here in the United Kingdom the amount of government-controlled activity declined steadily after 1979 as the Conservative governments elected after that date were all committed to private enterprise. Despite this there is still a wide range of public enterprise in the United Kingdom and for that reason we say that this country has a *mixed economy* – it contains both sorts of business activity.

1.3. Answer the following questions with at least a full sentence, or by writing out the missing words.

2. What is the main difference between market and planned economies?

3. Explain the phrase 'mixed economy'.

4. Central government passes _____ which affect business activity.

1. What is the difference between local and central government?

Business ownership

In the mixed economy of the United Kingdom business ownership can be placed in one of two groups:

The private sector, where businesses are owned by private individuals or groups of private individuals.

The public sector, where businesses are owned by local or central government.

The two sectors are represented in the following diagram.

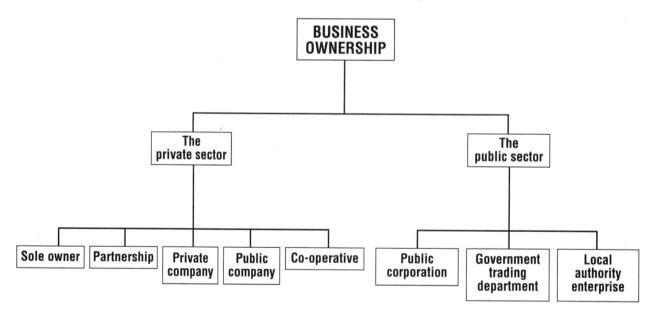

How the private and public sectors can be broken down
(Note that a definition of each term is given below)

You might ask why there are so many different types of business. The answer is that each type of business has its own legal rights and responsibilities so that individuals wishing to own a business may choose the type which best suits their own financial and personal circumstances. The advantages and disadvantages of each type of business are discussed below.

The private sector

As we have seen, the private sector covers those areas of business activity carried out by individuals or groups of individuals. There are several types of business in the private sector:

The sole owner

This sort of business is owned by one person, sometimes referred to as the *sole proprietor* or *sole trader*. Corner shop owners, small builders, hairdressers or electricians may be sole owners although they may have some employees.

Advantages of sole ownership.

- Easy to set up in business. There are no expensive legal procedures to go through.
- The owner of the business can give personal attention to staff and customers. This can help to keep a high level of personal service which many customers appreciate.
- All profits belong to the owner.
- Decisions can be made quickly as there is no need to consult or get the approval of others.

Disadvantages of sole ownership.

- Legally the business is not separate from the owner. Because the business is not a *separate legal entity* the owner can be held personally responsible if in the course of its business activity the business breaks any laws. For instance, if health and safety laws are broken the owner may have to pay fines imposed on the business.
- The owner has *unlimited liability*. This means that if the business fails the amount the owner stands to lose is unlimited. For example, if Michelle Callaghan invests £5000 in a small shop which fails with debts of £7000 she must sell the shop and its contents to pay the debts. If, after having done this, there is still £2000 to be paid she must pay it, even if this means selling her car, home or other personal possessions which are unconnected to the business.
- Responsibility for finding the money to start the business rests entirely on the owner. The finance may be raised from savings or loans from friends, relatives or a bank.
- If the owner is ill the business may be threatened.
- The business ends on the death of the owner.

The partnership

Partnerships tend to be restricted to doctors, dentists, solicitors and other professions. This type of organisation represents a useful way for a sole owner to expand, as it allows more capital and

If the owner of a business has unlimited liability then they must be liable for any debts.

different skills to be brought into the business. The Partnership Act of 1890 recommends that a *partnership agreement*, sometimes called a *deed of partnership*, is drawn up between the partners. This is a written agreement which states how much each partner will be paid, how much they have invested, how profits and losses are to be shared and the trading name of the business. Two major disadvantages of partnerships are unlimited liability and not being a separate legal entity. The unlimited liability partnership, or general partnership, which has just been described, can be made into a limited liability partnership under the rules of the Partnership Act, 1907. These *limited partnerships*, as they are sometimes called mean that most investors' liability is limited to what they invest in the business. So, if Michelle Callaghan were to put her £5000 into a limited partnership she would only lose that money, no matter what the debts of the business were when it failed. The law requires that at least one partner remains a general partner, which means that that person's liability is unlimited. Those partners with limited liability are not allowed to take part in the running of the business and because of this are known as *sleeping partners*.

Advantages of a partnership.

- Still retain a large degree of personal control.
- Access to more finance than a sole owner.
- Can bring in a wider range of skills than a sole owner.
- Partners with particular talents can concentrate on what they are good at, which makes the business more efficient.
- Losses are shared with other partners.
- The other partners can carry on the business if a partner is ill or on holiday.

Disadvantages of a partnership.

- Decisions may be delayed by disagreement amongst the partners.
- Partners may have unlimited liability (unless a limited partnership is established).
- Capital is still restricted to the combined wealth of a few partners.
- A new partnership agreement is required if a partner leaves or dies.
- In some circumstances the actions of one partner may be legally binding on the others.

The private company

Private companies are usually larger than businesses controlled by sole owners or partnerships. Any number of people may contribute to the business by buying shares although the company cannot advertise to the general public to buy shares. A partnership which was seeking to expand and raise more capital would do well to consider becoming a private company as shareholders have limited liability and the business is a separate legal entity. In order to warn people trading with the business that they may not be paid in full if the business fails, because of the limited liability of the owners (the shareholders), private companies must always have 'Limited' after their name.

Advantages of a private company.

- Limited liability means that if the business fails only the money invested is lost and personal possessions are not at risk.
- The separate legal identity of the business means that the owners (shareholders) cannot be held personally responsible for the actions of the business.
- The business is usually considered more secure than a partnership or a sole owner and so may find it easier to borrow money from banks.
- The owners can take a personal interest in the business and write the internal rules (Articles of Association) to restrict how shareholders may sell their shares. This means that it is more likely that the company has only those shareholders it feels are desirable.

Disadvantages of a private company.

- The increased size of the business may mean that the owners can no longer give personal attention to detail.
- Each year accounts must be presented to the Registrar of Companies, who is responsible for making sure companies keep within the law in their business dealings. The accounts are then made public, which may not be in the owners' interests, particularly if the firm is not doing well.
- Decisions may be slow because the size of the organisation hinders good communication.

1.4. Answer the following questions with at least a full sentence, or by writing out the missing words.

1. Who owns public sector businesses?

2. Why are there different types of business organisation?

3. It is _____ to set up in business if you are a sole proprietor.

4. The sole owner may have to give up his/her possessions because of _____ _____ .

5. The _____ _____ is a document containing details of how profits will be shared.

6. A partner who cannot take part in the business is a _____ partner.

7. Explain the phrase 'separate legal entity'.

Voting at a shareholders' meeting

Public company

The public company is the largest sort of business in the private sector. It is an ideal sort of business organisation for businesses which require large amounts of capital, as the business can advertise its shares for sale to the general public. The public can then sell the shares easily through the Stock Exchange, where buyers and sellers of public company shares can usually find a ready market. Just like the private company, the public company must warn people who may be owed money by the company (creditors) that they might not get back all that is owed to them if the business fails. This is done by adding PLC after the company name. PLC stands for Public Limited Company. Notice that the public company is in the private sector. This is because the public company is owned by a group of private individuals, not the whole population. Sainsbury PLC and Boots PLC are examples of public limited companies, although they both started as sole owners.

Advantages of a public company.

■ Limited liability means that shareholders are more likely to invest. This makes it easier to raise capital for large projects.

■ The separate legal identity of the business is also attractive to shareholders as it means that they cannot be held personally responsible for the actions of the business.

■ Banks and other financial institutions who lend money may consider the public company more secure than other types of business and be more willing to lend to it.

■ The job security and resources available in a public company means that it will find it easier to attract highly-qualified specialists such as computer programmers or personnel officers who will make its work more effective.

Disadvantages of a public company.

■ The large size of the business means that personal attention to detail by the owners is not possible. Employees and customers may feel out of touch with the firm. This can have a bad effect on sales and employee efficiency.

■ The business is very expensive to set up as there are several legal processes which have to be completed. (We look in more detail at how to set up a company in Chapter 8).

■ Decisions may be slow because the organisation's size hinders good communication. Several committees or managers may have to be consulted before an important decision can be made.

The board of directors of a company are required by law to present a report each year for their shareholders. This must also be sent to the registrar of companies. The report should show the profit and loss account and balance sheet. Other information that must be given includes details of political donations, the names of the directors, how much dividend is to be paid and a description of the main activities of the company and the overall state of its business.

The co-operative

We said at the start of this chapter that the motives for being in business vary. All of the types of business we have discussed so far exist only to make a profit for the individuals who invest their money in them. The people who work in the businesses we have looked at so far, or buy their goods and services, are unlikely to be shareholders in the business, although some companies, for example ICI PLC, encourage their staff to buy shares which are sold to them cheaply. In co-operatives customers or staff are the shareholders. There are two types of co-operative, the producer's co-operative and the consumer's co-operative.

- *The producers' co-operative* These are businesses whose shares are owned entirely by the people who work for the business. They will usually be small businesses, perhaps engaged in crafts such as printing or shoe and garment making. The largest and most successful producers' co-operatives are to be found in farming. These co-operatives exist to buy things like seeds and animal feed for their members or to help them sell and distribute their production. Agricultural co-operatives are widespread in Europe, particularly in France. During the last decade or so there have been many workers' co-operatives formed in Britain. Generally these were formed to provide employment for their members. They are mostly small businesses existing in the services or retail sectors of the economy.

- *The consumers' co-operative* The Co-op is recognised all over Great Britain by its familiar blue and white symbol. The Co-operative Movement is really a collection of individual, co-operative societies who have agreed to adopt the same identity to make advertising and joint purchasing from manufacturers more efficient. The first successful co-operative started in 1844 in Rochdale when 28 working men joined together to set up shop to provide good quality goods at fair prices to members of their society. Profits were distributed to members in proportion to their purchases with the society. Anyone over 16 years of age may buy a share in a consumer Co-op which entitles them to vote and take part in the various cultural, social and political activities of the organisation. Recently in some towns and villages people have joined together to buy goods in large quantities and to re-sell them amongst themselves at less than usual shop prices or to ensure that local people have shopping facilities following the closure of a private shop. This is another example of a consumer co-operative at work.

Advantages of a co-operative.

- A co-operative aims to be run in a democratic way.
- Members' loyalty gives the business stability and may limit workers' industrial action or consumers shopping elsewhere.
- These organisations may try to implement what they consider to be worthwhile social or political aims.

A modern Co-op store

Disadvantages of a co-operative.

■ By being democratic unpopular decisions may be 'dodged'. This can make the business inefficient.

■ Those people elected to positions of responsibility may not be the most able to do the job.

■ Not all shareholders take an active part in the business, which allows small groups of active members too much power.

1.5. Answer the following questions with at least a full sentence, or by writing out the missing words.

3. Describe two advantages and two disadvantages of a public company.

1. PLC shows a company is a ___ ___ ___.

4. Detail one advantage and one disadvantage of a co-operative.

2. What is it about a public limited company that might encourage investors to invest?

5. Name two types of co-operative.

The public sector

Much of the public sector is not concerned with making a profit. Instead, these sections aim to provide public services such as health or education. They have been included here because they use factors of production to provide goods and services. The public sector differs from the private sector in the following ways:

- It is owned and controlled by central or local government.
- Some sections do not aim to provide profits but to give essential services such as health, education or defence.

Public sector businesses are owned by the public. This means the population of the country, or the population of the local government area if it is a local government enterprise.

The public corporation

The public corporation is a separate legal entity from the government. Another way of saying it is separate is to say that it is a corporation or *corporate body*. British Coal and British Rail are examples of public corporations. These public corporations were once collections of several individual private and public companies but have been taken over by governments since the end of the Second World War. This was because the success of these businesses was essential to the British economy's recovery from the war. The government, at the time, thought that they should be managed with this in mind, rather than making a profit for private individuals. Businesses which are taken over in this way are sometimes called *nationalised industries*. Some public corporations, such as the British Broadcasting Corporation (BBC) and London Regional Transport did not exist in any form until the government established them, and cannot really be described as nationalised industries, because they were not *taken over* by the government.

Organisations like British Gas and British Telecom were once public corporations. The government thought they would be more efficient if they were public companies whose aim was to make a profit. In order to make them public companies, shares were sold and the businesses moved from the public sector into the private sector. The selling off of public businesses is called *privatisation*. Since the end of the Second World War, British Steel has been nationalised, privatised, nationalised again, and then privatised again.

Each public corporation is controlled by a board which is linked to a government department headed by a minister. The minister appoints the members of the board. The Prime Minister appoints each of the ministers to a different government department. British Coal, for example, is responsible to the Department of Energy. The minister must answer questions and provide information to parliament, as well as the Prime Minister, for the workings of the corporation.

Arguments in favour of public corporations.

- Some industries are too important to be left in the hands of private individuals whose main aim is to make a profit.
- Competition amongst several firms may mean that factors of production are wasted as services are duplicated or used in avoidable advertising. For example, two buses from competing firms might run half-empty on the same route when one bus could be running full and the other used elsewhere.
- State control prevents one firm becoming too powerful and charging very high prices.
- Large, single units can operate more efficiently than several smaller, competing units. This is known as the benefits of *economies of scale* (see page 119).

Arguments against public corporations.

- The size of the corporation slows down decisions as communication is more difficult.
- As financial losses do not necessarily lead to the closure of a public corporation it might not be as keen to avoid waste and inefficiency as a public company.
- Political considerations might prevent important decisions being made. An inefficient steel works, for example, might be kept open because closure might give high levels of unemployment in an area.

Local authority enterprise

Every local authority uses the factors of production to provide services such as parks, roads, schools and libraries. Most of these do not make a profit but some, such as sports centres or theatres might earn money for the local authority. Local authority enterprises might have two aims:

- To provide a public service, e.g. parks and schools.
- To earn money to spend on other services, e.g. sports centres or theatres.

Local authorities are controlled by a city, town or county council according to the type of area concerned. The council consists of elected councillors, ordinary women and men who have an interest in serving the local community. Most councillors belong to political parties who help them to campaign to be elected to the council. Each council has sub-committees to look after each area of the council's work, for example an Education sub-committee, a Recreation sub-committee, a Housing sub-committee. The members of each sub-committee are chosen by the council and assisted by full-time paid officials of the council, such as the Director of Education. The councillors also choose from amongst themselves someone to be chairperson of each sub-committee. The chairperson or 'chair' of each committee is responsible for its smooth running. The Chair of Education will work closely with the

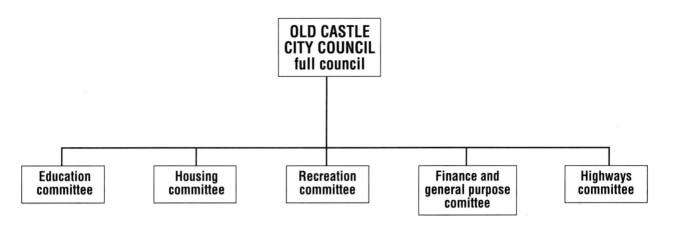

An example of a council's committee structure. Each committee may set up its own sub-committees. For example, the education committee might have a schools sub-committee and a Further Education and Adults sub-committee.

Director of Education, for instance, to ensure a good education service is provided. In some areas certain council services, such as school cleaning or waste disposal, are provided by private sector firms and not the council's own employees. These services have been *contracted out*. This is another form of privatisation.

Local authorities get income from the community charge or poll tax, from the charges they make for some services, and from central government. Just under half of all local authority income comes from central government.

Businesses pay a Uniform Business Rate (UBR) to the council (which is set by central government) and will have to apply for permission to build or alter premises. Most councils have a Trading Standards and Environmental Health section to ensure that businesses are trading fairly without polluting or damaging the environment. Local councils provide buildings and other work for private firms. Clearly, local councils have an important impact on business.

Government departments

Her Majesty's Stationery Office (HMSO) is a government department which trades with the public by selling government publications such as Acts of Parliament (the laws of the land), government reports on matters of interest, and statistical material. This sort of information is useful to business as it needs to provide goods and services within the law and will use statistical information to become more efficient. For example, by knowing the size or age of the population in a particular area a business can calculate possible sales and how much to produce.

The Export Credits Guarantee Department (ECGD) is part of the Department of Trade and Industry. The ECGD provides insurance cover for British firms against non-payment of debts by overseas customers. This sort of insurance is too risky for many commercial insurance companies to offer and by providing it the government is encouraging firms to trade overseas, which helps the British balance of payments (see Chapter 13).

Most government departments are concerned with the administrative affairs of the country and engage in little commercial activity.

Apart from the features outlined above, it should be remembered that local and central government are an important source of income for business. Together they provide about seven million jobs, and so seven million wage packets will be spent on the goods and services provided by business. Also local and central government will spend money on goods and services such as cleaning, catering and building which business provides.

1.6. Answer the following questions with at least a full sentence, or by writing out the missing words.

3. How are local government departments controlled?

1. Put forward two arguments in favour of public corporations.

4. Explain how business is affected by government.

2. Put forward two arguments against public corporations.

5. Describe two sorts of privatisation.

5. How do goods and services differ?

6. What two problems might a sole owner face?

1. In what ways are skilled, semi-skilled and unskilled labour different?

7. What sort of undertakings might a public company be suitable for?

2. In business studies what two meanings does the term 'land' have.

8. Why are there different sorts of business?

3. Explain the difference between fixed, and liquid capital.

9. Which form of business ownership is best suited to making quick decisions?

4. If a firm describes one of its assets as 'liquid', what does this mean?

10. Name at least one business which is controlled by central government.

STIMULUS RESPONSE QUESTIONS

1. Read this article 'Sharing the company with the employees' and then answer these questions.

   a) What does ESOP stand for? *(1 mark)*

   b) How did Mr Bright try to implement his beliefs? *(2 marks)*

   c) In what ways would a producer's co-operative appear to be different from an ESOP scheme? *(10 marks)*

   d) What are the advantages of the workers owning shares in their company
   (i) To the workers? *(4 marks)*
   (ii) To the company? *(4 marks)*

That everybody in a business should be of equal status, other than salary, is one of the firm beliefs of Mike Bright, chairman and managing director of Brighton-based Flexible Manufacturing Technology, which makes machine tools. In the early 1980s, Mr Bright began to implement his beliefs by abolishing a dual-status canteen and car park at the company, then part of the Vickers group known as KTM. He has since introduced a programme aimed at harmonising employee and management benefits. There are plans to abolish clocking-in and to standardise the working week at 37½ hours. But when last year Mr Bright led a successful £7 million management buyout of KTM, he saw the opportunity to extend his principles further. He was determined to hand over a slice of the equity to the employees, though he was not quite sure what mechanism to use.

A solution emerged when Granville, the company's financial advisers at the time of the buyout, introduced FMT to Unity Trust, the trade union bank, which has pioneered the concept of Employee Share Ownership Plans in Britain.

An ESOP gives employees a financial stake in the success of their company. A trust is set up to acquire company shares, which then go tax efficiently to employees through a share participation scheme. Eventually the employees can sell the shares back to the trust or, if the company is floated, on the stock market.

Seven leading financial institutions – Barclays de Zoete Wedd, Chemical Bank, Continental Bank, Kleinwort Benson, Manufacturers Hanover, Security Pacific and Unity Trust – are now putting their muscle behind the ESOP movement in the United Kingdom. They have jointly made funds of up to £100 million available for ESOP schemes. So far 18 ESOPS involving 20,000 employees have been launched in the UK. But the idea is catching on so rapidly that Malcolm Hurlston, who heads the London-based ESOP Centre, predicts that within five years some two million employees in Britain will be involved.

FMT placed 16.9 per cent of its shares into a trust to distribute to employees. An initial allocation of half the shares was made at the end of last year to employees with at least a year's service. A second allocation will be made this year.

A total of 227 employees – all but two of those eligible – have opted to participate. The proportion is high but refusal is unlikely when the shares are being given away.

"The allocation is primarily related to basic pay but we build in an element based on length of service because we were under a lot of pressure from our union representatives to do so," says Mr Bright. Another important element of the FMT scheme is performance-related. "We are a pretty organised sort of a company. We have our annual plans which set down the targets for the year and we determined the ESOP allocation would be made against the business plan criteria – essentially profitability".

It is to early to say whether FMT's workforce has become more motivated as a result of the ESOP. Robert Brotherton, FMT's personnel director, has modest expectations: "It's one of a number of measures all designed to encourage and build on the co-operation and flexibility of everyone trying to achieve our objectives".

He also says that there is a major weakness in an ESOP that could have the opposite effect to that FMT is seeking. After the second allocation of FMT shares it could be some time before shares sold back to the trust build up sufficiently to justify a new distribution. This could cause resentment among new employees denied access to the scheme.

THE GUARDIAN, MONDAY AUGUST 7TH 1989

2. Privatisation
   'It is the government's view that the sooner we can get rid of these large public

corporations the better it will be for all of us', said the government minister to applause from the audience at his election meeting.

a) What is privatisation? *(1 mark)*

b) In what ways will privatisation be better 'for all of us'? *(5 marks)*

c) What are the arguments against privatisation? *(5 marks)*

d) How does the government control public corporations? *(5 marks)*

e) Name two privatised companies *(4 marks)*

3. Business Expansion

Terry could not understand it. Although he was good with engines he was not very good on car electrical systems. Mind you, if he had that new piece of electronic testing equipment he had seen advertised he might have been able to fix the fault by now. There again, if he had typed the letter fast enough he could have caught the post yesterday and stopped Mr Evans coming for his car. Instead Mr Evans was due at any moment and the car was far from ready. This had happened a lot over the last few months as business had improved. Being self-employed wasn't all it was cracked up to be. What could he do?

a) What type of business organisation does Terry have? *(1 mark)*

b) What are his two main problems as shown by this situation? *(2 marks)*

c) What sort of business organisation should he change to? Explain why you think this is a good idea. *(10 marks)*

d) Despite the problems of self-employment, many people find it satisfying. What advantages of self-employment are there
(i) for the self-employed person?
(ii) for their customers? *(7 marks)*

1. Contact your local council offices. Ask for information about the range of services they provide and how they are paid for. Prepare a wall display of your findings.

2. Banks provide services for business. Contact The Bank Information Service (10 Lombard Street, London EC3V 9AS) and ask them to send a speaker to talk about the service banks provide for business. They will also give information about careers in banking. Classify the available jobs into skilled, semi-skilled and unskilled.

3. Write to a Public Limited Company that you have heard of. Ask if they can supply information about what the firm does and how it has developed over the years. They may also be happy to supply you with advertising literature and a company report.

4. Choose two or three sections of roughly the same size in your local *Yellow Pages*. Which section has the most Public Limited Companies? Can you suggest reasons why there should be more in one section than another?

5. Write a class letter to a public corporation asking for information about the history and main services of the organisation. Prepare a wall display of your findings.

ON ASSIGNMENT

Using a large-scale map of your area, a copy of the local *Yellow Pages* and your own local knowledge:

Mark on the map, in different colours, where examples of the different types of business organisation are to be found. You should number the different firms and show them clearly in a key.

Examine your results and see if you can find what types of business activity there is most of and least of. Why do you think this is? What sort of business activity is missing in your area? Why is this? Write an account of your results, answering these questions and explaining any other findings.

CASE STUDY

The pop group's battered Ford transit van pulled up outside the Westbourne Working Men's Club and the four arguing members of The Moderators jumped out, followed by Kevin, their driver. They had been unable to find the club at first because each person thought that somebody else had got directions from the club secretary when the booking was made. Things were not helped by the fact that they had been double booked because two members of the group had made a booking with two different clubs. It was unlikely that the other club would have them back again after being let down at such short notice – as if work wasn't hard enough to find! They still had to decide how tonight's fee was to be shared out after they had finished. There had been an awful row last night when Gordon had demanded the largest share because he thought that his three years at music college made him a better musician than the others. They began to unload various amplifiers, drums, guitars, sheet music, drums sticks, lights

and microphones, equipment which they had built up together. The stairs were badly lit, but under the leadership of Karen, their drummer, the equipment was soon assembled on the stage, even though two of the band did nothing but stand drinking at the bar. It was only 4 p.m. but they decided to play one or two of the new songs they had introduced into the act, to get them just right. Then disaster struck. As they rehearsed, two of the strings on Gordon's guitar snapped and he found that there weren't any spares. 'Nip out to the shopping centre and buy a set, Kevin,' he said to the driver. 'Go yourself,' snapped Kevin, 'What do you think I am, your slave?'. 'Listen mate, if it wasn't for my guitar playing there would be no work for an unskilled layabout like you'. 'OK, calm down you two', said Karen as it began to get nasty, 'We've all put the same amount of money into this band so let's all sort this out., but as you've asked me to be leader I'll decide.' 'I didn't agree to that' protested the unhappy guitar player. 'Yes you did!' said one of the others. 'When? Tell me when! what did I say then? I don't remember' shouted Gordon. After more argument about who said what, when and to whom, Karen spoke up. 'Gordon, you go, we cannot rehearse until the strings are replaced so there's nothing else for you to do, but if Kevin stays he can check the equipment, while the rest of us practice the words of the new songs'.

Eventually, after a lot of argument which wasted valuable rehearsal time, the strings were replaced. At last the unhappy Moderators took the stage. As the applause following their introduction died away the group launched into their first song. After about two bars the audience started booing and jeering at the awful noise coming from Gordon's direction. 'Your guitar is out of tune , you idiot' hissed Karen, trying to smile at the audience. 'Oh' said Gordon 'I don't know why. It was OK when I bought it!' As the group walked off the stage in disgrace they began to mutter about breaking up and 'getting rid of that idiot Gordon'.

Answer the following questions individually or in groups.

1. How might the group's work have been better organised?

2. What sort of business organisation do you think would have been best for The Moderators? Explain how this sort of business organisation might have helped them deal with some of the problems they had.

3. Do you think Gordon was right to ask for more money than the others because he had had more training? List the arguments in favour and the arguments against.

4. Divide the sort of equipment this group might have into fixed capital and circulating capital.

5. Give at least one example of how The Moderators might have used the following business services: banking, insurance, advertising.

In order to get the greatest use from the factors of production it uses, a business must pay attention to the following activities which are the six basic business functions:

Personnel

A business must ensure it has the right number of suitably-trained people when it needs them. It is important that employees are kept up to date with developments in their area of work. All employees must be employed according to the laws affecting employment.

Finance

The firm's capital must be used in a way which gives maximum benefit to the firm. Slow-paying customers must be speeded up, fraud and theft should be prevented. The firm's accounts must be prepared according to the requirements of the law and all taxes owing should be calculated and paid.

Purchasing

In order to produce its goods and services a firm must buy raw materials and equipment. The purchases made must be at the right price and at the right level of quality. The firm needs to seek out reliable suppliers who will meet the agreed delivery dates.

Production

The raw materials and equipment must produce the highest quality, lowest priced goods or services possible. The production of the firm must be planned in a way which makes the best use of all the factors of production but also which keeps within health and safety regulations and other laws.

Marketing

The finished goods or services have to be sold. Marketing is about informing potential customers about products and persuading them to buy. As well as keeping existing customers, marketing is about finding out what new products or services customers might want and ensuring the firm supplies them. The firm will need to gather information about its competitors.

Research and development

Research and Development, or 'R and D' as it is sometimes called looks at new technology, techniques, processes and products as they become available. R and D tries to relate them to the firm's production with a view to improving the business's products, performance and profit. Only by constantly improving what it does can the firm hope to compete and succeed in staying in business.

Each firm will carry out the six basic business functions in a way which best suits that firm. One sole owner might carry out all six functions alone, another might carry out five personally and pay someone to look after the financial function. Large organisations will have separate departments to look after the six basic business functions. The numbers and titles of the departments will vary from firm to firm. For example, the personnel function might be called the Personnel Department in one firm and the Human Resources Section in another. Sometimes functions are subdivided. The marketing function may be split between an Advertising Department and a Market Research Department. Transport is an important part of the marketing function, but this is a separate department in many firms, often called Distribution.

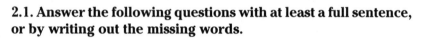

CHECK THIS OUT

2.1. Answer the following questions with at least a full sentence, or by writing out the missing words.

1. The six basic business functions are ___, ___, ___, ___, ___ and ___ and ___ .

2. Explain the marketing function.

3. Describe the personnel function.

4. What is the purpose of the finance function?

5. In what ways can the organisation of the six basic business functions vary from business to business?

Organisation charts

Firms will often show how they are organised by using simple diagrams called organisation charts. These charts show how each part of the firm is connected to the other parts. An organisation chart for a company might look like this:

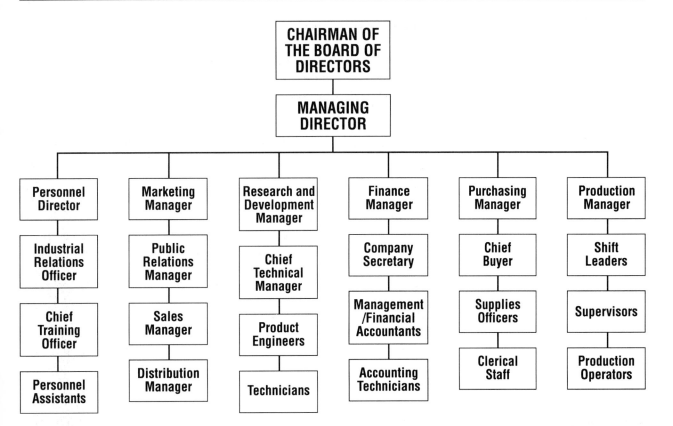

Under each manager is a line of staff for whom the manager is responsible. This gives rise to the phrase *line management*. In our diagram the supervisors, for example, are responsible to the leader of their shift (Shift Leader), who is in turn responsible to the Production Manager, who in turn must answer to the Managing Director. The Managing Director must explain his or her actions to the Board of Directors through the Chairman of the Board of Directors.

As well as the formal structures we have looked at, it should be remembered that businesses have informal structures. Individual personalities, habits and traditions all contribute to the business's informal structure. In the informal structure individuals may have access to information or be able to influence decisions in a way which is not usual to their particular level or job.

Individuals may have access to information

The informal structure is about what actually happens in an organisation as opposed to what the written structure says should happen. Good managers are aware of the informal structures and use them to help the working of the organisation.

Communications

Common sense tells us that the Managing Director, or any other manager, cannot carefully supervise the work of more than a few people. The limit to how many people someone can control is called the *span of control*. Managers rely on others to carry out tasks which they give them. Giving people responsibility and work to do is known as *delegation*. Managers will delegate responsibilities to staff within their span of control. The number of people directly reporting to a manager or supervisor will vary according to the sort of work being done. Narrow spans of control are usual if work has to be carefully checked. Wide spans of control may be used if the staff involved are experienced, well qualified and responsible. If people are working in the same building or office it is possible to have a wide span of control, but if they are spread over different offices a narrow span of control is better. This is because the problems of communication make a small, spread-out group harder to supervise than a large centralised one. The most common span of control is six or seven.

Diagram showing span of control

You will notice that each manager or supervisor has a span of control at their level of responsibility. In other words, the types of responsibilities differ at each level of the organisation. Line management makes sure that work is delegated so that the aims of the organisation are met.

In order to work efficiently, business organisations need to be able to pass on information between workers and to customers, the press, government and other interested organisations. Passing on information or *communication* will include:

- Passing on factual information
- Putting forward opinions and trying to persuade others
- Giving instructions

The method of communication used will depend on who is being communicated with, the cost of the communication, the urgency of the communication, if a record of the message is required, how confidential the message is and who is sending it. For example, urgent messages to the Managing Director could be telephoned to his/her portable telephone and a message to supervisors about a meeting in three weeks' time could be passed on by a poster on a notice board in the canteen. Communication happens in many ways. The main methods of communication are:

- Letter
- Memo (properly called a memorandum)
- Report
- Notices
- Spoken (verbal communication)
- Non-verbal communication
- Meetings

2.2. Answer the following questions with at least a full sentence, or by writing out the missing words.

1. What is an organisation chart?

2. How do formal and informal structures differ?

3. What factors affect a business's informal structure?

4. The limit to how many people someone can control is called the ___ of ___ .

5. Giving responsibility to others is called ___ .

6. What are the three main purposes of communication?

7. Six factors which effect the method of communication used are ___ .

8. Name six methods of communication used in business.

Letters

Letters are used by the firm to communicate with people and organisations outside the firm. Letters are not used for communication within the firm. High standards of presentation, grammar and spelling are important if a letter is to make a good impression on people outside the firm. For this reason the letter will be typed or word-processed on high quality paper. Most firms have their name, address and business symbol (logo) printed at the top or bottom of the letter. Often the name of the company chairman or the main directors are included. Paper which has the company details printed on it is called *headed paper*.

James Davis
Wedding Photography

12 West Street, Cheltenham, Gloucester GL50 2UQ

Tel: 0242 512000
Fax: 0242 512101

An example of a letter heading

As the sample letters opposite show, the address of the person receiving the letter is always typed on the letter. The title of the person receiving the letter should be used, in addition to their name, for example Mr G. Smith, Dr P. J. Patel, Lord Lucan, Ms M. Callagan (Chief Personnel Officer), etc. The address on the letter should match exactly the address on the envelope. The address should always have the town printed in capitals and include the post code.

Many letters have a reference number or code on them. This is used to identify who wrote and typed the letter but may include any reference numbers the firm uses, such as the person's credit account number.

The person receiving the letter is known as the *addressee*. If possible the letter should start with the addressee's name, for example Dear Mr Goggins, Dear Mrs Malik, Dear Peter, Dear Sue etc. This opening to the letter is called the *salutation*. The term comes from the word 'salute' meaning 'to greet with respect'.

After the salutation comes the body of the letter. The *body of the letter* contains the message. This part of the letter is broken down into paragraphs to deal with each of the points or lines of argument being made. Paragraphs break down the information into manageable parts and so aid understanding. The letter should not contain slang. Jargon which the other person might not understand should be avoided. Sentences ought to be short but clear. Politeness and courtesy are important, but if the letter contains some criticism it should not be phrased so politely that the addressee does not realise they are being criticised. It should be obvious by the end of the letter what the sender wants the addressee to do, for example to write a reply confirming the delivery date, attend a meeting in two weeks' time, send a refund for faulty goods.

The letter ends with the *complimentary close*. This is usually 'Yours faithfully' if the letter starts with 'Dear Sir' or 'Dear Madam'. If the letter starts with the person's name in the salutation (e.g. 'Dear Miss Smith', 'Dear James') then 'Yours sincerely' should be used. Space should be left for the sender's signature and their name should be typed underneath, followed by their job title or *desig-*

nation, for example John Whitley, Credit Controller or Reema Salim, Finance Director.

If something, such as an application form, leaflet or price list has been sent in the same envelope as the letter, 'Enc' is typed about two centimetres below the signature. 'Enc' is short for enclosure and tells the addressee that something has been included with the letter.

The presentation of a letter can create the first, and lasting, impression.

P., P. and J. White, Solicitors, 133 Nine Elms Road, Oldham OL45 67Q.

```
Messrs Sue, Grabbit and Runne
Solicitors
34 Letsbe Avenue
Heaton
NEWCASTLE UPON TYNE
NE6 3HB


Dear Sirs

Mrs B Booth

We are acting on behalf of our client Mrs B Booth to whom
you recently wrote claiming that she had collided with your
client's car. Mrs Booth has asked us to point out that in
her discussion with your client, Mr Brayson, he said that he
had been involved in a car crash before.

As this clearly shows that he has a record of careless
driving we would ask that you send us a cheque for £454 to
settle the loss suffered by Mrs Booth as a result of this
incident.

We have enclosed a written statement from an independent
witness who was passing at the time of the incident, a
Mr R Booth. This confirms our client's account of the
collision.

Yours faithfully



Mr P White

Enc
```

P., P. and J. White, Solicitors, 133 Nine Elms Road, Oldham OL45 67Q.

```
Messrs Sue, Grabbit and Runne
Solicitors
 34 Letsbe Avenue
Heaton
NEWCASTLE UPON TYNE
NE6 3HB


Dear Sirs

Mrs B Booth

We is acting on behalf of our clint Mrs B.Booth to whom you
recently wrote claiming that she had collided with your
client's car. Mrs Booth has asked us to pint out that in her
discussion with you client, Mr Brayson, he said that he had
been involved in a car crash before. As this

As this clearly shows that he has a record driving we would
ask that you send us a  check for £454 to settle the loss
suffered by Mrs Booth as a result of this incident.

We have enclosed a written statement  from from an
independent wotniss who was passing at the time of the
incident, a Mr R Booth. This confirms our client's account
of the collision.

Your faithfully



Mr P White

Enc
```

Memos

A memo is the most common form of written communication used *within* a business. Memos are not sent to people outside the organisation; a letter is used instead. A memo is used to pass on a message from one part of the business to another. The firm will have a specially-designed memo form. Memos are usually polite, brief, direct and to the point. Longer memos may have numbered paragraphs, or each point made numbered. Notice that memos are not usually signed, nor do they begin with 'Dear...'. In some firms memos are initialled at the end by the sender. Memos may be typed or word-processed. They may be handwritten to save time and money.

MEMORANDUM

Sue, Grabbit & Runne Solicitors

FROM: G Grabbit
DATE: 19 September 1991

TO: L Runne
REF: GG/AT

SUBJECT: Mrs B Booth

I have received a letter from Mr P White claiming damages on behalf of his client, Mrs B Booth. Please investigate this by getting Mr Brayson's side of the affair and report back to me in three days.

Each business has its own rules about the layout and style of letters, memos and reports which staff are expected to follow. This style is called the *house style*. Letters and memos have the advantage of providing a record of what has been communicated and they allow for preparation and presentation to be practised before the message is sent. The disadvantage of these methods of communication is that both the time it takes to send a letter or memo and the time taken to receive a reply make them unsuitable for situations requiring swift action.

CHECK THIS OUT

2.3. Answer the following questions with at least a full sentence, or by writing out the missing words.

4. Why would the term 'enc' be used in a letter?

5. What form of communication is most often used for internal communication?

1. In business, who would you communicate with by letter?

6. A memo is usually ___, ___, ___ and ___ the _____ .

2. What is headed paper?

7. Give two advantages of letters and memos.

3. The person receiving a letter is called the
   _____ .

8. Give one disadvantages of letters and memos.

Reports

When detailed consideration of a subject is needed it is usual for a report to be produced. An individual, or a group will be asked to produce a report for a particular date. This date is the *deadline*. It is important that deadlines are met as failure to do so may delay the work of others. Each business will have a house style for reports but it is common to find the following features:

- Each paragraph will be numbered

- A title explaining the purpose of the report, for example 'A report on the reasons for reduced sales at the Nuneaton branch during the last year' or 'A report to investigate the most suitable word processor for the new Wallsend office'.

- Terms of reference. A paragraph explaining what the people preparing the report were asked to do and who the report is to be presented to. For example 'Joe Brayson, Carol Smith and Suliza Hashim were asked to investigate word processors costing less than £1000 to find which would be the most suitable for the new Wallsend office. The report was to be presented to Peter Anderson by Friday 23rd July'.

- Procedures followed to complete the task. Who was interviewed? What books were consulted? What was done in the course of the research? Which firms were asked to supply price lists? This section will normally take more than one paragraph.

- Results of the investigation. A straightforward factual account of the results. For example, who said what, costs of each of the alternative word processors being considered, facilities of each machine, cost of servicing, ease of operation, if they can be linked to other machines etc.

- Conclusion. What the results lead you to believe. For example, that Wing word processors are cheap but Stradam's are more reliable while Amigo do not produce a word processor to suit the needs of your business, and FRXs can be used with other computers but are difficult to learn.

- Recommendations. For example, after having considered the various machines, which machine is recommended for purchase.

- Appendix. If there are a lot of complicated details these may be presented in a section at the end of the report called an appendix. It is important to refer to the appendix at suitable points in the results and conclusion sections of the report.

- Summary. If the person receiving the report is likely to be too busy to read it all or if the report is very long a summary is common. The summary is a short section at the front of the report which gives brief details of the investigation, the recommendations and the reasons behind them. It sums up the report.

Notices

Notice-boards should be kept tidy and have outdated information removed regularly. If this is done, notices can be an effective means of communicating non-confidential information to a large number of people.

Notices should be eye-catching and convey only essential information. Notices that are too detailed are hard to read. Remember, most people read a notice-board in passing. They will have little time to absorb chunks of unnecessary information and will be reading from a distance of, perhaps, several feet. It is good practice to make sure a notice is signed and dated by the person responsible for its display. Clear headings and pictures are effective ways of holding the readers' attention. Notices calling a meeting should always have details of the date, time and place of the meeting and explain, briefly, what is to be discussed. If the notice invites enquiries then the name, address and telephone number of the person to contact should be displayed.

2.4. Answer the following questions with at least a full sentence, or by writing out the missing words.

1. What is a deadline?

2. Name the nine common features of a report.

3. What are terms of reference?

4. Notices must be eye-catching as they are often read _____ _____ .

5. What are effective ways of making a notice hold the reader's attention?

6. Notices calling a meeting should give details of the _____ , _____ and ____ of the meeting.

Spoken communication

Spoken or verbal communication can take many forms. It may occur in an interview, a meeting, a television or radio broadcast, or could simply be a passing comment. Clear speech is important. Slang should be avoided, and so should jargon unless it actually helps others to understand. 'Jargon' means specialist terms or phrases used in a particular industry such as computing or nursing. The background of the person listening should be kept in mind. Spoken communication has the advantage of being fast and immediate. A response or *feedback* is almost instant. This form of communication allows questions to be raised and answered quickly. Verbal communication also speeds up the consideration of different opinions through discussion. The disadvantages of verbal communication methods are that they do not allow the same detailed level of preparation and presentation as written methods and an accurate record is hard to obtain. The telephone is important in spoken communication as it allows rapid communication over long distances. It has the disadvantage of being more expensive than most written methods of communication.

Non-verbal communication

A person's expression, the way they walk or sit and the number of times they smile or frown give clues about how they feel. They are communicating without speaking, hence the term non-verbal communication. The phrase *body language* is also used to describe this form of communication. As most body language occurs without thought it can give a real clue as to how a person is feeling. Care must be taken to avoid jumping to the wrong conclusions about a person, but being aware of body language can help to avoid being insensitive and help to bring out the facts behind what others think. Watch part of a film on television with the sound turned off. Often it is still possible to have an idea of what feelings the actors are communicating.

Body language can say a lot about a person

Meetings

Meetings are a combination of verbal, non-verbal and written communication. Many meetings are between managers or their representatives to consider reports or other written documents and to reach a decision. Meetings vary in size, from two people upwards. Business meetings are usually small and a meeting of more than 50 people is rare. Small meetings tend to be more efficient than larger ones. It is, however, important that all the people who need to be involved are involved. Meetings combine the advantages of spoken communication and overcome the disadvantages of written communication. A disadvantage of meetings is that they may be used too frequently and take staff away from other work. It is a bad habit to call meetings when other forms of communication can do the job just as well. For example, it is better to write a memo than to call staff together to hear a routine announcement. The order of items to be discussed is written down in an *agenda*. The agenda is usually sent out in advance of the meeting and contains details of the time of starting and finishing, date and place of the meeting. If an agenda is not sent, then details of the date, time and place are sent in a *notice of meeting*. The layout of the agenda and other documents used in formal meetings will depend on the house style.

Most *formal meetings* have a chairperson or 'chair' whose job it is to see that the meeting goes smoothly and that everyone has a chance to contribute. Usually the chair will restrict the number of times a person can speak on any one topic. There is also someone to take a record of the meeting's decisions (usually a secretary).

This record will be used to produce the *minutes of the meeting*, the official record of what occurred at the meeting. *Verbatim minutes* are a written record of what each person said at the meeting. *Resolution minutes* record what was decided without giving details of the discussion.

East Gridlington Social Club
Finance Committee

AGENDA

Meeting of the Finance Committee on 3rd November 1991, in the Committee Room of the club.

1 Apologies for absence

2 Minutes of the meeting held 3rd October 1991

3 Matters arising from the minutes

4 Treasurer's Report

5 New Year's Eve disco

6 Any other business

7 Date of next meeting

The following points appear on all formal agendas:

- *Apologies for absence*. This item indicates that the names of people who cannot attend will be announced at the meeting and recorded in the minutes of the meeting.

- *Approval of the minutes* is on the agenda so that the members of the meeting can agree that the minutes are an accurate record of the previous meeting. At this stage any inaccuracies can be corrected.

- The next item on the agenda is *matters arising*. Anything discussed at the last meeting can be raised briefly at this point, usually in the form of a question or a short verbal report. However, if the item is on the agenda again, discussion must wait until that point on the agenda is reached.

- The second to last item on the agenda is often 'Any Other Business' or AOB, as it is sometimes written. This item gives members a chance to raise short minor points which were not important enough to get a place on the agenda.

- At the end of the meeting it is usual for the group to decide when to meet again, or for an announcement to be made about the next meeting.

The advantage of formal meetings is that they provide an accurate record of decisions and allow discussions to occur in an orderly way. They have the disadvantage of being time-consuming and involve a lot of preparation and reading in advance.

Informal meetings are not as structured as formal meetings, although they will have someone to lead the discussion (like a chairperson). They tend to be shorter and restricted to one or two particular issues. When the issues are resolved the group will stop meeting. Groups that meet on this basis are called *ad hoc* groups. Informal meeting may have the disadvantage of lacking a formal record. The spontaneous nature of such groups may mean that certain individuals get overlooked. This can breed resentment and lead to delays.

The business' Annual Report (see page 12), advertising (see page 170) and statements to the press are other important methods of external communication.

2.5. Answer the following questions with at least a full sentence, or by writing out the missing words.

4. Verbal communication can speed up consideration of different _____ and allow people to ask _____ .

5. What is body language?

6. Meetings are a combination of _____, _____ and _____ communication.

1. Avoid ___ and ___ in spoken communication.

2. Feedback is a _____ to a communication or action.

3. Describe a disadvantage of verbal communication.

7. What is a disadvantage of meetings?

8. What is a chairperson?

9. What is an agenda?

10. How do these two types of minutes differ?

Problems in communication

The diagram shows the four important ingredients in the process of communication.

The most successful communication occurs when the transmitter chooses the medium appropriate to the type of message and the receiver. For example, sensitive information about the results of a person's medical examination should not be communicated in complex medical language over the firm's loudspeaker system! A face-to-face meeting or straightforward letter is far better. An important element in communication is feedback. This is the response of the receiver to the message. Feedback can be in the

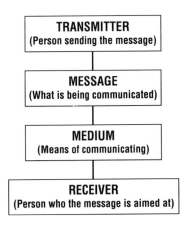

One-way communication

form of a letter, a shrug of the shoulders or any other response to the message. The transmitter should watch for feedback in order to be aware of the impact of the message. There is more feedback in situations where people are encouraged to participate in decisions about their work. This *two-way communication* is normally found with democratic or participatory-style management (see page 50). *One-way communication* is found in authoritarian, non-democratic styles of management such as in the army. The lack of feedback in one-way communication increases the risk that the message might be misunderstood or not even received. Problems or *distortion* in communication can arise for several reasons:

Emotional reasons

For example, personal stress or hostility between transmitter and receiver makes individuals less likely to share information. Possible solutions might include help or advice from colleagues or supervisors. If necessary help from a doctor or the firm's Personnel Department might be needed (see page 46). It is important not to 'bottle up' emotional problems or stress as this can make the problem worse.

Social reasons

An employee might think that the new boss expects too much of him. This might stop him being open about problems related to the job. Insecure managers might be too formal with their staff and restrict the communication between them. These sort of problems can only be overcome if all staff are made to feel secure in their jobs. Staff training on how to work with others might ease the problem. A particular social communication problem is the 'grapevine'. This refers to the informal, unofficial way gossip and information is passed through an organisation. Problems arise when there is too much unnecessary secrecy in an organisation which makes people feel suspicious and believe any information is better than no information. Poor security of confidential documents can lead to unauthorised access to information. This can feed the grapevine. The grapevine can often contribute to some of the emotional reasons for communication breakdown.

Geographical reasons

If workers are in offices throughout the world communication is made more difficult because there is less feedback than in a face-to-face situation, as well as time differences making contact by telephone hard to arrange. Delays in the postal service, rail strikes or motorway hold-ups can make communication difficult within a country. Even in an office, changes in the layout can make it easier for staff to contact each other and so ease communication problems.

Language reasons

If two people speak different languages swift and effective communication will be impossible without a translator. Skills in other languages are becoming important as the reduction in trade regulations between European countries in 1992 makes international trade more profitable. Poor use of language can also be a barrier to communication. Slang, jargon and poor grammar can often serve to confuse the receiver. Staff training can help to overcome language problems.

Technical reasons

This covers a wide range of problems. At a simple level, the error might be to choose the wrong medium to send a message. For example, sending an urgent letter by post when both transmitter and receiver have access to a fax machine would be an error. If a transmitter is unsure of a firm's structure and what the line management structure is, he might not inform all of the individuals who need to know a piece of information. Technical problems of this sort can usually be overcome with good training and preparation.

There are three basic principles to remember in any type of communication; clarity, concentration and correctness.

- *Clarity* Transmitters must be clear about what they want to say and make sure their message is logically structured with no room for misunderstanding. Receivers must be sure they know what the message is and decide what it requires of them. If the receiver is unclear about what the message says or requires this must be communicated to the transmitter – feedback is required.

- *Concentration* Both the receiver and the transmitter of a message should give it their full attention. Failure to do so might mean an individual has to spend a long time putting right an error. Examples of lack of concentration could include not writing down a telephone message because of the distraction of watching a computer screen or not checking a memo before sending it. Missing out a word like 'not' in a letter or adding a zero to a figure can have a big effect on the receiver!

- *Correctness* The correct medium for the job should be chosen. For example, when a rapid telephone call might prevent unnecessary work being done, sending a letter would be an error. The correct medium can aid the clarity of the message. For example, a large notice with a picture might have the effect of communicating a complex idea more effectively than a long and wordy memo.

CHECK THIS OUT

2.6. Answer the following questions with at least a full sentence, or by writing out the missing words.

1. Name the four ingredients in the communication process.

2. What is meant by the phrase 'medium of communication'? Give an example of a medium of communication.

3. Feedback is most common in situations where there is ___-way communication.

4. Give two reasons why communication might be distorted.

5. What is the grapevine?

6. The three basic principles of communication are ___, ___ and ___.

Information technology in communications

The development of the silicon chip in 1971 changed the way in which technical equipment was used in business. The silicon chip, the main component in calculators, computers and many other business machines, led to the development of new machines for handling and communicating information. The term *information technology* (IT) refers to all of the new machines we use to handle information. The main advantages of information technology over traditional methods of handling information are that it is faster and takes up less space. As we shall see, information technology also allows us to use information in new ways, ways that in the past were thought impossible because of the amount of time needed to analyse and check information. These advantages mean that, properly used, information technology is playing a major part in making business organisations more efficient. Machines that are important in IT include:

A main-frame computer in use

Computers

According to their size, we can identify three types of computer:

Main-frame

This is the largest type of computer. It is capable of storing the equivalent of several large libraries full of information. Many users can *access* (obtain) different information, all at once, by using computer keyboards called *terminals*. Terminals can be linked to a main-frame from different parts of the same building or even different parts of the world. In order to link computers in different parts of the world, a message is sent through a telephone line as a series of high-pitched noises produced by the computer. Only the largest business organisations find it worthwhile to purchase a main-frame as the high cost of such a computer puts it out of the reach of smaller organisations.

Mini-computers

These operate in the same way as main-frames but are not as large. Access by many users is possible as mini-computers can link up with computers in other parts of the world.

Micro-computers

These are the most common type of computer. They can be used at home and in many types of business. This book was written on a micro-computer. Micro-computers are becoming more and more advanced and are doing today what mini- and main-frame computers were doing a few years ago. They have brought the advantages of information technology within the reach of many people and organisations. At the most simple level, computers can process information in several ways using three sorts of *computer program* or *software*:

A micro-computer

- A *database* is a store of information – data. The information is usually in the form of words and letters but numerical data is also stored. A database is made up of many *records*. Each record is a set of information about a particular item, for example a customer, make of car, club member. A customer record might contain the name and address of the customer, the value of their last order, if they have any bills outstanding etc. This information could be kept on paper, but to find information on a complete set of records would mean an individual reading through all the files. A database can be searched by telling the computer what information is required. The details will be produced on screen or on paper. For example, a firm with 2000 customers wishes to find out which customers owe it money. In a paper system it might be necessary to look at each customer's file. A computer database system eliminates the need for this by looking through the records and providing the necessary details. Customers who live in a particular county or town can be listed so that sales representatives can visit them. This all saves time, which staff can use to do other things.

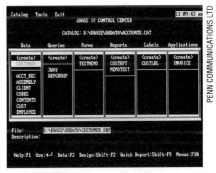

A database in operation

- A *spreadsheet* is used mainly to analyse numerical information. It can add, divide, multiply, subtract and sort figures into order much more quickly than any individual. Spreadsheets can also carry out complex statistical calculations. The spreadsheet can avoid the need for figures to be re-calculated. For example, if a firm's paper costs rise by ten per cent the computer can be told to do the calculation to show the overall effect on profits. Not only does this facility save time but it allows complex forecasts to be made. Different possible prices and costs etc

A word processor in use

can be speedily calculated to show the effect of possible decisions the business might make.

■ A *word processor*. This is the most common business use of computers. Word processing allows work to be typed on to a computer screen – the VDU or *visual display unit* – before it is printed. Blocks of text such as a paragraph or phrase can be moved around on screen, thus avoiding the need for complete retyping. Many word processors now have a feature which will check the spelling in a piece of work to show up errors and typing mistakes. Again, retyping is avoided.

As we will see when we look at the work of the departments of a business, computers have other uses and several firms have programs especially written for their own purposes.

CHECK THIS OUT

2.7. Answer the following questions with at least a full sentence, or by writing out the missing words.

1. What is the main component in computers and calculators?

2. What is information technology?

3. How does a main-frame computer differ from a micro-computer?

4. Explain how a database differs from a spreadsheet.

5. VDU stands for ___ ___ ___ .

6. Describe two ways in which word processing reduces the need for re-typing.

The Observer Prestel News Service being used

Viewdata systems

Viewdata systems are an important development in the use of computers. They are sometimes called teletex. A viewdata system has a series of colour images and text messages stored on a central computer. These can be read by a distant computer, with a modem. This is short for MODulator-DEModulator. The modem is a small box connected to the computer and to the telephone line. It prepares outgoing signals for transmission (modulates) and interprets incoming signals (demodulates). Modems can be used for any communication between computers, not just for teletex. Users have a password to obtain access to the information. A password is allocated once the user has paid a membership subscription. Cost is based on the length of time the user is connected to the service. Prestel is the best known viewdata service. It is a database which contains over 300 000 pages of information. This includes advertisements, airline timetables and details of ferry services. These pages are provided by advertisers, called *information providers*, who can amend their message as necessary. People using the service can transmit messages to information providers, such as a request for further information or a booking.

Viewdata provides a quick way to obtain up-to-the-minute information. Information providers can regularly update their messages and make contact with the users of the service.

An important additional advantage of computers is that, provided information is entered correctly in the first place, they make far fewer mistakes than humans. Computers do not get tired, angry, excited or fed up. All of these contribute to human error through loss of concentration.

Facsimile transmission

A fax machine

A facsimile is an exact copy of a drawing, picture, plan or piece of writing. A *facsimile transmission machine* or *fax machine* as it is usually called is a way of sending exact copies of plans, drawings or documents to other places. A fax machine works in a similar way to a photocopier. Instead of the copy appearing out of the machine the original was placed in, it appears in a far-off machine. This is because the image has been sent over the telephone lines. Fax numbers are dialled, just as on a push button phone, and the receiving machine sends a message to the sending machine to say it is ready to receive. Fax machines are numbered type one, two, three or four. The higher the number, the faster the machine can send and receive images. Fax machines can be bought for under £1000. They are fast, simple and fairly cheap to run. By allowing the transmission of material that, in the past, would normally have been sent by messenger or post, they save a great deal of time and money. Several firms are now selling fax machines with a built in telephone and photocopier.

Telex

Telex is an abbreviation for TELegraphic EXchange of messages. Like a fax machine, telex uses the telephone system to communicate with other telex machines. Telex machines are dialled in the same way as fax machines and telephones. Telex messages have to be typed in by a trained operator. This can be expensive if two machines are connected or *on line*, as the charge for the service relates to the time taken. However, messages can be prepared *off-line*, when the computer is not connected to other computers. Telex is a faster method of communication than traditional letter post. Like fax, telex messages can be received when the office is closed. One advantage of telex over fax is that there are more telex machines in use so there is a greater chance of establishing contact via telex. The improvements in fax, along with the steady drop in price makes it unlikely that this advantage will remain.

A telex machine only provides the telex service, but some computers can provide telex in addition to their other functions. A piece of information technology equipment which can only be used for one purpose is called a *dedicated* machine. Computers which can provide telex facilities are not dedicated and so are more flexible.

2.8. Answer the following questions with at least a full sentence, or by writing out the missing words.

3. Computers reduce error as they do not get —, —, — or fed up.

4. Why would you use a fax machine?

1. What is the best-known viewdata service?

5. What advantage does telex have over fax?

2. What are information providers in a viewdata service?

6. Explain what is meant by a 'dedicated machine'?

The way the six basic business functions are carried out varies from firm to firm. No textbook can describe how every single firm operates. It should be noted that a business can only be effective if all of the firm's departments communicate with each other. For instance, production needs to communicate with personnel to ensure that suitable staff are employed, although they can only be employed if the finance section makes clear that they can be afforded. In order to simplify matters, we will look at how a typical firm might be organised and treat the six basic business functions as separate departments. You should always remember that how firms organise these functions will vary. Each function or department has been given a separate section in the book.

6. How do memos and letters differ?

7. How do minutes and agenda differ?

1. List the six basic business functions.

8. Give another term for non-verbal communication.

2. What is the purpose of R and D?

3. Why are organisation charts useful?

9. Describe two problems of communication and how they might be overcome.

4. What is the most common span of control?

10. Detail at least three advantages of using computers in business.

5. Explain what is meant by levels of responsibility.

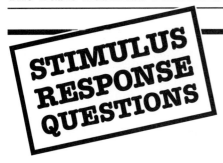

STIMULUS RESPONSE QUESTIONS

1. *Over 30 million letters and half a million parcels are posted every working day. We do our best to ensure that they arrive safely, and the vast majority do. ... The ordinary inland letter and parcel services will often meet your everyday requirements. They are not designed for sending valuable items like money or jewellery.*

   (POST OFFICE INFORMATION SHEETS)

   a) Name three alternative methods of communication apart from letters that a firm might use to contact other businesses. *(6 marks)*

   b) Explain to someone who was unsure how a letter should be written and say what points the writer should consider. *(14 marks)*

2. *Developing computer software essentially involves the enormous challenge of creating the 'middle man' between the simple logic of the computer and the business solutions required by the complex human beings who use it.*

   (IBM, 'MAKING INFORMATION TECHNOLOGY WORK IN EUROPE')

   a) Name three types of computer software. *(6 marks)*

   b) Describe three advantages of using computers to process information rather than traditional methods. *(6 marks)*

   c) Computers are used to provide viewdata systems. Explain what these are and how businesses might use them. *(8 marks)*

3. *After waiting twenty minutes for the meeting to start, Bill decided that there had been another breakdown in communication and that he might as well go back to his office rather than waste his time hanging around for a non-existent meeting.*

   a) Give three factors that might cause a communication breakdown and explain how they might be overcome. *(12 marks)*

   b) What is feedback, and in what sorts of organisations is it most likely to be found? *(6 marks)*

   c) How can the grapevine hinder good communication? *(2 marks)*

LEARN IT YOURSELF

1. As a group arrange a meeting to decide how to organise one of the tasks in this section. You will need to prepare an agenda, keep minutes, choose a chairperson and conduct the meeting efficiently so that the work to be done is agreed and shared out fairly.

2. In groups contact three businesses. Ask for information about how they are structured. Ask them to send you an organisation chart if one is available. If not, prepare an organisation chart from the information you get.

3. Draw an organisation chart for your school or college. Comment on the levels of responsibility and spans of control that you see.

4. Prepare a wall display entitled 'The use of information technology in business'. Collect brochures, leaflets and information about information technology as well as reading suitable books and magazines from the library.

5. Collect as many different letter headings as you can. Make a list of the things they have in common (e.g. use of colour, firm's address, etc.)

Prepare a questionnaire for local businesses to complete about how they use Information technology. Details you might investigate could include: What information technology equipment they have, how often it is used, why they bought it, what advantages and disadvantages they have found. Include other points that you think are useful. Present your results as a report, using the correct layout.

Fatima looked at her desk and frowned. As the new deputy manager of Brotherton's the builders she had just got this memo from her boss and was a little worried:

MEMORANDUM

Memorandum

From: Monica Simms

Date: 17 October 199-

To: Fatima Hussain

Subject: Various

I have to go out for the rest of the week to the Luton branch. Please sort out these odds and ends for me.

1 Get the plans for the Manchester housing estate to the Manchester branch by 18th October.

2 Prepare an agenda for my meeting with Richard Lacey, the Regional Director, and his staff on 25th October. The main item is the review of September's sales figures but he wants it in a proper agenda layout. Don't worry about the figures as they've already been sent; just do the agenda!

3 Write a memo to the new secretary. She has no idea about how to lay out memos and letters. You will have to draw diagrams for her showing her how it is done. You had better write a memo explaining the main points as well.

4 I've booked Archie's bistro (Fountain Street) for the Christmas do! It will cost £10 each and I've arranged it for 20th December as agreed. The do starts at 8.00 p.m. and I need a fiver deposit by 22nd October. Please do a poster for the staff notice board.

5 Richard Lacey is worried about competition. Please look through the Yellow Pages to find out how many other builders there are in the area and what services they are offering, and write a short report on your findings. Early November will do for this.

a) Arrange these tasks into priority order.

b) Complete each task as if you were Fatima Hussain. In the case of task one it is sufficient to say which method of communication you would use and why.

SECTION TWO

Personnel

CHAPTER 3

INTRODUCTION TO PERSONNEL MANAGEMENT

A firm's labour force, staff or personnel is probably its single most important factor of production. In order to make good use of the other factors of production (capital and land), a business must strike the right balance of skilled, semi-skilled and unskilled labour. The country's labour force is over 20 million people. It includes those people, between 16 and 65 years old, who are employed, unemployed or in the armed services. The successful firm needs to be able to select the right people for the jobs it has and ensure that its *employees* – the people who work for the firm – work well and are content. The part of the business which deals with matters relating to the workforce is the personnel department. In some organisations it may be called a different name such as human resource department, manpower section or staffing department.

A personnel manager conducting an interview

The business may have a *centralised* personnel system where a particular part of the firm deals with personnel matters. Some firms have a *decentralised personnel system* where sections of the firm deal with their own personnel matters. Decentralised systems tend to duplicate effort, be inefficient and lack specialist personnel staff and techniques. Whatever name or system is used, each organisation needs to devote some of its efforts to looking after its staffing or personnel needs. This chapter will examine the main work of a typical personnel department.

What does the personnel section do?

The personnel department must link up with the other parts of the organisation and work with them to make sure that the right sort of personnel are being recruited and that they are managed properly. The personnel department will be concerned with all aspects of the workforce including recruitment, training, redundancy, discipline, promotion, welfare, industrial relations and pensions administration. To carry out its work the personnel department draws on legal skills to make sure it meets the requirements of the law. In order to ensure that the workforce is working efficiently and effectively it also uses skills relating to psychology – how individuals think and act – and sociology – how individuals think and act in groups. In order to ensure that employees are as effective as possible, work and rewards need to be organised in a way which helps individuals to meet their own needs, as well as the needs of the firm. The personnel department has an important role in helping to *motivate* or encourage the workforce to work to the best of its ability.

Three important researchers who influence much of the work of the personnel department are Abraham Maslow, Fredrick Hertzberg and Douglas McGregor.

Abraham H. Maslow argued that individuals had a pyramid or hierarchy of needs. They would be happier and so work more effectively the more these needs were met.

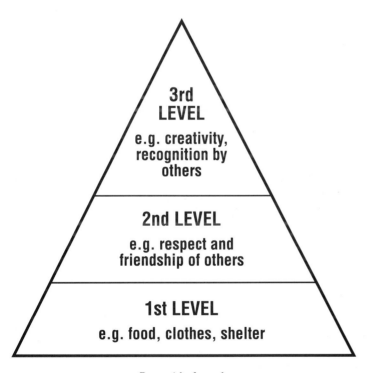

Pyramid of needs

The basic or first level needs of food and shelter are essential before any of the other needs can be met. Social or second level needs, including respect and acknowledgement of family or friends,

Pay is not the only important factor at work

can be met if the firm provides not only suitable financial rewards but a job which is seen to be worthwhile. Personal or third level needs involve status, recognition and responsibility. Promotion and suitable job titles, as well as suitable pay, can help to meet these needs. However, finding individuals' strengths and developing them in a creative way can meet these needs more effectively. We can conclude from Maslow's argument that individual recognition is an important factor in motivating individuals.

This view is supported by the research of Fredrick Hertzberg. He found that working conditions, company policy and wage levels can contribute to people's unhappiness at work. However, even in situations where these things were satisfactory they did not serve to motivate staff to work well. He called these features – working conditions, company policy and wage levels – *hygiene factors*. Hertzberg concluded that no matter how satisfactory these hygiene factors were, other factors were important in motivating workers. Factors such as achievement, recognition, responsibility and the quality of the work itself were more important. If Hertzberg is correct, then these factors need to be built into jobs if workers are to be well motivated. You will notice that these features are similar to the top layer of Maslow's pyramid. From this research we can see that the way in which the workforce is managed is very important.

3.1. Answer the following questions with at least a full sentence, or by writing out the missing words.

1. Explain the term labour force.

2. The personnel department is concerned with all aspects of the workforce including _____, _____, _____, _____, _____, _____, _____ _____ and _____ administration.

3. Name the three levels of need identified by Maslow.

4. According to Hertzberg, which things are more important than pay?

The way in which the workforce is managed has a bearing on how well the employees work. Just as individuals have different ways or styles of playing tennis or dressing, there are different styles of management. Douglas McGregor's research identified two extreme styles of management. These styles were based on the managers' view or theory of their employees' attitudes to work. The two types of manager were called Theory X managers or Theory Y managers according to which of the two theories they agreed with.

- Theory X managers believe that the workers will seek to avoid work and need to be forced or financially encouraged to work hard. In this view money is the main motivator, although insecurity can produce effort. Workers have little interest in the work and prefer to be directed rather than given responsibility. The workforce has limited imagination.

- Theory Y managers believe that people can enjoy work and find it satisfying. Workers can be encouraged to accept responsibility and can be creative and clever. Employees are capable of imposing self-discipline and working in an undirected way to agreed targets. In Theory Y employees are believed to benefit psychologically from the challenges of work.

Theory X and Theory Y can be seen as extreme views, with most managers and supervisors falling in between these extremes according to their beliefs.

Theory X   **Theory Y**

McGregor's styles of management

Research, such as that carried out by Maslow, Hertzberg and McGregor, has led firms and individuals to develop styles of management and has a key role in putting these management styles into practice once employees have been appointed.

We can summarise management styles as being similar to one of the three approaches below:

- Autocratic – In this style of management the manager is the unquestioned boss. Everything which is done has to be approved by him/her and there is little discussion about how the work is organised. Employees work as individuals answering to the boss and there is little encouragement to co-operate with others. This can lead to disagreements. Only the boss's ideas are used. Communication (see page 36) is 'top down'. In other words, the manager gives the orders and instructions and there are limited chances for employees to have their say. This style of management can lead to lack of interest amongst workers and poor quality work because they feel uninvolved in what is going on. This style of management is based on ideas similar to McGregor's Theory X.

- Democratic – The democratic manager allows employees to have a say in how work is organised. Workers belong to a group and are encouraged to co-operate with each other. The employees are given opportunities to make decisions about what they do. Communication is two way. This means that not only do the employees hear what the manager is saying, but the manager also listens to the employees. By allowing staff to participate they feel involved and so are motivated to produce better quality work. There is greater job satisfaction than in the autocratic style of management. Discussion and consideration of workers' views can be time-consuming and so lead to less output than in the autocratic style of management.

- Laissez faire – This French phrase means 'do as you please'. This approach leaves the workers to 'get on with it'. There is almost no supervision. Work is disorganised as the manager will only get involved as a last resort. The lack of leadership means that individuals work on their own and there is no sense of group identity. The amount and quality of work will be variable. Communication will also be disorganised.

Well-managed firms and good managers will not follow one particular style but will use the approach best suited to a given problem or situation.

3.2. Answer the following questions with at least a full sentence, or by writing out the missing words.

2. Name three other management styles.

1. How do Theory X managers differ from Theory Y managers?

3. How do democratic and autocratic managers differ?

Population

We have already said that people are important to the success of a business. This is because people are the *work force* and the *customers* of a business. It is not possible to understand business without having some understanding of population. The total population of the United Kingdom is approximately 56 million people. The population is measured in detail every ten years through a *census* carried out by the government. This takes the form of a questionnaire sent to each home in the country which must, by law, be completed and returned. It is predicted by the government that by the year 2000 the population will be 59–60 million. The size of the population changes because of a combination of three things. These are:

- Deaths. The *death rate* is the number of people who die per thousand. Since 1900 the death rate has dropped because people have lived longer as a result of better healthcare and improvements in conditions at work and at home, and there have been fewer infant deaths. Better quality food and improved sanitation have also played a part.

- Births. The *birth rate* is the number of people who are born per thousand. In 1901 the birth rate was 35.5 whereas now the figure is about a third of this. Once again, improved health care and sanitation are important reasons for this (babies are likely to survive today, so less are born),but other reasons include increased acceptance of contraception and more women going out to work. For example, in 1951 only 22 per cent of married women had jobs outside the home. By 1981 this figure was up to 50 per cent. Changes in the average size of family from five or six children in the early part of this century to less than two children now reflects the drop in the birth rate.

- Migration. This is the difference between those leaving a country *(emigrants)*, and those entering a country *(immigrants)*. Since 1960 the general trend in the United Kingdom has been for migration to be negative. This means that more people have left the country than have entered it. The countries in the European Community (EC) and Africa have been the source of most UK immigrants, while emigrants have headed mainly for the United States and the EC countries.

3.3. Answer the following questions with at least a full sentence, or by writing out the missing words.

1. The _____ takes the form of a questionnaire sent to each home in the country which must, by law, be _____ and _____ .

2. Give two reasons for the drop in the death rate.

3. Give two reasons for the drop in the birth rate.

4. Explain how emigration and immigration differ.

In order to better understand how the population affects business activity, population statistics can be broken down in several ways: the working population, the distribution of the sexes, age, geography and occupation.

The working population

This refers to the number of people working or available for work. It includes the unemployed. The working population is approximately 29 million. This is because people below the age of 16 years and those over retirement age are excluded from the calculation.

The working population and the population as a whole can be broken down into further groupings for the purpose of analysis.

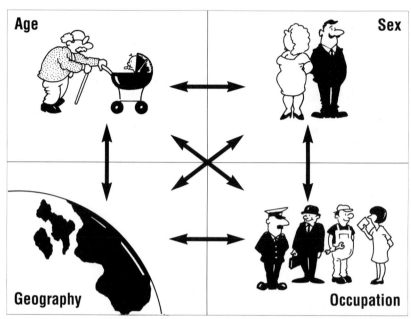

By examining the different parts of the population and how they are distributed we can understand and predict changes in the population

The distribution of the sexes

The relative number of men and women has an effect on the birth rate, and so on the size of the population. As women tend to live longer than men, 77 years on average as opposed to 71 years, there are more women in the population than men. The increasing number of women at work is thought to be due to several factors: changing attitudes towards the role of women in society, the increased use of contraception and more demand for women's skills as the workforce diminishes. The decline of heavy industries and the rise of service industries and electronics industries has also had an affect on the number of women going out to work.

Age

The reduction in the birth rate and death rate mean that the UK population is, on average, getting older. Twenty per cent of the population are over 60 years of age. This has an impact on the future size of the workforce, and demand for goods and services such as housing and health care. If this trend continues it will result in the government having to use the taxes of a relatively small workforce to pay for the pensions and care of an aging population.

Geography

Well over two thirds of the population live in seven major urban areas. From the smallest to the largest, these are:

1 Tyneside

2 Merseyside

3 West Yorkshire

4 Central Clydeside

5 Greater Manchester

6 West Midlands

7 Greater London

The relative size of these areas reflects the fact that for most of this century people have tended to move to the South as the traditional industries of the North (e.g. engineering, shipbuilding and mining) have declined. This movement or *geographical mobility*, has led to several developments. One is concentration in the South, leading to congestion, pollution and strain on facilities, reflected in rising housing costs. Benefits have include the development of leisure facilities to meet the rising population. In the North there has been a decrease in young workers with the right skills and a decline in living standards, relative to the South.

Occupation

A person's occupation refers to the job they do. The three basic categories of employment are primary, secondary, and tertiary (see Chapter One). Throughout this century the proportion of the working population involved in primary industry has been the smallest of the three groups. Currently about three in every 100 employees is involved in the extractive industries (three per cent). Since the 1960s the tertiary sector of production has become the main employer as manufacturing has declined. Roughly two-thirds of all employees are involved in the tertiary sector. As technology develops and consumer tastes change it is likely that employees will undergo several changes of job during their working lives. This *occupational mobility* will require training and changes in attitude to career development.

CHECK THIS OUT

3.4. Answer the following questions with at least a full sentence, or by writing out the missing words.

1. Explain how the age structure of the population has changed.

2. Over two thirds of the population live in ____ major _____ areas.

3. The _____ sector of production has become the main employer as _____ has declined.

Unemployment has become a feature of the twentieth century. In the past twenty years unemployment has risen from two per cent to over twelve per cent. While recent years have seen a drop in unemployment we are, at the time of writing, some way from returning to two per cent. Unemployment in the economy can be classified in three ways:

Frictional unemployment

This refers to the number of people unemployed as a result of changing jobs. They have left one job and are waiting to take up another. They may be hampered by lack of information about other jobs which exist.

Structural unemployment

Unlike frictional unemployment, structural unemployment refers to those unemployed whose skills are not in demand. This can arise as a result of changes in the structure of the economy. For example, the decrease in engineering industries and the rise in service industries affects those with engineering skills. Structural unemployment can only be overcome through geographical or occupational mobility.

Cyclical unemployment

This type of unemployment arises through temporary reductions in the demand for products or services. It is assumed that there will be some fluctuation in demand for goods and services as time passes and that when the increase in demand occurs this sort of unemployment will be reduced.

3.5. Answer the following questions with at least a full sentence, or by writing out the missing words.

1. How do structural and frictional unemployment differ?
2. _____ unemployment arises out of temporary reductions in the demand for ____ or ____ .

It is only by understanding the size and structure of the population that a firm can produce products which are affordable and desired and at the same time recruit and train the right sort of employees for its purpose.

SHORT QUESTIONS

1. How do centralised and decentralised personnel systems differ?

2. Name two skills that are important in personnel work.

3. Describe ways in which a firm can help an individual meet the three levels of need identified by Maslow.

4. Explain what is meant by 'hygiene factors'

5. McGregor identified the Theory ____ and the Theory _____ approach to management.

6. What is meant by a 'laissez faire' approach to management?

7. A disadvantage of democratic management is that it can be _____ .

8. In autocratic organisations communication is _____ .

9. In democratic organisations communication is _____ .

10. Good managers use the approach best ___ to a particular ____ or situation.

STIMULUS RESPONSE QUESTIONS

1. *'All these workers are interested in is money, money, money!' said the angry personnel officer after pay talks had broken down.*

   a) Apart from money, what other factors motivate employees? *(10 marks)*

   b) Explain what style of management might help the personnel officer to find out what motivates the firm's employees. *(10 marks)*

2. *Being in charge of the Research and Development team meant that Nina was responsible for a team of highly qualified and well-motivated staff. The latest book she had read on management styles suggested that an autocratic approach would get the most out of her team.*

   As the Personnel Officer for Nina's company, write a memo to her containing your recommended approach to managing this team of staff. The subject heading should be 'Management Techniques'. *(20 marks)*

LEARN IT YOURSELF

Write a class letter to the personnel manager of a large local company, or to the local branch of the Institute of Personnel Management (see the telephone directory or *Yellow Pages*) and ask if they would be prepared to send a speaker to talk about 'Approaches to Personnel Management in the 1990s'.

ON ASSIGNMENT

Interview twenty people about how their managers or supervisors treat them at work. Find out if they are happy, what is done to encourage them, what sort of rewards are available and how much opportunity they have to progress and to affect what happens where they work. See if you can classify the management styles you find as autocratic, democratic or laissez faire, or whether it is better to find their place on the Theory X/Theory Y diagram. Write up your findings as a formal report.

CASE STUDY

When Robert McKeown looked at the figures for last week's production he was more than worried. They showed that output was down but that the amount of absenteeism was increasing. The amount of damaged equipment and the faulty goods gave him the impression that nobody really cared about what was happening any more. It had been a happy section until the new manager had been appointed. He was well-qualified in engineering and his references from the army were very good, but the staff here didn't like his approach. As one of the mechanics had said 'The new bloke won't let anybody else get a word in, and when they do they're always wrong according to him. If you argue he tells you not to be rude and refuses to take any other ideas into consideration'.

As the new manager's boss he knew he had to do something, but what?

a) What style of management has the new manager introduced?

b) What style of management do the staff seem to have been used to?

c) As Robert McKeown, write a memo to Bill Sanders the new manager.

Explain why you are worried about his style of management and what changes you would like to see.

CHAPTER 4
RECRUITMENT AND SELECTION

As we have seen, it is very important that firms choose the staff which suit their needs. A firm with the best equipment, products and premises will not be successful unless it employs people who can make the best use of its resources. For this reason the selection of staff is very important and an activity which takes up a great deal of time for the average personnel department. We can divide the recruitment and selection process into several key stages:

Evaluation

Before a firm fills a vacancy it has to make sure that it needs to be filled. New, more advanced equipment might, for example, mean that individuals with different qualifications are needed. If there have been improvements in efficiency the post can be left unfilled without affecting production. It may be that a *part-time* appointment is sufficient. This means that the person is employed for only part of the working week, and paid accordingly. A *full-time* employee works for the full working week. The personnel department needs to work with the section of the firm which is seeking to fill the vacancy to establish how and if the post should be filled. Part of the evaluation might consist of an *exit interview*; in other words, a discussion with the employee who is leaving to find their views about the needs of the job. Once the personnel department and the section's manager or supervisor have completed this evaluation and decided to fill the vacancy the recruitment process can start.

Job description

If it is agreed that the post should be filled, a list of the main duties will be prepared, together with other information, such as who the post holder will be responsible to and where they will work. This information is a job description and can take many different forms according to the type of job and the firm concerned. Job descriptions can be written using information from the previous post holder, the section manager, and direct observation of the job in question. Different types of job involve different pay and working conditions. This means that trade unions (see page 89) may be involved in the process of arriving at a job description. This ensures that the rate of pay for the job is agreed.

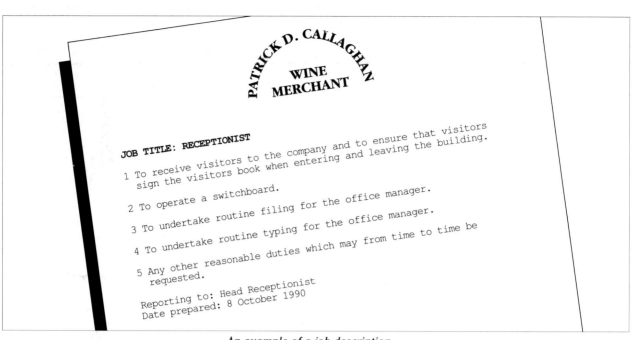

An example of a job description

Job specification

The personnel department will help to identify what sort of skills, qualifications and experience are required in order for the job to be done well. This information is called a *job specification* or *person specification*. The job specification is used to judge the suitability of applicants (those applying for the job) during the process of selection. A job specification for a typist might require that applicants can type at 45 words per minute while a requirement for a porter might be that they have good health and can lift heavy objects.

An example of a job specification

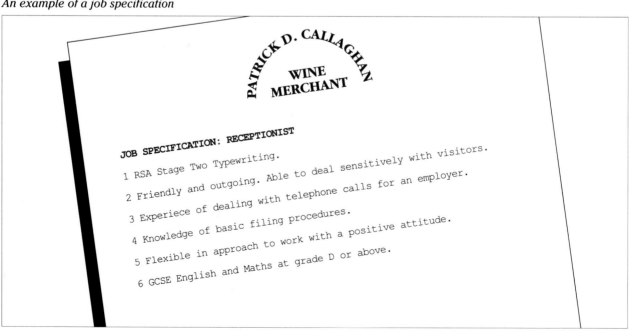

4.1. Answer the following questions with at least a full sentence, or by writing out the missing words.

2. What is a job description?

3. How might a job description be arrived at?

1. Why might a firm choose not to fill a vacancy?

4. A job specification is used to judge the _____ of applicants.

Attracting applications

Newspaper advertisements, employment agencies, job centres and school or college careers services are all used by firms to draw the attention of members of the public to vacancies. In some cases – perhaps in the case of posts above the firm's basic pay grades – people already working for the firm might be encouraged to apply, and the position might only be advertised inside the firm. This is called *internal advertising*. Most vacancies are filled by advertising in newspapers or magazines. The job's level of responsibility, skills and pay involved will affect how it is advertised. For example, un-skilled jobs may be advertised in local newspapers when the firm knows that locally there is a plentiful supply of suitable applicants. More skilled or highly-specialised jobs might be advertised in na-tional newspapers or specialist magazines, in order to attract as many people as possible. For example, the newspaper *Computer Weekly* carries advertisements for jobs working with computers.

54

EMPLOYMENT

116 SITUATIONS GENERAL

TELE-SALES

Amongst the best telesales opportunities available in Manchester

£350 +

Each and every week, made up of basic, commission and bonus

Bright, articulate and assertive people will enjoy well above average income and pleasant working conditions.

EXPERIENCE NOT ESSENTIAL

Phone now:

061 839 1234

Mr John Smith

A-Z CARRIERS LIMITED

Requires

Two Exp HGV Fitters

For their busy workshop

EXPERIENCED

CHARGE HAND CABINET MAKER

Ace Displays Ltd

061 680 2144

Contact Mr East or Mr Varney

International Security Company

Requires full & part time

SECURITY OFFICERS CONTROLLERS & SUPERVISORS

To be situated in the Manchester area. Good rates of pay and uniform provided.

Ring 061 905 2145

Leading international courier company require

SALES ASSISTANTS

RDV STOCKPORT

Urgently require

HGV DRIVERS
WAREHOUSE STAFF
FLT DRIVERS
PACKERS

(Male/Female – suit students)

For local contracts . Excellent rates

Tel JACKIE

061 422 1248 (Agy)

SUPERDRIVE PLC

Is driving your profession? Do you like variety and not routine? If so why not try SUPERDRIVE PLC?

We need:

EXPERIENCED HGV and 7.5t DRIVERS IMMEDIATELY

Usually the advertisement will give the name of the firm, a description of the main duties of the post, information about pay, and how to find out further details. It is usual to indicate the closing date for applications. The Sex Discrimination Act, 1975 makes it illegal to treat one person more favourably than another on the grounds of their sex. Job advertisements can only ask for a specific sex if there is a legitimate reason or *genuine occupational qualification* (GOQ) as it is called. For example, a woman might be needed to supervise a residential home for elderly women and a man required to model male clothes. In other words, an employer can only discriminate against a sex for reasons of decency or where features typical of only one sex are required. It is illegal to discriminate on the grounds that customers prefer staff of one sex. For example, public houses and clubs can no longer legally advertise for barmaids. The Sex Discrimination Act also rules that it is illegal to pay men and women different rates of pay for work of a similar nature. If someone believes that they have been discriminated against on the grounds of their sex, they may seek help from a trade union, solicitor, Citizen's Advice Bureau (CAB) or the Equal Opportunities Commission (EOC), (see page 97).

The Race Relations Act, 1976 makes it illegal to discriminate on grounds of race. Refusing someone a job on the grounds of their race is called *direct discrimination*. The 1976 act makes it illegal to lay down conditions which are not necessary to do the job but might discriminate against someone of a particular racial group. This is called *indirect discrimination*. For example, a job in which a person works mainly on their own with little need to communicate with others cannot legally be advertised as a job requiring a good command of English. It is possible to require certain racial characteristics in particular circumstances. For example, a Chinese restaurant can advertise for a Chinese waiter. If someone believes that they have been racially discriminated against, they may seek help from a trade union, Citizen's Advice Bureau (CAB), solicitor or the Commission for Racial Equality (CRE), (see page 97).

The owner of a business is legally responsible if his/her staff discriminate on grounds of race or sex. This is because the employee who discriminates is legally acting on their behalf, even if the employer does not know about it. Discrimination in this way is called *vicarious discrimination*.

Applications for the job

Those people who request details of the post will normally receive a job description, an application form, and some background information about the organisation offering the job. Most firms request applicants to complete an *application form* giving details of their employment and educational record, date of birth, name and address and other information the firm will need to consider the application. Applicants will often be asked to write a *letter of application* which should say why they want the job, why they think they could do the job and their ideas about doing the job. Often this letter is part of the application form. The applicant must provide all the information requested and follow any instructions given in the application form (for example, to complete it in black ink or to type the answers).

CURRICULUM VITAE

Name: Jennifer White

Date of Birth: 31st October 1975

Address: 41 Gresty Crescent
CREWE Cheshire CW1 1DU

Telephone: 34567

School Attended: John Partington Comprehensive
Littlehampton Road CREWE CW3 5TT

Date of leaving: June 1991

Examination Results:
GCSE Business Studies A
GCSE English Language C
GCSE Biology D
GCSE French D

Hobbies: Gymnastics - I represented my school for three years.
Music - I sang in the school choir.

Previous Experience: I worked as a Saturday Sales Assistant in a shoe shop for two years.

Referees
Mr H Tomlinson
Headteacher
John Partington Comprehensive
Littlehampton Road
CREWE CW3 5TT

Ms J Brady
Manageress
Tite Fit Shoe Shop
Market Street
CREWE CW4 6KK

APPLICATION FORM

PATRICK D. CALLAGHAN WINE MERCHANT

Please complete this form in black ink or type.

Post applied for: _____

Name: _____

Address: _____

Telephone No: _____

School/College attended	Dates	Qualifications and grades

Previous employers and addresses	Start date	Leave date	Salary	Duties	Reason for leaving

Please give details of any hobbies or interests.

Please give the name and address of two referees. One should be your current or most recent employer.

Please add any other points to support your application in a covering letter.

Where did you see this post advertised? _____

I declare that the information given in this application is accurate.

Signed: _____ Date: _____

A CV can be laid out in a number of ways but it is important that it is neatly typed and contains relevant information.

Sometimes firms will not provide an application form and instead ask applicants to write a letter of application and provide a *curriculum vitae*. A curriculum vitae, or CV as it is sometimes called, is a summary of a person's employment and educational record. It should contain most of the information usually requested on an application form, but it is laid out according to the applicant's preference. Whichever method is used to provide information, the applicant must follow the instructions of the firm offering the job, particularly the closing date for receiving applications.

3. What is meant by genuine occupational qualification?

1. Name four ways in which a vacancy can be drawn to the attention of the public

4. Laying down unnecessary conditions which discriminate is called ____ ____ .

2. Advertising inside the firm only is called ____ ____ .

5. Explain the difference between a CV and an application form.

The selection process

Once the closing date for applications has been reached, the selection process starts. The personnel section works with the department which has the vacancy. The first stage of selection is *short-listing*. The purpose of short-listing is to decide who to interview (to include on a short list), and who to reject. At the short-listing stage the people involved in the selection process examine the applications and compare them to the job specification. Some organisations will grade each application against each point in the job specification while others will give an overall grade or make a decision to interview based on the overall quality of the application in relation to the job specification. Those applicants whose application meets the requirements of the job specification are then invited for interview.

The interview

The interview is really just a conversation between the applicant and the firm's representatives in which they find out more about each other. This helps them to decide if they are suitable for each other. It will not feel like this at the time of the interview for the person being interviewed! Because interviews can be stressful it is important that both the applicant and the interviewer are well prepared. Applicants should:

- Arrive a few minutes early. Check bus and train times well in advance.
- Dress comfortably but smartly.
- Find out as much as they can about the organisation before going for interview. This will help them to understand what is said and to ask sensible questions.
- Have some questions about the job and the firm in mind. This shows that they have taken the trouble to prepare for the interview.

- Try to anticipate some of the questions. They can then prepare better answers. Applicants should avoid answering with only a 'yes' or a 'no' and give detailed answers if possible. They should say if they do not understand a question.

- Mind their manners! They must be polite, shake hands, wait to be invited to sit down and not smoke unless invited to.

Interviewers should:

- Make sure that they have read the application forms in advance of the interview.

- Prepare a list of questions relevant to the job which an applicant can reasonably be expected to answer.

- Put the applicant at their ease. Interviewers should avoid being aggressive, encourage the applicant to answer each of the questions fully and should not interrupt an answer. They should also make sure that the interview is not interrupted by other business.

- Make sure that questions are answered and not avoided.

- Take notes of the applicant's answers for later consideration.

- Allow sufficient time for the interview to find out all the relevant facts. The other applicants should not be kept waiting.

On the day of the interview, interviewees are often shown around the building where the successful applicant will work. This provides a chance for the applicants to meet some of the people who work there. This informal 'guided tour' allows firm and applicant to make judgements about each other in a way which would not be possible at the interview.

Jobs requiring particular skills might involve a test in addition to the interview. Typists, for example, might have to type a piece of work to show how fast and accurate their typing is. Would-be bus conductors might complete a maths test to demonstrate their ability to calculate fares and give the right change. Some firms use personality assessment for certain types of jobs. For example, organisations which sell pensions and insurance might require individuals being considered for jobs in the sales force to complete a questionnaire. This test, written by psychologists, asks questions about a person's attitudes and ambitions which help the firm to judge their suitability for a job involving selling.

Most application forms will ask the applicant to name at least two *referees*. A referee is someone who will be prepared to write to the employer giving details about an applicant. Employers might expect to be told about the applicant's appearance, reliability, time-keeping, politeness, and any particular skills the applicant might have. This information is called a *reference*. Sometimes potential employers ask referees to write a letter about you, sometimes they list questions they would like the referee to answer. The way in which references are used varies from firm to firm. Some firms will use references to decide who to interview, some will decide who to interview and then ask for the references and some do not use references until after the job has been offered.

Typists might be asked to take a typing test

In this situation the references are used to check that the applicant was telling the truth. If the applicant lied, the job offer can be withdrawn. An advantage of this use of references is that, unlike the other methods, applicants cannot be held back if a referee provides a reference biased against the applicant for reasons unconnected with their ability to do the job. This is very important as most firms will expect you to use your previous employer as a referee and will be most suspicious if you do not do so. Other referees might be a school teacher, college lecturer, vicar, priest, imam, rabbi, youth club leader, scout or guide leader, Saturday or part-time job employer. Close relatives should not be used as referees because employers will expect them to give a biased reference!

Once the interview and any tests are completed, the firm is able to make a decision about who should be offered the job. If none of the applicants did very well in the interview and did not meet the job specification the firm might decide not to offer anyone the job and start the recruitment process again. Usually a suitable applicant will be chosen and offered the job. Depending on the firm and the sort of job involved the offer may be made in a letter or telephone call some time after the interview, or the offer may be made at the interview. The person offered the job will accept or reject the offer. If the offer is rejected the next suitable applicant may be offered the job, or the firm may choose to advertise again. If the offer is accepted the person will start the job at a time suitable to the firm. If the person offered the job is already in employment they will have to resign from that job and work their *notice*. This means the period of time between resignation and actually leaving. This allows time for the firm they are leaving to find a suitable replacement. Notice periods can be anything from a week to a month or even longer, depending on the sort of job involved.

4.3. Answer the following questions with at least a full sentence, or by writing out the missing words.

3. Name two things that a person conducting an interview should try to do.

1. What is the first stage of selecting an employee?

4. What is a referee for a job?

2. Name two things that a person being interviewed should try to do.

5. The time between resigning from one job and starting another is called the _____ of _____ .

SHORT QUESTIONS

1. How does a job description differ from a job specification?

2. What three factors affect where a job is advertised?

3. What is the purpose of the Sex Discrimination Act, 1975?

4. What is the purpose of the Race Relations Act, 1976?

5. Explain what is meant by shortlisting.

6. Describe the purpose of the selection interview.

7. Why should you find out about an organisation before being interviewed?

8. Why does it help interviewers to take notes at an interview?

9. Describe the sort of information a referee will provide.

10. What is the purpose of notice periods?

STIMULUS RESPONSE QUESTIONS

1. *As the youth club committee meeting came to a close Michelle said to Norman, the secretary, 'Please make sure you get the advertisement for the new full-time youth worker into the newspaper by next week'.*

   a) What sort of information should the advertisement for the new youth worker contain? *(10 marks)*

   b) Would it be better to advertise the job in national or local newspapers? Why? *(10 marks)*

2. Look at the memorandum opposite.

   a) If you were the personnel officer what would you do to find an answer to the problem? *(5 marks)*

   b) Explain why this job should be advertised either locally or nationally. *(5 marks)*

   c) What skills and personal qualities would you look for in applicants for this job? *(5 marks)*

   d) Explain how sex and race discrimination laws will affect the filling of this post. *(5 marks)*

MEMORANDUM

From: Office Manager

Date: 12 June 199–

To: Personnel Officer

Subject: New Typist

I think we need a new typist in the sales section as Mandy is leaving. Now that we have the word processing system I find it hard to tell if the new person should be full-time or part-time or if we don't really need a replacement for Mandy. Can you please help?

LEARN IT YOURSELF

1. Collect ten job advertisements for school or college leavers. List the features that the advertisements have in common.

2. As a group contact the Commission for Racial Equality and/or the Equal Opportunities Commission. Mount a wall display about their work.

3. Collect advertisements for jobs you might be interested in and obtain the application forms and job descriptions. Compare them and note anything you might have to do to improve your chances of being shortlisted for this sort of job.

4. Visit your local Job Centre and note the details of 20 jobs you see. Write a report of your findings, including the average wage, hours to be worked, types of job available etc. Find out what services the Job Centre offers to employers wishing to fill vacancies.

5. Write a CV for yourself. It should give details of name, address, age, qualifications, hobbies, spare time jobs and any other relevant information. Arrange for it to be typed or word processed.

ON ASSIGNMENT

In groups, contact local firms and ask if they will help you collect information about the way in which they recruit employees. Find out if they rely on interviews or if they use any other sorts of tests. If so, what sort of tests are they? Who is involved in the interviewing process, and what sort of approach do they use for selection? See if you can find out the sorts of vacancies they have, what qualifications they require, what rates of pay and training opportunities are offered to new staff. You could entitle your assignment 'An investigation into the recruitment policy of ___ PLC'. Present your findings in a suitably organised folder.

CASE STUDY

The Union had complained three times now to Owen Evans the Personnel Director of Clark's Textiles PLC. The basis of the complaint was that every time the works manager, George Anderson, interviewed staff for jobs he left them frustrated, angry and upset. He did not seem to take notes,

interrupted the applicants and did not tell them anything about the job. Those appointments he had made had proved to be unsuitable as either the people were too well-qualified and left as soon as something better came along, or were not qualified enough and were inefficient and cost a fortune to train. Owen had just found out that there was no job description or job specification for the last person George had appointed! The job before that had not been advertised and went to someone George had met in a pub. When he tackled George about the situation he was told that as George had ten year's experience he had no need of 'all the paper work and the fancy procedures' and he knew a good man when he saw one. In any case, George had added, nobody had ever told him how to go about it so how was he to know what to do?

a) Why should Owen Evans get involved? In what ways is the firm likely to suffer because of George Anderson's approach?

b) Owen decides to write to Anderson about ways in which he should improve his appointment of staff. Draft the memo on behalf of Owen.

c) Draw a flow chart showing the procedure for appointment to accompany the memo.

d) Do you think that Owen should take some blame for the situation?

Starting work

Most firms arrange an introduction or induction for new employees. The purpose of the induction is to help new employees get used to the firm and its procedures. The length of the induction period will vary. In some firms the induction programme might last only a morning, in others it might last a week. During the course of induction the new employee will normally find out about routine matters such as meal break times, company rules and what goods or services the firm provides. Many organisations will provide new employees with a booklet describing the work of the business and outlining rules and procedures. It is usual in large businesses for the employee to be told how he or she fits into the whole organisation and what their section of the organisation does. ICI, for example, is a very large chemicals firm organised into several divisions dealing with different products such as pharmaceuticals or dyes. New employees will find out what their division does and how it relates to other divisions.

Other matters covered in the induction period might be health and safety regulations and an introduction to the trade unions in the firm. A firm's induction programme will usually involve visits to different parts of the firm, as well as talks and lectures. Although most conditions of employment will have been agreed before the employee started work the law (Employment Protection Act, 1978) requires that an employer issues a contract of employment to new employees within 13 weeks of them starting work. The contract must outline:

- The rate of pay for the job in question and how payment is to be made (i.e. weekly or monthly, in cash or direct to a bank)
- Hours to be worked
- Holiday arrangements and entitlement
- Arrangements for sick pay
- Length of notice to be worked
- Job title
- Grievance procedure – in other words, what the employee is entitled to do if he or she feels unfairly treated.

Clearly, one of the most important aspects of a job is the pay. As we saw in Chapter 1, wages are paid weekly and salaries are paid monthly. An employee's pay can be calculated in several ways:

Time rate - In this system, employees are paid according to the hours they work at so much per hour. If the employee works more than the normal working week then he or she is paid for the extra hours at a higher hourly rate called *overtime*. A firm may employ someone for a basic 35 hour week at £2.00 per hour. If the person works late and does a 38 hour week, they are paid at the overtime rate for the three extra hours. If the overtime rate is 'double time' the employee receives double the hourly rate for the hours worked over the usual working week. In this example they will receive £4.00 per hour (i.e. double £2.00 per hour) for three hours overtime. This will give overtime, pay of £12.00. Instead of paying overtime, some firms have a system of giving staff time off work equal to the amount of overtime worked. This is known as *time off in lieu*. Organisations which have a time-rate system have a method of recording the hours worked. This may involve *clocking in* where a time-keeping machine stamps the time on an employee's clocking-in card, or *signing in* a book to show the time of arrival and departure from work. As the time-rate system pays employees for the hours they work there is no financial encouragement for them to produce work quickly or to a higher standard. This lack of encouragement or incentive is a disadvantage from the employer's point of view. An advantage of the system is that it is fairly simple and cheap to operate.

Piece rate - Under a piece-rate system workers are paid for each piece of work they do. For example, machinists in a factory producing jeans will be paid for each pair of jeans they sew together to an acceptable standard. As long as the employee meets minimum standards of output (i.e. so many pairs of jeans to an acceptable standard each day), the amount of time taken is of limited importance. The piece-rate system is designed to encourage employees to produce as much as possible in the time available, and so overcome some of the problems of the time-rate system. It is more complicated to organise as each worker's output has to be monitored to ensure that work is of an acceptable standard and that each worker is paid in relation to what he or she produces. Under this system workers are often paid a *bonus* once they produce more than certain target levels. Bonus payments are greater than

Payslip

Staff No.	123456				
Name	J R Smith				
			Period	Week 31 02.11.90	
Nat. Ins. No. AB001234B				Deductions	3.62
					4.75
Tax and Pay Year to Date	Employee's Contributions	Gross Pay and additions		NATL INS 70.00	
Code No.	National Insurance	Basic Hours 35.00		P.A.Y.E. Tax 6.00	
300L	133.80	O/T Hours 3.00			
	Tax Free Pay	@ x 2			
Gross Pay	1793.00				
2176.00					8.37
Taxable pay				Total Deductions	
383.00				76.00	
Tax		Gross Pay	8.37	Company Name	
95.75		Total Deductions	67.63	ANY COMPANY LTD	
		Net Pay			

the basic piece rate and are intended to encourage the employees to meet targets so that they can then be paid at the higher rate.

Sometimes a bonus is used in the time-rate system to encourage hourly-paid workers to meet production targets. This is intended to overcome the lack of incentive to produce at maximum output.

Commission - If you have a friend or relative who runs a catalogue such as Avon, Janet Fraser or John Moore you may have heard them talk of the commission they receive. The commission is their payment for selling goods. The amount of commission is worked out according to the value of the goods sold. A commission of ten per cent means that the person running the catalogue gets ten per cent of the value of the sales they make. For example, if they sell goods to the value of £10.00 they will receive £1.00 commission.

Insurance sales people are paid commission according to the value of the financial services they sell. They are one example of a group of people who do not receive payment according to a time rate. Individuals who work on this *commission only* basis are similar to piece rate workers - what they earn depends on how successful they are. Commission payments are usually used to pay staff involved in selling a firm's goods or services. From the employer's point of view commission-only systems encourage hard work, while the employee has the prospect of unlimited earnings - if they are successful! Commission payments have to be carefully monitored in order to ensure that each employee receives the correct payment.

Mixed systems - It is not unusual to find organisations using combinations of the payment systems we have looked at. For example, employees in a department store could be paid on a time-rate basis but also receive commission on sales made. The percentage commission will be less than for someone working on a commission-only basis. Similarly, employers might choose to use a combination of time-rate and piece-work systems in certain industries.

5.1. Answer the following questions with at least a full sentence, or by writing out the missing words.

3. Name four things the contract of employment should state.

4. A payment system based on the hours worked is called ____ ____.

5. ____ ____ is a pay system based on what a person produces.

6. Payment based on the value of sales is called ____ .

1. The ___ helps new employees get used to the firm.

2. A contract of employment should be issued within ___ weeks.

See note 1-3

1 Income from trade, profession or vocation
6 April 1989 to 5 April 1990

Business name and address	Type of trade, etc.	Amount for year
		£
	Enterprise allowance	
	Balancing charges	
4	Deductions for Capital Allowances	

5-9   **2 Income from employment etc.: 6 April 1989 to 5 April 1990**

Income received for duties performed wholly in the UK including fees, bonus, commission, tips benefits, expenses, leaving payments and compensation.

Occupation and employers name(s) and address(es)	Amount for year
	£

Income received in respect of duties performed wholly or partly abroad

Employment concerned	Amount for year
	£

Dates absent from UK when working abroad. Enclose statement if necessary.

To claim dedn. enter an "X" here ☐

10-12   **3 Other Income: 6 April 1989 to 5 April 1990**

Property in the UK
* delete as appropriate

	Address	Gross income including premiums	Expenses (enclose statement)	Amount for year
*Unfurnished lettings *Furnished lettings *Furnished holiday lettings *Ground rents or Feu duties *Land				£

2

The first page of Income Tax form (P1)

The employer is required to deduct income tax from the employee's pay under the PAYE system (Pay As You Earn). This system avoids the employee having to pay tax in a lump sum each year. The amount of tax to be paid is indicated by the employee's tax code which shows how much they are allowed to earn without paying tax. This figure is based on the previous year's income, which is declared when a person fills in the P1 or income tax return. The P1 also outlines any financial commitments. The P2 is sent to an employee by the Inland Revenue, who deal with income tax for the government, notifying the person of their tax code (see page 223). At the end of each tax year (April 5th), the employee receives a P60 from the Inland Revenue which shows the total earnings for the year (the employer notifies the Inland Revenue of this), and the amount of tax deducted. This should be carefully checked in case there has been a miscalculation and too much or too little tax has been paid. On changing jobs or being dismissed the employee will receive a P45 which sums up the earnings and tax paid during the current financial year.

In addition to the pay an employee receives there may be other benefits provided by the firm. These benefits are known as *fringe benefits* or *perks*. They are rewards for employees in addition to any bonuses they receive. Common benefits include a staff canteen, company car, luncheon vouchers, sports or recreation facilities and discount on purchases of the firm's goods. Medical insurance and opportunities to buy shares in the firm at a reduced price are further examples of employee benefits. In some firms employees have to have been with the firm for a certain length of time before qualifying for fringe benefits. For example, bank employees may have to work at the bank for a minimum of one year before being allowed to borrow money at a reduced rate of interest.

Hours of work are an important consideration when starting a new job. Most firms will lay down the starting and finishing times, for example 8.30 a.m. to 4.30 p.m., with tea and lunch breaks at fixed times. An increasing number of firms are moving away from this *fixed-time* system to a system of *flexitime*. Flexitime means 'flexible time'. In a flexitime system, workers can start and finish work when they wish as long as they complete a certain number of hours per week or month. There are variations on the flexitime system but most require the worker to be in work between certain times, for example 10.30 a.m. and 3.00 p.m. This time is called the *core time*. From the employee's point of view this system has many attractions. It gives more freedom to organise things like collecting children from school, attending meetings, going shopping etc. Most flexitime systems allow employees to work more than the required number of hours in a particular week or month and have the time off in lieu at a later date. This increases the individual's control over their private life. If an employee works *less* than the required hours the time has to be made up the following week or month. Although flexitime can be difficult to organise from an employer's point of view it can lead to a happier workforce, working more efficiently at the times which suit them best. Flexitime is not suitable for all jobs, but jobs such as clerical work which involve limited contact with the public and other workers are well-suited to the system. Jobs involving frequent contact with other people (such as teaching) could not be done efficiently under a flexitime system as pupils would not be certain when teachers were available to teach them.

Manufacturing industries often use a shift system. This means one team of workers starts work as another finishes. Using equipment more or less continuously is more cost effective from the firm's point of view. Shift work gives employees free time during the day, but some people find a night shift unpleasant. An *unsocial hours* payment is often made for shifts done outside the normal working day.

With flexitime you might choose to start work very early

5.2. Answer the following questions with at least a full sentence, or by writing out the missing words.

1. What is the difference between the P45 and the P60?

2. What does PAYE stand for?

3. Extra rewards for employees, in addition to pay, are called _____ .

4. Explain what flexitime is.

5. Why would an employee receive an unsocial hours payment?

The *grievance procedure* of a firm is the agreed way in which an employee can resolve disagreements with a manager or workmate. It is normally an agreement made between the employer and the trade union in a particular place of work.

If the employee's work or behaviour gives cause for concern then the *disciplinary procedure* will be used. This is the method agreed between union and management for dealing with employees who are thought to have broken the firm's rules. Ensuring that workers are well paid, well trained, motivated and suitable for the jobs they have been given is important in reducing the number of times a firm has to use the disciplinary procedure. Disciplinary arrangements vary from firm to firm but usually if an employee breaks a rule (for example, poor time-keeping, not following correct procedures), then they will receive a verbal warning. If there is no improvement a written warning may be given. These warnings indicate that unless there is an improvement the employee might be suspended from work or dismissed. If there is no improvement after two or three written warnings the employee will be invited to explain their behaviour to a senior manager who will have the power to dismiss or suspend the employee. At this type of hearing the employee usually has the right to be accompanied by a trade union representative who will help the employee to put their case forward. In serious cases, such as theft or drunkenness, employees can be dismissed without warning, although there is usually an opportunity to appeal against the decision at a hearing like the one just described.

5.3. Answer the following questions with at least a full sentence, or by writing out the missing words.

1. Explain what a firm's grievance procedure is.

2. What is the disciplinary procedure?

Employee training and development

Successful businesses develop their goods and services so that customers' demands are anticipated and satisfied. To be able to develop goods and services it is important that a firm's employees are kept up to date with changes and developments which affect their careers. This not only benefits the firm but also the employees' future job prospects. The personnel department is involved in the process of staff development.

Training is a major part of the staff development process. Training can be of two basic types:

■   On the job. This is where the employee learns new skills while at work. Usually this sort of training will involve the trainee watching someone carrying out the work they have to learn to do and then copying them. This sort of training provides the chance to discuss work with other employees. On-the-job training has the advantage of being cheaper to provide than other sorts of training because production is not disrupted as it would be if the employee went outside the firm to learn new skills. A disadvantage of on-the-job training is that the product being produced by the trainee might, at least at first, be sub-standard or result in high amounts of wastage. On-the-job trainers might not be particularly skilled unless they have had training in how to teach others.

On-the-job training

■ Off the job. Employees develop new skills by being taken out of work, perhaps to a college or the firm's training centre. Off-the-job training allows the trainee to develop skills and knowledge without the distractions of work. It is usually carried out with specialist staff who can provide more detailed knowledge about the work being done. This sort of training can be expensive as specialist staff salaries have to be paid and the production rate goes down while the employee is away from work. Off-the-job training is commonly organised on a *day release* basis or a *block release* basis. Day release trainees are released from work one day a week for their training while block release trainees might be trained for days or weeks at a time before going back to work. Some employees have off-the-job training at night classes organised by colleges in the area where they live.

A firm's decision to use on or off-the-job training will be affected by details such as cost, the type of work involved, the sort of skills which have to be learned and other practical details. In all cases a firm's decision about training will be guided by the contribution training makes to improving the firm's future prospects. Most young or junior staff will be expected to undergo some sort of training when they start work. Many school leavers will have their training provided by the Youth Training scheme (YT). This is a two-year training scheme run by a government organisation called the Training Agency. YT for 17-year-olds lasts one year. All 16 and 17-year-olds are guaranteed a place on YT. The Training Agency pays employers, local councils and private training organisations to provide work experience and training. These organisations are known as *managing agents*. The trainee is paid a weekly training allowance and, in approved cases, help is given with travelling expenses.

Before YT was introduced many employers provided *apprenticeships*. An apprentice was trained for a particular job, for example an apprentice welder. The apprenticeship system involved the employer in paying all the costs of an apprentice's training while the apprentice became qualified in a particular job. YT has tended to replace the apprenticeship system as the government meets the cost of training and trainees gain an introduction to a wider range of skills.

The Training Agency also runs the Employment Training scheme (ET). This is a scheme designed to help unemployed adults develop new skills and find a suitable job. Like YT, ET pays a training allowance and gives help with travel costs. There will also be help with the costs of child care. ET is intended to be tailored to the individual's needs and can last up to a year. Restart is another adult training scheme organised by the Training Agency. It is aimed at the long-term unemployed. Restart aims to give the unemployed the necessary basic skills to find work.

5.4. Answer the following questions with at least a full sentence, or by writing out the missing words.

1. What is the difference between on-the-job and off-the-job training?

2. What is the difference between block release and day release?

3. Name three factors which will affect the decision to use on or off-the-job training.

4. What is the YT scheme?

5. What other schemes does the Training Agency run?

Training is not the only way of improving the performance of staff. Some organisations use a system of *appraisal*. This means that employees' standards of work are discussed and assessed by the employee and his/her manager. The aim of appraisal is to help the workers improve in their jobs, to the benefit of both firm and worker. There are different methods of appraisal but they have several features in common. The employee might fill in a questionnaire before the appraisal interview. The questionnaire then becomes the starting point of the discussion. Points dealt with in any appraisal system might include how well the employee works with others, what they think their strengths and weaknesses are, what their career ambitions are and any ideas they have for improving the way their part of the firm works. It is usual for the manager to write a report of the discussion. Sometimes this report is read by the employee, who checks that it is an accurate record of what was discussed. The report is placed on the employee's file and can be the starting point for discussion at the next appraisal interview, when any developments and improvements in the employee's work can be discussed. The appraisal report will usually summarise the discussion between the manager and the employee and will list any goals that were agreed, for example the employee might agree to try to improve their timekeeping and the manager to organise a place on a training course. In some organisations the appraisal report will be taken into account when considering employees for promotion or salary increases.

An appraisal interview

Appraisal interviews usually take place annually but a good manager will regularly review the work of his/her staff in order to anticipate any problems. The advantage of appraisal interviewing is that it allows managers and employees to discuss, in a constructive way, any problems the employee might be having and allows the employee to put forward ideas and suggestions. Such discussions can create a good working atmosphere, thus ensuring that the organisation is working as well as possible. A disadvantage of appraisal interviews is that they are time-consuming, usually lasting at least half an hour, and take the manager and employee away from other work.

Another way of developing employees' skills is *job rotation*. This means that workers regularly swap jobs with other people in their section. Job rotation can prevent boredom, and helps the employee to understand how other parts of the organisation work. This makes them feel more involved with the firm as they can understand how their work fits in with what other people in the firm do. It leads to a more flexible workforce as individuals are capable of doing several different jobs. Being able to do several jobs means that the employee has a wider range of skills to offer should they choose to seek promotion or work for a different firm.

Job enrichment is where employees are given more responsibility for their own work. They can be left to organise many aspects of their job without having to refer to managers or supervisors. Not only does this make the work more personally rewarding but it also increases the skills employees have, which benefits the business.

Job satisfaction and employee development can increase with *job enlargement*. This means that employees are given more to do but at a similar level of responsibility and difficulty. The wider range of tasks can make a job more interesting and challenging.

5.5. Answer the following questions with at least a full sentence, or by writing out the missing words.

1. What is appraisal?

2. What is the appraisal report used for?

3. Explain what is meant by job rotation.

4. _____ _____ is where employees are given more responsibility for their own work.

5. Job enlargement is where employees are given more to do at the same level of _____ and _____ .

1. Describe some of the things which might be covered during the induction of a new employee.

2. What details should be included in a contract of employment?

3. What are the advantages to the firm of paying workers on a piece-work basis?

4. How does double time differ from time off in lieu?

5. Give three examples of perks.

6. What does the Inland Revenue do?

7. Describe the advantages of flexitime.

8. In what ways is off-the-job training better than on-the-job training?

9. What is the difference between job enlargement and job enrichment?

10. Why might job rotation be introduced?

1. *Town Hall chiefs threatened by a staffing crisis, want to introduce a lucrative 'perks' package.*
   They claim that Stockport Council is not only losing staff to the private sector, but to other neighbouring authorities because pay levels are so low.
   The problem is not just confined to the top ranks, promising

youngsters are also becoming harder to attract.

Town Hall bosses fear that unless something is done quickly, vital services like education and social services could suffer.

Now with the backing of the council's personnel sub-committee, a package of proposals have been drawn up designed to stop the brain drain.

They include pay rises and a car leasing scheme for the high-flying principal officers. There would also be better re-location allowances, interest-free car loans, mortgage subsidies, creches and short-term salary increases for hard-to-fill posts.

Councillors also want to see more job sharing: "There must be a large number of professional women who would gladly return to work, including solicitors, accountants and social workers, exactly the type of people we are trying to recruit". said Councillor Peter Wharton during lengthy discussions at Monday's personnel sub-committee.

The package of perks is now awaiting approval from the full council.

(STOCKPORT EXPRESS AND ADVERTISER, 24TH AUGUST 1989)

a) Why has Stockport Council introduced perks? *(2 marks)*

b) Which council sub-committee dealt with the matter? *(2 marks)*

c) Describe three perks the council have introduced. *(3 marks)*

d) Would it, in your view, be possible to introduce flexitime for some council workers? Say why some jobs would have to be excluded from the scheme. *(5 marks)*

e) Apart from increased pay, in what other ways might the quality of work be improved for council employees? *(8 marks)*

2. *Nazir was excited about starting his new job. Even though it was a YT scheme he looked forward to developing his skills as a mechanic at the small garage near his home.*

a) Which government organisation is responsible for YT? *(2 marks)*

b) Where might Nazir go to receive off-the-job training and why might his employer send him there? *(8 marks)*

c) Why will it help Nazir and his employer if he has an induction course? *(8 marks)*

d) If he is taken on permanently Nazir will receive a contract of employment. Describe four items of information it should contain. *(2 marks)*

1. Contact a local college to find out what courses they run to help young people prepare for work. Pay attention to areas of work you might be interested in and find out what qualifications, if any, are needed and if there are grants or allowances available. What work will be done on the course?

2. Ask your careers officer for information about the YT scheme and prepare a poster EITHER to encourage young people to join it OR to discourage them.

3. Look at the job advertisements in local or national newspapers and make a list of the perks being offered. Write a short paragraph explaining what each of the terms used means. Which perks are most common and which are least common? Do certain types of perks seem to be common to certain types of jobs?

Collect 25 advertisements for the type of job you might be interested in (e.g. typist, receptionist, clerk, car mechanic, computer programmer, etc.). Record wages, hours worked, perks and assistance with training. Present your findings, which should include graphs and tables, showing which firms are offering the best and worst employment opportunities from your point of view. This research can be presented in the form of a formal report.

Mary looked at the three CVs in front of her. They were from applicants trying to get the job of clerk-typist in her travel agency. The problem was she could not decide who to employ.

CURRICULUM VITAE

Name: Mary Davis

Date of Birth: 3rd December 1975

Address: 18 Roach Road
                   WESTON-ON-SEA
                   Essex CM23 1DW

Telephone: 34567

School   Sandford Comprehensive
Attended: Francis Road, WESTON-ON-SEA
                   Essex CM23 2RJ

Date   June 1991
of leaving:

Examination   GCSE Business Studies   A
Results: GCSE English Language   C
                   GCSE Biology   D
                   GCSE French   D

Hobbies: Squash - I represented my school for
                   three years.
                   Music - I sang in the school choir.

Previous   I worked as a Saturday Sales Assistant
Experience: in a newsagent's for two years.

Referees   Mr F Terry
                   Headteacher
                   Sandford Comprehensive
                   Francis Road, WESTON-ON-SEA
                   Essex CM23 2RJ

                   Ms J Finch
                   Manageress
                   Local News
                   High Street, WESTON-ON-SEA
                   Essex CM23 1AA

Name and Address
Mr. T T Races
34 Weston Drive
Weston on Sea
Essex CM45 1QW

Age: 22 years

Previous Employment:
Shelf packer - Superspend Supermarket, 6 months
Warehouse hand - Goodley Wholesalers, 9 months
Filing clerk - Astley Insurance, 2 months
Unemployed - 10 months, despite several
                   applications

References:
G. Bolt
Youth Worker
St. John's Youth Club
22 St. John's Road
Weston on Sea
Essex

Terry Races

Jean Donaldson   20 years old
Address
13 Seagull Drive
Weston on Sea
Essex CM23 5KL

Career History:
1986-1987 ~ Sales assistant in Ridley's
                   Ladies Wear shop.
1987 ~ now ~ Sales supervisor Barlow
                   Fashions.

Qualifications:
O level French ~ Grade C
O level Geography ~ Grade A
O level Maths ~ Grade D
O level English ~ Grade B
Interests: Travel ~ I have been to
            Tunisia, France and Spain
            Sport ~ I support Manchester
            United and play netball.
References can be obtained from:

Mr. G Ridley   Mr. BGT Barlow
Ridley's Ladies Wear   Barlow Fashions
222 The High Street   89 London Road
Weston on Sea   Weston on Sea
Essex CM34 8PP   Essex CM55 6ER

---

a) Look at the three CVs and decide who is best for the job. Explain why you think this is the case.

b) Would you interview all three? Give reasons for your answer.

CHAPTER 6

ENDING EMPLOYMENT

The swift pace of economic and technological change means that most people will change jobs several times in their life. There are four main reasons why an employee might leave a job. These are:

- Retirement
- Dismissal
- Redundancy
- Personal reasons

Retirement

In most industries the retirement age is 65 years old for men and 60 years old for women. Legally, women are entitled to be treated the same as men. This means that under the Sex Discrimination Act 1987, women can work until 65 years of age if they choose to. *Early retirement* allows employees to leave work before the official retirement age if they are in poor health or their jobs are no longer required by the firm. Firms will pay the retiring employee's pension contributions to enable them to claim a full state pension. This payment is called *enhancement*. In most cases people who retire early receive a payment, a *lump sum*, which they often invest. The proceeds of the investment help them to manage financially during retirement. The advantage to the firm of early retirement is that it is more considerate to long-serving staff – and often cheaper – than redundancy, or paying the wages of staff it no longer needs. Employees benefit through a longer retirement and may find employment elsewhere.

Dismissal

An employee is dismissed or 'sacked' when they are told to leave their job. Usually a dismissed employee is *given notice*. This means that they are allowed to work for a certain period of time before their employment ends. According to the Employment Protection Act, 1978 the minimum notice period is one week for every year worked over two years. However, an employee's contract of employment might state that more time must be allowed. Sometimes dismissed employees might be paid for the notice period but not required to work. This is called *payment in lieu of notice*.

Employees will be *dismissed with notice* if they prove to be incapable of doing the job. The organisation's recruitment and selection procedures should weed out unsuitable candidates but unsuitable appointments are still made. Employees may be judged incapable of the job if their attendance is poor, if the work they do is not up to standard or if their attitude or behaviour is below the standards expected by the firm. Employers must be able to give employees reasons for why they are unsuitable for the job. A clear job description is important in helping to do this and in avoiding misunderstandings. Before the employee is dismissed with notice their employer should give advice and help to enable the employee to improve, together with sufficient warnings about the situation. An employer who fails to provide these could face a claim for unfair dismissal (see below).

Misconduct, such as repeatedly failing to obey instructions, is another reason for dismissal. In rare cases an employee might be dismissed without notice. *Gross misconduct* such as theft, fighting or drunkenness can lead to dismissal without notice.

Constructive dismissal occurs when an employer changes an employee's working conditions or job so unreasonably that the employee feels pressurised into leaving the job. To prove constructive dismissal the employee must prove that the changes were unreasonable.

Unfair dismissal is a dismissal which, as far as the law is concerned, is unreasonable. While each case is judged on its own merits, dismissal for trade union membership, being of a particular race or religion, or being homosexual are examples of acts of unfair dismissal. It is only possible to have a claim for unfair dismissal considered if the employee has been working at least 16 hours per week for a year with the same employer. In some jobs for example in the army and police force, this aspect of the law does not apply.

If there is a dispute about whether a dismissal is fair employees can seek advice from, and be represented by, a trade union. The union might, if necessary, help the employee put a case to an *industrial tribunal*. Industrial tribunals have been set up by parliament to resolve disputes concerning matters of employment. Instead of a judge there is an independent, legally qualified person appointed by the government to act as chairman. The other two members of the tribunal are nominated by the trade union and the employer.

An industrial tribunal hearing

These people consider cases put before them and give a verdict. Although industrial tribunals have similar powers to a court in employment matters they are less formal in their approach. If the employer or employee disagrees with the industrial tribunal's interpretation of the law they may appeal to an employment appeal tribunal.

There is an industrial tribunal in most major cities and towns. When business is conducted the public are allowed access, as they would be to a court.

6.1. Answer the following questions with at least a full sentence, or by writing out the missing words.

1. What are the four main reasons for leaving a job?

2. The legal retirement age for men is _____ .

3. The minimum notice period for a dismissed employee is one ____ for every ____ worked, over two years.

4. For what reasons might someone be dismissed without notice?

5. Explain the term 'constructive dismissal'.

6. Describe the work of industrial tribunals.

Redundancy

Redundancy occurs when the job an employee is doing is no longer required. This can be because the employer closes down a factory or office. It may be because the particular skills that an employee has are no longer required because the work of the firm has changed or the job can be done by fewer employees using new equipment or new processes. Rather than make an employee redundant an employer might offer a similar job elsewhere in the organisation. If it is a reasonable offer made within four weeks of the employee's contract of employment being concluded and the employee turns it down the entitlement to redundancy pay could be lost. Redundancy pay is paid by the employer with help from the government through the Redundancy Fund. Some employers may add to the payment the redundant employee receives depending upon the employer's financial state and negotiations with the trade unions involved. Employers have a legal responsibility to provide the trade union with information about proposed redundancies and negotiate with them with a view to minimising the effects of the redundancy. The amount of redundancy pay is linked to the age of the employee and the length of time they have been with the employer. To qualify the employee must have been with the firm for at least two years after the age of 18 and have worked a minimum of 21 hours a week.

- A redundant employee between the ages of 18 and 21 will receive a minimum of half a week's wages for each year worked.

- A redundant employee between the ages of 22 and 40 will receive a minimum of one week's wages for each year worked.

- A redundant employee between the ages of 41 and 65 will receive a minimum of one and a half week's wages for each year worked.

All payments are up to a maximum of 20 years' employment and up to a maximum amount fixed by the government, in line with any increase in the cost of living. The calculation is based on the last week's basic wage. Overtime and other payments are not included unless they are part of the normal pay or salary. Piece-rate workers are paid on an average of the last twelve week's earnings. If the employee has a disagreement about the amount of redundancy pay they receive they can take advice from a trade union which will, if necessary help them take a case to an industrial tribunal.

Personal reasons

Employees may leave a job for reasons that have little to do with the employer. Some may move to a different part of the country to be with their wife or husband, boyfriend or girlfriend who is perhaps starting a new job. Domestic reasons such as marriage or divorce may mean a person has to leave work.

Some employees will leave to start their own business. After a period of six months' unemployment they can become eligible for the government's *Enterprise Allowance*. This scheme allows anyone with £1000 and a business idea with a chance of success to claim over £40 per week from the government and to keep any money their business earns, subject to taxes and expenses. Under the Enterprise Scheme free guidance in legal and financial matters is given to help the businesses get started. Businesses which have started under this scheme include comedians, kissograms and pop groups as well as photographers and other traditional types of business.

It is important to find the cause of high staff turnover

Other common reasons for leaving a job are that the employee has found another job elsewhere, has been promoted or been moved to a different job within the same firm. The rate at which employees leave a business and are replaced is called the *labour turnover* or *employee turnover*. The higher the rate of employee turnover the more expensive it is for the firm. Not only does the firm have the expense of advertising for replacement staff but it also loses the production that would have taken place had the people involved in interview and selection been involved in something else. It is expensive to train new staff as longer-serving employees have to leave their work to explain to the newcomer what has to be done. During the training period new staff are not as productive as their longer-serving colleagues, even though they may be receiving the same wage or salary.

If a firm experiences a high rate of labour turnover it should try to find the cause. Common causes are bad management or supervision, poor communication leading to frustration, poor pay levels in relation to similar firms or the job being too complicated or too boring. The causes can sometimes be discovered through observation of the section of the firm experiencing high employee turnover. A more revealing method is to conduct an exit interview. The employee who is leaving meets with their supervisor and the employee's work with the firm is reviewed and their feelings about what they have been doing are discussed. Employees with a job to go to may talk freely as they no longer have to rely on the employer conducting the interview. Care has to be taken when looking at the results of the exit interview as years of frustration may produce a distorted and unreliable picture if an employee is bitter or unhappy with the firm when leaving it. A system of appraisal interviews (see page 75) should highlight growing problems.

6.2. Answer the following questions with at least a full sentence, or by writing out the missing words.

1. When does redundancy occur?

2. Who pays redundancy pay?

3. A person must have been with a firm for ____ years after their eighteenth birthday to qualify for _____ pay.

4. Between the ages of 41 and 65 years a redundant employee will receive a minimum of ___ weeks' wages for each year worked.

5. Give three personal reasons why a person may give up their job.

6. _____ _____ is the rate at which employees leave a firm.

7. Give two reasons for high labour turnover.

1. How do dismissal and redundancy differ?

2. What is payment in lieu of notice?

3. Under what circumstances might an employer face a claim for unfair dismissal?

4. Describe the three people normally found on an industrial tribunal.

5. What three factors determine the level of an employee's redundancy pay?

6. What is the Enterprise Allowance?

7. Why would a firm wish to avoid a high level of labour turnover?

8. Describe the causes of high labour turnover.

9. How can high labour turnover be avoided?

10. Why should the results of an exit interview be considered cautiously?

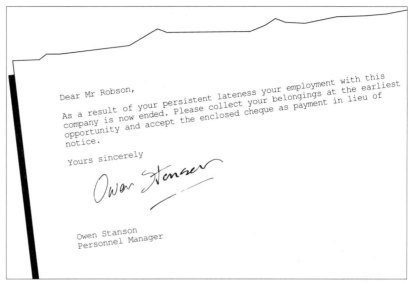

Dear Mr Robson,

As a result of your persistent lateness your employment with this company is now ended. Please collect your belongings at the earliest opportunity and accept the enclosed cheque as payment in lieu of notice.

Yours sincerely

Owen Stanson
Personnel Manager

1. a) John Robson had not been told that his employers were concerned about his lateness. Does this affect the situation and if so, why? *(5 marks)*

b) What should Owen Stanson have done if he was concerned about John's lateness? *(5 marks)*

c) Assuming the firm will not change its mind, what possible courses of action are open to John Robson and which would you recommend? Say why you make this recommendation. *(10 marks)*

2. *If the report in front of Jayne Border were true - and several witnesses had confirmed it - Ian Gower had been drunk when he came back to work earlier this afternoon. She was worried about safety and damage because he drove a fork lift truck. It seemed that his work had been going down hill for weeks as a result of domestic problems. As Personnel Officer, she had to do something.*

a) Would Jayne be within her rights to dismiss this man on the spot? Explain your answer. *(5 marks)*

b) Jayne was unhappy about Ian Gower trying to organise a union branch in the factory and wondered if she would be on firmer ground sacking him for that.

Explain if she is. *(5 marks)*

c) How could the situation have been avoided? *(5 marks)*

d) Up until now Gower's work had been satisfactory. What are the arguments for not sacking him? *(5 marks)*

Charterhouse Auto is a long-established Midlands company making car parts for larger manufacturers like Ford and Rover. It has a good industrial relations record. In recent years the company has fallen onto hard times. The board of directors has agreed to make 35 men and women redundant from its work force of 200 because future orders are lower than they have been for years. They are discussing the best way to handle the situation . . .

'The union won't like it,' Bob James (the Personnel Director) muttered hesitantly. 'Perhaps we should leave it a few weeks before we tell them how bad things are and not do anything now'.

'Choose 35 out of a hat and put the notices in next week's wage packets. Let's get the thing over with,' said Peter Bates (the Finance Director). 'The quicker we get rid of them, the sooner we start saving some money. It's not a charity we run here, is it? A short sharp shock is what they need. If we tell the union too much they will want to know everything, so let's take them by surprise.'

'We need to prepare them for it' said Stella Evans (the Public Relations Director). 'Why don't I have a word with a few local journalists and get the news into the papers. That should frighten them a bit'.

'Yes, and the next thing you know we'll have a strike on our hands and then where will we be? I know these people, I've worked with them. Why not get them into the office and tell them how big a mess the company is in? I'm sure they'll understand,' suggested Charles Raymond (the Production Director) . . .

After an hour's heated discussion the Board decide to choose 35 names out of a hat and put the redundancy notices in the following week's wage packets. They decide not to tell the union beforehand but to leak it to the local newspaper the day before pay day, so that the workforce can read about it before they come to work.

Answer the following questions individually or in groups:

a) What does the company's approach to its labour force tell you about its methods of communication and style of management?

b) Write a memo to Peter Bates explaining why his way of handling the problem might not be to the company's advantage. Explain how you think the problem should be approached.

c) Describe the sorts of effects the closure of a factory like Charterhouse Auto might have on the area where the factory is situated.

d) You are the District Secretary of the Transport and General Workers' Union, which has 150 members at Charterhouse Auto. You have received the following letters. Write, type or word-process a reply to each of them:

Flat 45
The Albany
Whiteside
Nuneaton NU4 7XC
4/5/90

Dear Sir

As a result of my unfortunate redundancy (not my fault) I would be grateful if you would let me know what you think my pay off from the firm should be. I am 24 years of age and have been with the firm for three years in the general office. My wage for the last twelve weeks has been £140 per week.

Best wishes

Jill Saunders.

6.5.1990
53 Broomfield Road
Moor Heaton
Nuneaton

Dear District Secretary

Those swines at Charterhouse have put me on the dole at my age, 53 years old. Where am I going to get another job now. Our shop steward says that you need to know our last twelve weeks wages so that you can work out our redundancy pay. Well, its none of your business but if you will keep quiet here is the information. I earned £180 each week but in the last two weeks had an extra £25 each week because I withdrew my Christmas club money. I joined this firm when I was 15 years of age and I think its a right disgrace what they have done to us.

Yours

A. Grimes

567 Lightside Street
Nuneaton
5.5.1990

Dear Sir or madam

I am informed by my shop steward, Eddie Marks, that if I give details of my last twelve weeks earnings you will be able to calculate my redundancy pay. I got a basic pay of £155 per week but my productivity bonus has been in each of the twelve weeks:

£34, £33, £40, £43, £39, £37, £40
£39, £32, £32, £38, £37

I am 34 years old and have been with this firm for 10 years

Yours faithfully

Winston Cummings

(Assembly Worker)

22 Alberta Terrace
Nuneaton
6.5.1990

Dear Sir/Madam

The firm I work for, Charterhouse Auto, have decided to make me redundant. I am 17 years old and have come off the YTS to take a proper job with them. I have worked for them for nine months and get £89 a week. Please let me know how much redundancy pay I will get.

Thank you

Tracey Mitchell

PS please send me some advice about how to invest the money I will get.

CHAPTER 7

INDUSTRIAL RELATIONS

Industrial relations is an important part of personnel work. *Industrial relations* refers to the process of discussion between representatives of the firm and representatives of the firm's employees. Usually the employees are represented in these discussions by a trade union official. However, some firms will not *recognise* or negotiate with trade unions. Sometimes these *non-union firms* as they are called agree to talk to a staff association or committee, often paid for by the firm.

Industrial relations involves negotiation about such things as:

- Wage and salary rates
- Health and safety at work
- Working conditions
- Holiday entitlements
- Retirement arrangements
- Procedures for settling grievances or disciplinary matters
- Procedures for dealing with redundancy
- Hours of work

Trade unions try to improve all of these things for their members. As well as trying to influence employers, trade unions try to influence government. This is done in many ways. Trade unions will pay for research into problems which affect their members and put forward suggestions to the government about how the problem might be dealt with, for example they might do research on the effects of chemicals in agriculture on farm workers. Committees such as the National Economic Development Council (NEDC – sometimes called 'Neddy') give unions a chance to discuss issues with government ministers. NEDC is concerned with the country's economy and gives trade union representatives a chance to have their say about how the economy should be run. The amount of notice that is taken of the unions depends on the attitude of the government of the day.

Another way unions try to influence the government is by *sponsoring* Members of Parliament (MPs). This means that a union contributes to an MP's expenses and supports him or her at election time by campaigning on their behalf. For example, Neil Kinnock, the leader of the Labour Party, is sponsored by the Transport and General Workers Union (TGWU).

JOHN HARRIS, INTERNATIONAL FREELANCE LIBRARY LTD

Neil Kinnock, leader of the Labour Party

7.1. Answer the following questions with at least a full sentence, or by writing out the missing words.

2. List four things that trade unions negotiate.

3. Describe three ways in which trade unions might try to influence government.

1. What is meant by industrial relations?

Some employers have an agreement with the trade union(s) representing their employees that they will not employ anyone who refuses to be a union member. This arrangement is called a *closed shop*. This means that the firm's work*shop* (or anywhere else for that matter!) is *closed* to non-union members. Employers agree to this situation because communication and the carrying out of negotiations is easier if all employees are in a union. Trade unions argue that as all employees benefit from the negotiations carried out by union representatives, all employees should contribute financially and take part in union affairs. Some people believe that the closed shop is an unjustified restriction of the individual's freedom. What do you think?

Types of trade union

There are about 350 different trade unions, with a total of ten million members. Just less than half the working population belong to a trade union. As self-employment, unemployment and the number of small businesses have risen, the numbers in trade union membership have declined. Nearly two-thirds of all trade union members belong to the ten biggest unions, which have over a quarter of a million members each. Examples of the biggest unions include the Transport and General Workers Union (TGWU) and the General, Municipal Boilermakers and Allied Trades Union (GMBATU). There are four different types of unions:

- Craft Unions: Membership is open only to those with recognised qualifications in a particular skill or occupation. Craft unions tend to be amongst the smallest unions.

- Industrial Unions: The National Union of Miners (NUM) is an example of an industrial union. Membership of this sort of union is open to anyone working in a particular industry. Anyone working in mining can join the NUM. Craft unions and industrial unions will compete for members in particular industries. Their financial well-being depends on the number of members they can gain as each member must pay a subscription or membership fee to join and remain a member.

- General Unions: These are the largest type of union. We have already mentioned two examples, the Transport and General

A union demonstration for more pay

Workers Union (TGWU) and the General, Municipal Boiler-makers and Allied Trades Union (GMBATU). These tend to represent unskilled and semi-skilled workers (see page 4), regardless of what industry or craft they are in. While the large size of these unions makes them powerful, the fact that they are so large and spread over several industries tends to be a weakening factor as there may be a conflict of interest amongst the membership.

■ White Collar Unions: The National Union of Teachers (NUT) and the National and Local Government Officers Association (NALGO) are examples of white collar unions. White collar unions represent clerical, managerial and professional workers. As a group they are the fastest-growing type of union. This is because the amount of manufacturing work in Britain, in which general, industrial and craft unions are strong, has declined. At the same time there has been a growth in financial, scientific and other service industries in which white collar unions are represented.

CHECK THIS OUT

7.2. Answer the following questions with at least a full sentence, or by writing out the missing words.

1. Explain the term 'closed shop'.

2. How does an employer benefit from a closed shop?

3. Who can join a craft union?

4. An _____ _____ represents all workers in a particular industry.

5. The TGWU is an example of a _____ union.

6. What sort of workers are represented by white collar unions?

7. Which is the largest type of union?

8. Which is the smallest type of union?

9. What is the fastest-growing type of union?

10. Why have general unions declined in strength?

How trade unions are organised

Each union has its own particular structure and methods of organisation. In the workplace the union will be represented by a *shop steward*. The shop steward is an ordinary employee elected to represent the views of the union members. They receive no payment from the union for this work. There is often an agreement with the employer that the shop steward can devote some of his/her time to union duties. These duties include collecting membership subscriptions, organising or attending meetings and dealing with individual problems. Large workplaces may have several shop stewards representing the same union in different parts of the works.

If there are several recognised unions the shop stewards may form a *shop steward's committee*. In this committee the different unions' shop stewards try to agree similar approaches to the management, co-operate with each other and share information. In the newspaper and printing industries shop stewards are, for historical reasons, known as *fathers or mothers of the chapel*.

Voting at a union mass meeting

Each union member belongs to a union branch. If the place of work has sufficient union members there will be a works' branch. In the newspaper and printing industries branches are known as *chapels*. Most branches are based on a particular town or city or part of a town or city. Any union member can attend a branch meeting and has the right to speak, ask questions and put forward ideas. Branch meetings allow employees to find out what is going on with other employers and the union locally and nationally. The decisions of a branch meeting are represented by the shop stewards or branch officers (for example a chairperson or secretary) to the local employers. The branch officers meet as a committee to carry out the wishes of the branch and look after branch affairs in between meetings.

Branches elect representatives to put forward their views at the regional and national level of their union. The union will have a National Conference, usually each year, in which the policy of the union for the coming year will be decided. The union's senior national officers are the general secretary, treasurer and president. The general secretary is usually a paid employee of the union, although subject to a five-yearly election, and is the union's main representative. These officers, together with other elected representatives, form the union's national executive. It is the job of the national executive to carry out the wishes of the national conference and represent the union's views to the government, newspapers and other trade unions. Trade unions have a staff of full-time officers to help, advise and represent branch officers and members. Usually some are based at union headquarters and others in each of the union's regions or districts.

As long ago as 1868, unions realised it would be in their best interests to co-operate with each other. For this reason the Trades Union Congress (TUC) was formed at a meeting called in Manchester in that year. Since then the TUC has met more or less every year to decide policies to be put forward to the government, newspapers and trades unions in other countries. At present about 95 of the largest and most influential unions are members of the TUC and send representatives to the annual congress or meeting each September.

Although every union is independent, the aim of the TUC is to help unions reach agreement in cases of dispute amongst themselves. For example, *demarcation disputes* between unions are not uncommon. These disputes are over which union's members should be allowed to do particular types of work. As well as ensuring its members' work is not taken by other unions' members, a union will try to protect wage *differentials*; that is, it will try to make sure that the differences between its members' wages and other lower paid workers is maintained. It will, of course, try to reduce differentials with workers who are paid more than its members. Another aim of the TUC is to form a united front when speaking to the government or employers about economic policy or industrial relations.

The TUC annual congress in session

7.3. Answer the following questions with at least a full sentence, or by writing out the missing words.

3. TUC stands for ___ ___ ___ .

1. In the workplace, the union will be represented by a ___ ___ .

4. The aim of the TUC is to help unions reach ___ amongst themselves.

2. Who has the right to attend union branch meetings?

5. What does the TUC speak to the government about?

Employers' organisations

Employers have also realised that a united response to trade unions is the best way of representing their views. For this reason, several employers' organisations have been formed which put forward the views of employers to trade unions; rather like the way trade unions put forward their members' views. Each of the employers' organisations is based on a particular industry, for example the Engineering Employers Federation, the Road Haulage Association, the Building Employers Confederation. As well as helping and advising members, the employers' organisations also represent their views to trade unions, government and the newspapers.

In the same way that unions have tried to use the TUC to speak on behalf of all trades unions, the employers have formed an organisation to represent all employers. This organisation is called the Confederation of British Industry (CBI). About a quarter of a million firms of all sizes in all lines of business belong to the CBI. The CBI has local committees as well as an annual conference to decide its attitudes to economic and industrial relations matters. The Institute of Directors is another employer's organisation that represents the views of employers from all parts of industry.

Industrial relations in practice

The way in which employers and trade unions negotiate will vary from employer to employer and industry to industry. Industrial relations take place at two levels, national and local.

National level

Wage rates, hours of work, holidays and pensions are examples of things which tend to be agreed at this level between national representatives of the employers and trade unions.

Local level

Negotiations at a workplace or *plant* level are carried out between regional officers with local representatives of the shop stewards and branch committee and particular employers.

Local or plant discussions often deal with piece rates, bonus payments, staff facilities and health and safety matters. These discussions are known as *collective bargaining* because the representatives of employers and unions are speaking on behalf of their *collection* of members who will respect the outcome of the discussions. When disputes arise they are settled by negotiation in 90 per cent of cases. When disputes cannot be settled in this way they are said to be *deadlocked*. The trade unions might take various sorts of *industrial action* to support their case. These actions can include:

■ Work to rule – The workers refuse to do anything that they are not strictly required to do, according to their contract or job description. This slows down work and can produce practical problems for the employer if all the tasks required by the firm have not been written into job descriptions. It has the advantage that workers paid on a time-rate basis do not lose any pay.

■ Go-slow – By doing their jobs slowly workers can reduce production and so cost the employer money. This also has the advantage that workers paid on a time-rate basis do not lose any pay.

■ Overtime ban – As the name suggests, the workers do nothing more than their basic hours. Firms that rely on overtime to maintain production or to meet a delivery date can be badly hit. The disadvantage of this tactic is that poorly-paid employees may need the extra earnings from overtime and suffer financially.

■ Strike – A strike is where employees refuse to work. Strikes are quite rare in Britain (although usually well-publicised by newspapers and television), and are only taken as a last resort. The law requires that a secret ballot of all members involved in a strike has to be taken before the strike can go ahead. The strike must follow within 30 days of the ballot result. A strike which is approved by the national union is called an *official strike*. Workers in some situations may strike without union approval. This is an *unofficial strike*, sometimes called a *wildcat strike*. Unofficial strikes occur if a group of workers are frustrated by the union's lack of progress or if they feel some action by management requires an urgent and serious response. When an *all-out strike* occurs, all of the workers are called out on strike. Often they will not return to work until the dispute is settled. The term *indefinite* strike is used when no time limit is put on the strike.

To make up for the wages lost while on strike, members will receive strike pay, from the union's strike fund. The cost of all-out strikes to a union might mean that it chooses to use *selective strike* action. In this situation certain selected groups of the membership are called out on strike. These are often important groups of workers and the withdrawal of their labour is very disruptive.

In order to express disapproval or to show that an issue is taken seriously by the workers a *token strike* may be called. This form of action involves the workers striking for a short period of time: a day, half a day or even less. It is usually intended to show employers that the workforce are prepared to take longer strike action if necessary. In order to raise money to finance industrial action union members may be asked to make an extra contribution called a *levy*.

When a ballot for a strike is called and the vote is in favour of a strike, most workers accept the democratic decision of their workmates. Some people do not and continue to work in defiance of the decision. Strikers and their supporters will use the

A union picket

term *scab* or *black-leg* to describe these workers. To try to persuade people not to weaken their strike by going in to work,
the union will mount a *picket-line*.

The group of pickets stand outside the entrances to the workplace to persuade others of their case. The union might also
try to persuade workers in another business to go on strike in
their support. For example, workers on strike at a factory making tin cans might try to persuade the workers at the firm
supplying the tin to come on strike with them. If they were to
succeed the tin suppliers would be taking *secondary strike
action* and any pickets at the tin suppliers would be *secondary
pickets*. The Employment Act, 1980, made secondary action of
this nature illegal and the union could be taken to court by the
firm affected by the secondary action. If the union chooses to
ignore the court ruling its funds can be taken from it or *seques-
trated*.

One way workers in other places can help strikers is to *boycott*
or *black* goods or equipment produced by non-strikers. They
refuse to work with or co-operate with the non-strikers. It is also
common for other unions or branches of the same union to
send money to support strikers.

In certain very serious cases, for instance when a factory is
threatened with closure, workers may stage a *sit-in* or *occupation* of the premises. This means that they refuse to leave the
building and hope to prevent goods or equipment being taken
away. This can also result in legal action against the union by the
employer who wishes to continue his/her business elsewhere.

7.4. Answer the following questions with at least a full sentence, or by writing out the missing words.

1. Name four employers' organisations.

2. CBI stands for ___ ____ ___ .

3. Explain what is meant by collective bargaining.

4. Describe two sorts of industrial action.

5. What is the difference between official and unofficial strikes?

6. To try to persuade people not to work a union will sometimes mount a ____-____ .

Solving disputes

As we said earlier, strikes are rare and sit-ins even rarer. Most disputes are resolved by negotiation through the process of collective bargaining. Depending on the type of dispute, help can be sought from various outside bodies in order to bring the dispute to a close. Important organisations which can help the process of industrial relations include:

■ The Advisory, Conciliation and Arbitration Service (ACAS) was set up by the government under the Employment Protection Act, 1975. It is independent of the government, although paid for by the government. It is run by representatives of the TUC, CBI and independent members. ACAS has full-time staff whose job it is to help employers and unions settle industrial relations disputes. This is done in several ways:

They provide an *advisory* service. ACAS advises employers and unions on specific problems and it publishes leaflets and reports on particular topics. ACAS also produces *codes of conduct* advising how employers and unions should behave in dealing with certain industrial relations problems.

Conciliation means helping people who disagree to try to reach agreement. ACAS helps unions and employers put their case to each other in a way designed to help reach agreement. In some cases it will act as a 'go between' by relaying messages and helping to put arguments forward in a constructive way.

In some disputes a negotiated agreement cannot be reached. In order to resume production and employee earnings, unions and employers can ask someone to decide how the dispute should be settled. Both parties agree to follow the decision. When someone is asked to decide like this it is called *arbitration*. ACAS can call upon individuals with legal and industrial relations experience to make these decisions when employers and unions request it.

■ The Equal Opportunities Commission. The aim of the Equal Opportunities Commission (EOC) is to ensure that people are not treated less favourably because of their sex. The EOC makes sure that the requirements of the Equal Pay Act, 1970 are put into force. Under this Act it became illegal to pay women less than men for carrying out the same work. The Sex Discrimination Act, 1975 is another area of concern for the EOC. This Act required that women be treated equally not just in relation to pay but in other things, for example promotion and training opportunities. Advertisements for workers of a particular sex were made illegal under this Act unless there was a Genuine Occupational Qualification (see page 60). To help prevent disputes over equal opportunities the EOC provides advice and information to employers and employees. It provides *codes of practice* which are guidelines for dealing with particular equal opportunities situations. The EOC may, in certain circumstances, help employees who feel discriminated against to take the employer to court or an industrial tribunal. If it suspects that discrimination is taking place the EOC may issue a non-discrimination notice against the employer. This legal document warns the employer to improve the situation or face further legal action.

The following table shows how women are paid less than men in similar occupations and why the EOC is needed:

Type of job	Pay per hour Male (p)	Pay per hour Female (p)
Catering, Cleaning, Hairdressing	288	243
Transport	341	276
Clerical	390	316
Selling	419	254

■ The Commission for Racial Equality. Under the Race Relations Act, 1976 it is illegal to treat one person less favourably than another in employment on the grounds of their race, nationality, colour or ethnic group. This covers training, promotion, recruitment and conditions of service. The Commission for Racial Equality (CRE) was established to ensure the aims of the Act are met. To help prevent disputes over racial matters the CRE can provide advice and information to employers and employees. It provides codes of practice for dealing with particular situations where racial discrimination might occur. The CRE may, in certain circumstances, help employees who feel discriminated against to take the employer to court or to an industrial tribunal. If it suspects discrimination is taking place the CRE may issue a non-discrimination notice against the employer. This legal document warns the employer to improve the situation or face further legal action.

7.5. Answer the following questions with at least a full sentence, or by writing out the missing words.

3. The aim of the ___ ____ ___ is to ensure that people are not treated less favourably because of their sex.

4. What does the Commission for Racial Equality do?

5. ___ ___ ___ are guidelines for dealing with particular situations

1. What is the purpose of ACAS?

2. Explain what is meant by arbitration.

Clearly, the personnel department plays an important part in a company in dealing with industrial relations. Without a well-trained, motivated and managed workforce no business organisation can succeed. For this reason it is crucial that the personnel department establishes strong links with all other parts of the business organisation. Without these strong links the business cannot hope to benefit from good personnel practice as the personnel department will be unable to put its expertise into effect.

1. Explain the phrase 'industrial relations'.

2. Why might a union sponsor an MP?

3. Name four types of union and give an example of each.

4. What does a union's national executive do?

5. What is the name given to disputes over which union's members should do a particular job?

6. Describe the work of the CBI.

7. What is the difference between an overtime ban and a go-slow?

8. Explain the difference between all out, selective and token strikes.

9. What are secondary pickets?

10. Explain the meaning of the word 'conciliation'.

STIMULUS RESPONSE QUESTIONS

SALES STAFF REQUIRED

Wanted: Two young women to sell ballpoint pens in large department store in the centre of Bristol.

Married women and trade union members should not apply. Fluent Welsh speakers particularly welcome.

For an interview apply to Gwyn Evans on Bristol 3456 898.

1. a) Which two organisations could a male, non-Welsh speaker approach for help in persuading Gwyn Evans to consider him for this job? *(2 marks)*

    b) Point out four ways in which this advertisement might be in breach of employment law and explain why. *(8 marks)*

    c) Re-write this advertisement so that it does not break the law. *(10 marks)*

2.

'. . . and I believe that if we accept this pay offer of 5.3 per cent we will allow the wage differentials between our members and members of the TWMG to slip to an unacceptable level. Since we lost the demarcation dispute last year our position has weakened. Industrial action is the only way we can defend our rights . . .'

a) Explain what is meant by 'differentials'. *(2 marks)*

b) Explain what is meant by 'demarcation dispute'. *(2 marks)*

c) Describe four types of industrial action that could be taken in this situation. *(8 marks)*

d) In what ways could this union branch try to resolve its problems before taking industrial action? *(8 marks)*

1. Divide the class into groups and write group letters to different unions asking for information about their work. If possible, arrange for a speaker to talk to the class. Present your findings as a wall display.

2. Write a class letter to the CBI asking for information about its work. If possible arrange for a speaker to talk to the class. Present your findings as a wall display.

3. Collect five newspaper cuttings about industrial relations disputes. Mount them on a piece of plain paper and write an account of what the disputes are about. See if you can find any points they have in common and write about these at the end.

4. As a group discuss the idea that 'The closed shop is fair and helps employers and employees alike'. One person should argue in favour and one against in order to start the discussion. All members of the group should say something on the topic. Take a vote at the end to see if your group supports the idea of the closed shop or not.

5. If your school or college has a work experience scheme find out what unions there are where you go to work, how to join and what the costs and benefits are. See if you can collect any leaflets about the union. If there is no union at the firm, try to find out why.

Conduct a survey amongst 25 working people you know. Find out if they are in a union or not. What reasons do they give for joining or not joining? What benefits do those who belong to unions get? Use graphs and a written report to show your findings.

NOTICE

As from next Monday all afternoon tea breaks will be reduced from 15 minutes to 5 minutes. Any member of staff who breaks this rule will be dismissed.

N. L. Harris
(Works Manager)

Ruth Goldberg the senior shop steward stared at the notice from the new Works Manager. It was the first she had heard about this. She knew the firm was not doing very well and needed to boost production but in the past changes like this would have been discussed first. She knew it would have to be discussed at the shop stewards' weekly meeting that night.

a) Should Ruth do anything before the meeting?

b) Assuming that the new works manager will not change his mind, what should the employees do in order to persuade him?

SECTION THREE

Finance

Small businesses will often employ an accountant to look after their financial records and advise them on matters relating to finance. Often the accountant merely checks that records kept by the owner are accurate and meet the various government regulations relating to things like VAT (see page 224). The accountant may be part-time, working once a week or once a month. Larger firms will have full-time staff dealing with financial affairs as their financial resources are greater and more complex. The bigger firms will have a finance or accounts department. Within such a department we could expect to find the following staff.

Financial accountants

It is the responsibility of the financial accountant to keep a record of what the company has spent and how this has affected its profits. This means that the financial accountant has to produce regular reports showing how the company's money has been spent and what income has been received. This information is vital as it helps the managers of the business to plan future activity. Regular financial reports can show patterns of expenditure or income that can be controlled or developed. The financial accountant prepares the profit and loss account and balance sheet (see pages 122 and 124).

Cost accountants

As the name suggests, the cost accountant calculates the costs of the business's services and products. By showing which parts of the organisation are efficient, the cost accountant helps management make plans about how the work is to be organised. This is done by showing the costs of each part of the production process.

The cost accountant is able to show which products are the most profitable, which helps managers decide what to produce. The cost accountant needs to work closely with the other departments of the firm to ensure that costs are measured as accurately as possible. Cost accountants help managers make decisions about the most efficient ways of running the firm.

Management accountants

The management accountant deals with the actual income and expenditure of each of the firm's departments. Departments are allocated money to perform their various tasks. They are set financial targets. These allocations and targets together are called a *budget*. The management accountant advises managers on how well departments are doing in meeting their budgets. This allows decisions to be made before, for example, too much is spent. The management accountant may help the manager decide to increase a department's income.

Sources of finance

All business organisations need to find money to finance their activities. This is particularly important when the business is starting up and when expansion is being considered. Savings are a source of finance but generally firms do not want to delay their plans until they have saved enough money for them. Most business finance is borrowed in some way. In return for borrowing the money the borrower usually pays *interest*. Interest is a percentage added to the amount borrowed, for example ten per cent. This extra amount must be paid to the lender in return for having the use of the lender's money. The interest received is income for the lender. Interest is charged at an annual percentage rate (APR). The APR must be shown on all advertisements offering to lend money, for example *Borrow £3000 now at 13% APR*. Banks such as National Westminster, Barclays and Lloyds are important providers of finance to business.

Overdrafts

This is one source of finance open to business organisations. An overdraft allows the organisation to take out more money from their bank account than is invested, up to an agreed limit. Interest is paid to the bank only on the amount the account is overdrawn. This gives the business flexibility in how much they overdraw and the amount of interest they have to pay. Overdrafts tend to be used to finance short-term needs, for instance if a major customer fails to pay a large bill on time.

Loans

With a loan interest is charged on the full amount from the day it is borrowed, even if not all the loan is taken out of the bank account. This means that a loan is a less flexible means of borrowing than an overdraft. Loans are also used for short-term needs, often to buy a particular item of equipment which will, over time, earn enough to cover its own cost.

In certain cases loans will have to be *secured*. This means that the person borrowing the money must agree to give up some asset, worth at least as much as the loan, if they fail to meet the repayments. A *mortgage* is a particular type of secured loan. With a mortgage the asset which is secured is usually a building or piece of land.

Hire purchase

This tends to be an expensive way of finding finance to purchase equipment. It is a method used mainly by small firms unable to find alternative methods of making a purchase. Hire purchase has the advantage of allowing the firm immediate use of equipment which it might otherwise have to save up for. When the firm wishes to purchase the equipment it signs a hire purchase agreement with a *finance house*. A finance house is an organisation which makes profits by providing this sort of service. The finance house pays, in full, the firm selling the goods. The finance house now owns the goods but allows the organisation which has signed the hire purchase agreement to use the equipment. In return it receives regular payments which cover the cost of the item plus interest. At the end of the agreed period the finance house hands ownership of the equipment to the firm which has made the payments. Although the finance house owns the goods until the end of the repayment period it would face legal difficulties if it tried to take goods back once the hirer had paid more than one third of the cost.

8.1. Answer the following questions with at least a full sentence, or by writing out the missing words.

1. What is the difference between a financial accountant and a management accountant?

2. An _____ allows a business to overdraw its bank account up to an agreed limit.

3. How does a loan differ from an overdraft?

4. What is a secured loan?

5. Who owns goods purchased through hire purchase arrangements?

Leasing

There are two sorts of leasing arrangement, the *operating lease* and the *finance lease*. With an operating lease a firm has use of equipment but does not own it. The equipment is owned by the leasing firm. This arrangement avoids the *lessee* – the firm using the equipment – having to make a large payment. Payments can be made in small amounts over the period of the lease. By knowing how much it will have to pay over a period of time, the firm can estimate the real value of the equipment by judging what it contributes to the business in relation to what it costs. Staged payments help a firm to plan its finances accurately. With an operating lease the leasing company normally has responsibility for the maintenance of the equipment, thus releasing the lessee from some expense and inconvenience. By not requiring large sums of money at one time, leasing allows the lessee to use capital for other things which may earn money. As technology changes and equipment becomes more advanced, leasing arrangements allow companies to keep up to date and abreast of competitors by making it easy for them to install modern equipment without committing themselves to a major capital purchase. At the end of the lease period the equipment is either returned to the leasing company or the lease is renewed. At this stage the lessee may wish to lease different, more modern equipment.

A finance lease is similar to hire purchase – the lessee has the opportunity to purchase the equipment at the end of the lease period. This is because with a finance lease the lessee owns the equipment as a result of using the finance provided by the leasing company and only has to give it up if payments are not maintained – just like hire purchase. With an operating lease the ownership of the equipment rests with the leasing company which allows the lessee to operate the equipment.

Factoring

Factoring is a service provided by *factoring houses*. These organisations survive by 'buying' the debts of their clients. In other words, they make a payment worth about 80 per cent of a firm's outstanding debts. The factoring house pays the remaining 20 per cent when it has collected the money from the firm's debtors. It charges its clients a fee for this service. The client firm has the advantage of not having the cost and responsibility of chasing money owed to it. In addition it has almost immediate use of money it might have had to wait some time for.

Asset Sales

By selling something that it owns, for example equipment or shares in other businesses, the firm can raise capital. The disadvantage of asset sales is that the firm loses the use of the asset.

Credit

Most transactions between businesses are done by credit. That is to say payment is normally made after the goods have changed hands. Usually payment will be requested within a few days. By delaying payment of outstanding bills a business can use its money for other purposes which may be profitable or of more immediate importance. An advantage of using credit in this way is that it carries no extra charges of interest or fees. However, it might cause suppliers to refuse credit in future if the facility is abused. This can be very damaging for a business's reputation.

Government grants

In certain areas of the country called *assisted areas*, for example the North East, the government will provide finance or low interest loans to business. This sort of help is given in an effort to overcome problems of unemployment.

Ploughing back

Instead of spending the profits on themselves the owners of a business might spend them on things which benefit the business, for example new equipment. This is known as *ploughing back the profits*.

8.2. Answer the following questions with at least a full sentence, or by writing out the missing words.

1. Explain the term 'lessee'.

2. Who has responsibility for maintaining equipment used under an operating lease?

3. Why might a firm use a factoring house?

4. What are the advantages and disadvantages of delaying payment to suppliers?

5. Ploughing back profits means spending money on things to ____ the ____ .

Shares

As well as the methods described above, available to all business organisations, companies have other ways of raising finance. One way is to issue shares. This is usually necessary if there is to be any substantial expansion of a company. Investors buy shares in a company and receive a *share certificate* indicating the number of shares they own and, in return for the finance they have provided, they may receive a *dividend* on the shares yearly or twice yearly. There are different types of share which appeal to different types of investor. Some individuals may choose to take a share with more risk attached, but with the prospect of large returns; whereas others prefer a more secure, steady income. There are several sorts of share.

Ordinary shares

These are sometimes called *equities*. There is considerable risk attached to them, as they may not be repaid in full if the company closes down and the dividend is not fixed. The dividend income is paid only when all other claims on the profits have been met, but this income can be quite high if the company is doing well.

The price of the shares on the Stock Exchange may also climb rapidly if the earnings are high, until it is much higher than the nominal (par) value as shown on the share certificate. Shares which are less secure are sometimes called *risk capital*. Ordinary shares generally carry voting rights, unlike most other shares, and there is normally one vote per share, so that someone holding more than 50 per cent of these shares would control the company. Companies do not have to declare a dividend, for example in cases where a company makes a loss or only a small profit.

Preference shares

The owners of these shares receive preference over ordinary share-holders when the dividend is being paid, and also in the repayment of their capital if the company closes down. Normally, these shares carry a fixed rate and are useful for people who want a steady income. Preference shares are therefore safer than ordinary shares, but the share price does not increase very much because they do not have the chance of high earnings. Generally they have no voting rights. There are special versions of these shares:

- Share holders with *cumulative* shares have the right to any arrears of dividends from previous years when profits were insufficient. The fixed rate of dividend paid for each year means that the shareholders are normally certain of receiving a return on these shares unless the company goes into liquidation.
- Shareholders with *non-cumulative* shares do not have any right to arrears of dividend.
- *Redeemable* shares will be repaid by the company in the future, and they can be bought back from the shareholders either out of accumulated profits or from the money received from a fresh issue of shares. This type of share is used to help to start a company.

Deferred shares

Deferred shares are sometimes issued to the promoters or founders of a company. A family business may use them to give special rights and privileges to members of the family to ensure that they keep the controlling voting rights over ordinary shares. They may also ensure that their share of the profits is very favourable. These are also known as *founders' shares*.

New issues

Private companies are not allowed to advertise shares for sale, and this prevents them from raising money in this way. For this reason, an expanding private company may decide to convert to becoming a public company, or *go public*, as it is known. At the same time it may apply to the Stock Exchange to allow its shares to be dealt in on the Exchange. This will help make the shares more popular, as people know that they can sell them easily through the Exchange and that the company's background has been thoroughly investigated. Many companies, which are already public, are not listed on the Exchange, and these companies sometimes apply for a quotation which will make a new share issue attractive to investors and allow them to expand more readily.

Before the Stock Exchange Council will approve a new quotation, the company will first have to show evidence of a good trading record and sound financial prospects. The company must usually be worth at least half a million pounds before the Stock Exchange is likely to grant a quotation, as it is uneconomic to advertise small issues of shares.

The actual issue of new shares is a complex and expensive undertaking. Firms will usually employ the service of a merchant bank which specialises in new issues. These *issuing houses*, as they are called, undertake full responsibility for the issuing of the new shares and collecting payment for them. There are five basic methods which can be used when issuing new shares:

1. Rights issue

A rights issue allows existing shareholders in a company to buy up the new shares in proportion to the number of shares they already hold – for example, the right to buy one new share for every ten shares already held. An *open offer* does not limit the number of shares which can be bought by individual shareholders. Issuing by 'rights' has the advantage of being more economical to administer. Details of the share issue are sent to all existing shareholders, and they apply to purchase them directly from the company or through an issuing house.

2. Placing

If an issuing house believes that the shares on offer can be placed with a few large institutional investors or other clients, it will circulate details of the shares to them, often using the services of a stockbroking firm. As these institutional investors tend to buy shares in very large blocks, the issue can be disposed of, and finance raised, quickly and economically.

3. Prospectus

A prospectus can be drawn up and circulated, for example through stockbrokers to their clients, and it will often be published in the national press as well. A prospectus gives details of the company's development, past profits and prospects for the future. An application form is included, and if members of the public feel they wish to subscribe, they can apply. All applications are opened on the same day, *issue day*. This must be at least three days after the prospectus has been published.

4. Offer for sale

In this method, the issuing house first buys the shares and then resells them using a prospectus as in method 3 above. The advantage to the company is that it receives its finance without having to worry whether the share issue will be fully subscribed. This is now more usual than the prospectus method.

When methods 3 and 4 are used, the public also have the benefit of comments in the financial press as well as the information contained in the actual prospectus, before the issuing of the shares takes place.

5. Tendering

Very often the newly issued shares are sold again very quickly by speculators who wish to make a quick profit. These *stags*, as they are called, buy the shares at the issue price in anticipation that the price at which they are then quoted on the Stock Exchange will be significantly higher.

In order to limit this, the issuing house can invite tenders. The offer for sale or prospectus is again used, but it invites applications, not at a fixed price, but at or above a stated minimum price. This means that potential shareholders have to offer a price which they think is reasonable and which is.high enough to obtain some of the shares. When all the tenders or bids have been received, the issuing house looks at the prices offered and fixes a suitable price (the *striking price*) which will allow all the shares to be disposed of. Those people who *tender* at or above the striking price receive some of, or all of, the shares they wanted. Those whose bid is too low receive their money back. By using this method, the company ensures that the highest possible price at the time is obtained. This means that the financial benefits which the 'stags' might have had will come, instead, to the company.

Speculators

A speculator is a person who deals in shares with the intention of making a profit by buying and selling in a short period. Apart from the stags mentioned above, there are two other kinds of speculators, known as *bulls* and *bears*.

Bulls are speculators who believe that the price of certain shares will soon rise, and they buy shares so that they can be sold later at a profit.

Bears are the opposite of bulls and they sell shares for delivery at a future date, hoping that the price will fall. Since the bear does not actually possess the shares, but is hoping to buy some at a lower price in time for delivery, he can be said to be selling the bearskin before he has caught the bear!

1. The dividend on ordinary shares is not _____ and is paid only when all the other _____ on the profits have been met.

2. The owners of preference shares receive preference over _____ shareholders when the dividend is being paid.

3. Ordinary shares do not have a fixed dividend and the income can be _____ if the company is doing well, or _____ if the company has had a poor year.

4. Preference shares carry a fixed rate of dividend and are useful for people who want a _____ income.

5. A special version of preference shares is cumulative shares, which carry the right to any _____ of _____ from previous years when profits were insufficient.

6. Another version of preference shares is non-cumulative shares, which do not carry any right to _____ of _____ .

7. Because private companies are not allowed to advertise shares for sale and raise money in this way, an expanding private company may decide to become a _____ company.

8. A merchant bank, or _____ house will undertake full responsibility for issuing new _____ and collecting payment for them.

9. A prospectus gives details of the company's development, past profits and _____ for the future.

Debentures

This is another source of finance to a company. Debentures are loans to a company. Debenture holders are not owners of the company. A fixed rate of interest is paid each year to those who hold debentures. If the company goes into liquidation the debenture holders have a preferential right to repayment over shareholders. *Mortgaged debentures* are secured against a particular item of property. This makes them an even safer investment. Normally debentures are repaid – plus interest – after a fixed period of time.

We mentioned earlier that banks provide loans and other forms of finance. Banks provide a range of other services which help business. These include:

Current account

When a current account is opened the account holder receives a cheque book and a cheque guarantee card. When the number of the cheque guarantee card is written on the back of a cheque it means that the bank guarantees to pay the amount on the cheque to the person named. Usually this guarantee is up to a maximum of £50, but some banks are now issuing guarantees up to £100. An overdraft facility may be available with a current account. Current account holders receive monthly or three-monthly statements which give details of deposits and withdrawals. The current account helps a business by providing secure storage for its money and a convenient, secure way of paying bills. If the cheque book or cheque guarantee card is stolen a telephone call to the bank prevents anyone else being able to use the account. A disadvantage of the current account is that, usually no interest is paid on the amount in the account. However some banks have recently begun to pay interest on current accounts.

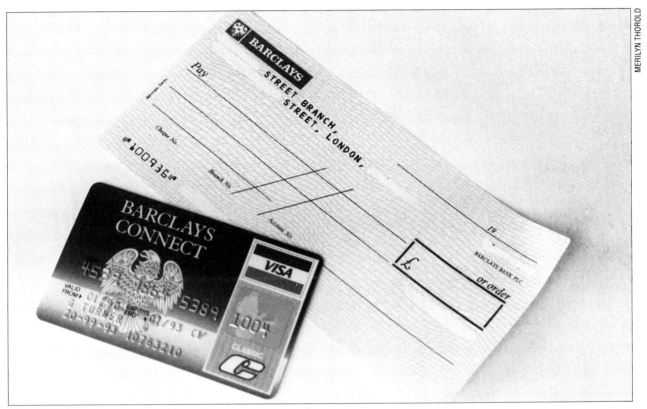

A cheque with a cheque guarantee card

Deposit account

This type of account has the advantage of paying interest but the disadvantage of being less flexible. There is no cheque book facility and *notice* or warning of withdrawal often has to be given. Payments and withdrawals are recorded in a *pass book*. The deposit account is a good way to keep money that may not be needed for some time.

Standing orders

Businesses may have to pay fixed amounts on a regular basis, for example a loan repayment of £100 per month for three years. A standing order is an instruction on a pre-printed form to a bank requesting that such payments are made. The firm does not then have the inconvenience of making out cheques or having to remember to make the payment. The bank will programme its computer to issue the payment as instructed, provided that there is money in the account to cover it.

STANDING ORDER MANDATE

BANK PLC

TO _____

ADDRESS _____

BANK	BRANCH TITLE (Not address)	SORTING CODE NUMBER — —
		ACCOUNT NUMBER

Please pay

BENEFICIARY'S NAME

for the credit of

AMOUNT IN WORDS

†the sum of

AMOUNT IN FIGURES		DUE DATE AND FREQUENCY
£	DATE AND AMOUNT OF FIRST PAYMENT	and thereafter every
*NOW	£	

commencing

DATE AND AMOUNT OF LAST PAYMENT	
£	

*until you receive further notice from me/us in writing

and debit my/our account accordingly.

*until

quoting the reference

*Delete if not applicable
†if the amount of the periodic payments vary they should be incorporated in a schedule overleaf

PLEASE CANCEL ANY PREVIOUS STANDING ORDER OR DIRECT DEBIT IN FAVOUR OF THE BENEFICIARY NAMED ABOVE, UNDER THIS REFERENCE

SPECIAL INSTRUCTIONS

ACCOUNT NUMBER

ACCOUNT TO BE DEBITED

DATE _____

SIGNATURE(S) _____

NOTE: The Bank will not undertake to   (i) make any reference to Value Added Tax or other indeterminate element
(ii) advise payer's address to beneficiary
(iii) advise beneficiary of inability to pay
(iv) request beneficiary's banker to advise beneficiary of receipt

Banks may decline to accept Instructions to charge Standing Orders to certain types of account other than cheque accounts.

BARCLAYS BANK

273 (2/86)

Direct debit

This works in exactly the same way as standing order. The difference is that it is used when the exact amount to be paid is not known in advance. The direct debit allows certain, trusted firms who are owed money to withdraw it from the accounts of their account holders. A firm which does not, for example, know what its gas bill will be might sign a direct debit to the gas board. This will allow the gas board to withdraw money from the firm's account to the value of the gas used. Direct debits and standing orders are usually used with a current account and the amounts withdrawn are shown in the account holder's statement.

Bank draft

We have seen how the cheque guarantee card guarantees payment of £50 or, in some cases, £100. Often firms have to settle bills far in excess of this amount. A bank draft can be made out, to the correct amount, by the bank of a person paying a debt. This can be handed over to the individual who is owed the money. It will be accepted because it guarantees payment of the amount written on it. It benefits the person paying the bill, who does not need to carry large amounts of money, while the person receiving the bank draft is guaranteed payment.

Night safe

By the time most businesses have closed for the day their bank is shut. To avoid the risk of storing cash on business premises overnight, banks offer a night safe service. Customers are given secure pouches into which the money is placed, together with written payment details. These can be 'posted' into the night safe, which is unlocked with a key, on the outside wall of the bank. The payment is processed in the normal way the following day.

Foreign currency

Firms which trade overseas can convert British currency, *sterling*, into the currency of the country of their choice. Payments in foreign currency can be converted into sterling. Banks can help firms make payment into overseas banks if this is requested by overseas contacts.

Status checks

As a lot of business transactions are done on credit it is important that firms know that their trading partners are able to repay their debts. Banks will provide references about a customer's *credit worthiness* or ability to pay.

Advice

Banks have a great deal of knowledge and experience about a wide range of business matters and overseas trade. They will offer this advice to their customers as the need arises.

8.4. Answer the following questions with at least a full sentence, or by writing out the missing words.

3. Describe how a direct debit and a standing order differ.

1. Name two banks.

4. What are two benefits of a banker's draft?

2. A _____ account does not usually pay interest.

5. Another name for British currency is _____ .

1. What does a cost accountant do?

2. Explain why a loan is less flexible than an overdraft.

3. What is a mortgage?

4. Explain how hire purchase works.

5. Describe the advantages of leasing.

6. Describe the work of factoring houses.

7. Why might a firm issue different types of shares?

8. Name five ways a firm could sell shares.

9. How do debentures and shares differ?

10. Why does the government give financial help to some firms?

Having reached an agreement with the bank manager on a secured loan for £1000 Ian was feeling quite pleased with himself. The manager had said that it would be 18 per cent APR, whatever that meant, when they worked out the repayments. Once he had bought the new enlarger he was sure his photography business would go from strength to strength.

a) What is interest? *(2 marks)*

b) What does APR mean? *(4 marks)*

c) Apart from the loan, in what other way could the bank have helped Ian to raise the money needed? What advantages would this method of finance have? *(10 marks)*

d) What is likely to happen if Ian cannot meet the repayments on his secured loan? *(4 marks)*

LEARN IT YOURSELF

1. Look at *The Financial Times* or the financial pages of *The Guardian* or *The Times*. See if you can find any news of a business selling shares. What points do the newspapers make about the share issue?

2. Contact your careers office or job centre and collect information on careers in accountancy. Your local college should provide information about accountancy courses. Prepare a wall display entitled 'Careers in Accountancy'.

3. Using *The Financial Times* or the financial pages of *The Guardian* or *The Times*, record the prices of the shares in three well-known companies for a week. See if you can find any reasons why they are going up or down.

4. Contact your local job centre to find out what help is available to people wishing to start their own business. What government help is available to existing businesses?

ON ASSIGNMENT

Using leaflets and other information from local banks, find out what help they provide to businesses. Present your findings as a project entitled 'How banks can help business'. You should cover both financial and non-financial assistance such as advice.

CASE STUDY

Despite being a well-organised business with sales of over £200 000, Megatoys PLC had always had financial problems. Things had got so bad lately that Rachel, John and Peter, the directors of Megatoys had asked their accountant to provide details of their problems. She had given them these two points:

i) Customers are too slow to pay their debts. This means that your business is often short of money. However, if you push too hard customers may feel pressurised and take their business to your rivals Bettatoys.

ii) Repeated breakdowns on the production line mean that delivery dates are being missed and you are having to give discounts to customers to compensate them. You need better equipment, but even if all your customers were paying their debts on time you would not earn enough to pay for it and would still be short of funds. If you bought this equipment you could produce more goods more cheaply, so the investment is essential.

Prepare a report for the directors of Megatoys PLC describing the options open to them. At the end state clearly which option you would choose and why.

CHAPTER 9

UNDERSTANDING FINANCIAL RECORDS

This chapter looks at techniques for understanding the mass of financial information produced by business organisations. Skilled managers and owners use this information as a guide to the decisions they make because they can calculate the effects of certain actions. In other words, financial records provide information that can be used to help plan activities, forecast the results of possible changes and predict what may happen in certain circumstances.

Cash flow

Planning the income and expenditure of a business is an important part of developing plans for the future. One way this is done is by use of a *cash flow forecast*. This is simply a table showing what income and expenditure the business expects in the coming months. Cash flow forecasts can cover long or short periods of time. Here is an example of a six month cash flow forecast:

Cash flow forecast for MLB paint manufacturers

	April	May	June	July	August	September
Income						
1 Bank Balance from last month	200.00	39.00	(84.00)	(175.00)	(260.00)	(236.00)
2 Sales	150.00	175.00	166.00	200.00	334.00	444.00
3 INCOME TOTAL	350.00	214.00	82.00	25.00	66.00	208.00
Expenditure						
4 Transport	68.00	60.00	34.00	66.00	65.00	67.00
5 Rent	20.00	20.00	20.00	20.00	20.00	20.00
6 Wages	150.00	150.00	150.00	150.00	150.00	150.00
7 Raw Materials	50.00	45.00	30.00	34.00	44.00	50.00
8 Electricity	23.00	23.00	23.00	23.00	23.00	23.00
9 EXPENDITURE TOTAL	311.00	298.00	257.00	293.00	302.00	310.00
10 END OF MONTH BALANCE	39.00	(84.00)	(175.00)	(268.00)	(236.00)	(102.00)

FIGURES IN BRACKETS ARE OVERDRAWN

By looking down the columns under each month you can get a picture of what money the business expects to spend and receive. You will see that income total (line three) is the total of lines one and two. Expenditure total (line nine) is arrived at by adding together lines four to eight. Line ten gives the end of month balance, which is line three minus line nine. In other words, line ten shows the difference between income and expenditure for that month. Figures in brackets are negative and mean that more has gone out of the business than has come in.

After having done these calculations, the accountant for MLB Paint Manufacturers would advise the owners to obtain money to cover the difference in income and expenditure from June onwards. In a case like this finance might be obtained through a bank loan or a bank overdraft. In order to improve the situation it is clear that MLB Paint Manufacturers need either to increase sales, or to reduce expenditure or to do both! Tackling the problem successfully is the responsibility of the organisation's managers. Unless it was likely that sales would improve or costs be reduced, there would be no point in this firm continuing to trade.

Costs and revenues

We can say that the money going out of the business is a cost while money coming in is revenue. In order to make precise forecasts and understand the firm's finances more fully costs and revenues can be broken down into several categories:

Fixed costs

These are costs which stay the same regardless of the level of production, for example rent will be the same regardless of whether the firm produces 10 pots of paint or 1000 pots of paint. Interest on the loan to buy equipment will be the same regardless of how many items a piece of equipment produces. Fixed costs are sometimes called *indirect costs*. This term is used as these costs have to be met regardless of whether production takes place and so they are only indirectly related to levels of production.

Variable costs

These change with the level of production. If the firm increases production to 1000 pots of paint it will need to buy extra chemicals to make the paint, and employ more staff which will mean more wages. As a result of being directly linked to production levels these costs are sometimes called *direct costs*.

It should be noted that some costs are hard to classify. For example administration costs will rise as output rises but will not be as closely linked to output levels as raw materials. Total costs can be thought of as a line with fixed and variable costs at opposite ends. Individual costs can be placed at some point on this line near to the fixed cost end or the variable cost end, depending on what they are.

FIXED COSTS   **VARIABLE COSTS**

Rent

Interest rates

**Labour costs,
raw materials**

*Some costs change more quickly than others as short-term changes in
production occur. Those costs which change most swiftly are called variable
costs. Fixed costs change much more slowly, if at all, in relation to productive
activity.*

Once a firm has started production the managers must decide what
the most profitable level of output is. The firm can only decide how
many more or less items to produce if it can find out the cost of
producing one item. The cost of producing one item is called the
unit cost or *average cost.* Unit cost is arrived at by dividing the total
cost of production by the number of items produced. If a firm makes
80 rubber ducks a week and total costs are £160 then the unit cost
is £2.00 (160 divided by 80).

Unit costs do not remain constant. As output increases each extra
item produced has to cover less of the fixed costs. This is because
the fixed costs are being spread over an increasing number of items,
each, as a result, having a smaller share of the fixed cost to carry.
Notice that each item has to carry the extra variable costs needed
to produce it. The following table demonstrates the point.

MLB paint manufacturers

Tins of paint produced	Fixed costs (£)	Variable costs (£)	Total costs (£)	Unit costs (£)
0	500	0.00	500	
1	500	1.00	501	501.00
10	500	10.00	510	51.00
50	500	50.00	550	11.00
150	500	150.00	650	4.33
600	500	600.00	1100	1.83
1000	500	1000.00	1500	1.50

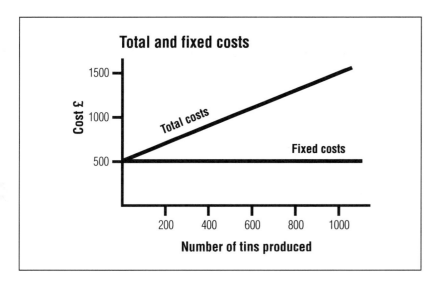

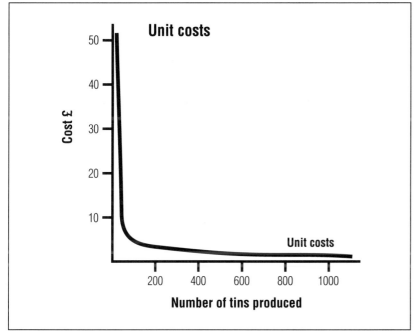

The figures used in the example can also be shown as graphs.

The table and graphs show that even though total cost is increasing unit cost is reducing.

Cost savings as a result of large-scale production are called *economies of scale*. Economies of scale occur in advertising a firm's products. This is because as more items are produced each item has to cover less of the advertising costs. The same applies to the costs of a firm's administration. The larger the size or scale of production, the greater the scope for savings or economies. The increase in output and size of a firm will eventually lead to *diseconomies of scale*. This means that the firm will have an increase in some costs as a result of its increase in size. Larger organisations tend to have problems associated with communication as a result of their size. Line management of large groups leads to inefficiencies.

The aim of a business is to be as efficient or productive as possible. This can be done by increasing output without increasing expenditure. Another way is to produce the same amount but for less cost. It is the aim of Research and Development to find ways of doing this (see page 216). New technology in production and administration is increasingly making firms more productive.

Revenue is the money coming into a firm. The bulk of an organisation's revenue comes from selling its products or services. Other revenue might come from investments or government grants. *Total revenue* is the total income an organisation receives. Average revenue is the revenue from each item the firm sells. Average revenue is calculated by dividing total revenue by the number of items sold (for example, if total revenue is £1400 and the firm sell 700 items average revenue is £2.00). We can represent revenue as a graph just as cost was represented in a graph.

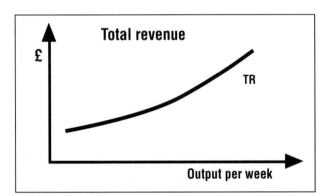

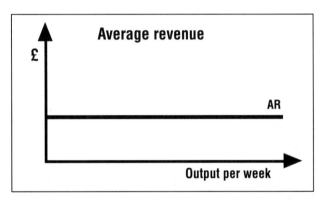

In most cases average revenue is the same as the price of the item sold. This is not the case if a supplier sells goods at different prices to different customers. For example, customers buying in bulk might get a reduction in price. In this case when average revenue is worked out it could be different from the price each customer pays for each item, or could vary at different levels of output.

9.1. Answer the following questions with at least a full sentence, or by writing out the missing words.

1. Explain what a cash flow forecast is.

2. How do fixed and variable costs differ?

3. Unit cost is arrived at by dividing the _____ _____ of production by the ____ of _____ produced.

4. Cost savings as a result of _____-_____ _____ are called economies of scale.

5. Money coming into the firm is called r_____.

6. _____ _____ is calculated by dividing total revenue by the number of items sold.

Breakeven analysis

A firm is said to *breakeven* when its costs are the same as its revenue. If costs are greater than revenue it is operating at a loss. If costs are less than revenue it is operating at a profit. Breakeven analysis is used to show how different levels of output can affect profits. It can also show how changes in price will affect profits at different levels of output. The following examples of breakeven charts use both total and average costs and revenues.

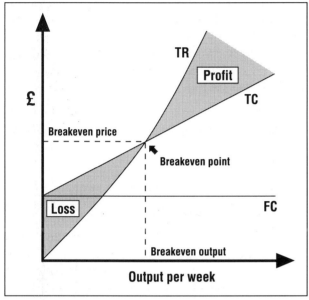

Breakeven chart using total costs and total revenue

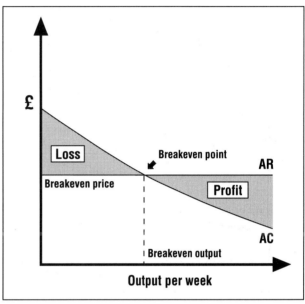

Breakeven chart using average costs and average revenue

Both charts show the same thing. By reading to the left of each line on the graph we find the value of costs and revenues. Where the lines meet we are able to find the revenue which matches the costs of the firm. By reading below this point we are able to establish the level of output required to bring this situation about. This level of output – where cost equals revenue – is called the *breakeven point*. Notice that at all levels of output fixed costs (FC) are the same. However, if existing capital equipment was working at full capacity and more equipment was bought the fixed cost line would rise by the amount the extra equipment cost. Breakeven analysis is a useful tool for analysing the effects of price changes on profit levels and for planning output levels.

9.2. Answer the following questions with at least a full sentence, or by writing out the missing words.

1. What does breakeven mean?

2. What is the breakeven point?

3. Why would breakeven analysis be used?

Keeping accounts

Most businesses are constantly buying and selling things in order to make a profit. The things the business owns are called *assets* (see page 4). Assets normally include land, buildings and equipment. *Fixed assets* are the least liquid of assets and include buildings and land. As we saw in Chapter 1 the more liquid an asset is the more easily it can be changed into cash. *Current assets* are those assets which often change (e.g. stock) and so are more liquid.

When the business owes money it is said to have *liabilities*. Liabilities might include bank loans or raw materials bought on credit. *Current liabilities* are those liabilities which have to be paid in a short period of time, usually less than a year. Current liabilities would include trade credit. *Long-term liabilities* are those debts which take longer than a year to pay. A mortgage is an example of a long-term liability.

The people to whom a business owes money are called *creditors*. A debenture holder is classed as a creditor, for example. The people who owe money to the firm are called *debtors*.

As we have seen, firms will employ accountants in order to keep track of their finances. The accountants will produce various reports and accounts to help managers and owners make decisions about their firm. Each year the accounts will be checked by accountants from outside the organisation. This is known as an *audit*. If the *auditors* - the people checking the accounts - are satisfied that they are accurate they certify them as providing a 'true and fair view' of the business's affairs. Two of the most important sets of figures are the *profit and loss account* and the *balance sheet*. We will look at each of them in turn.

Accountants help keep accurate records

Profit and loss account

This is sometimes called the *trading account* or *income statement*. The profit and loss account is a summary of the total of the business's purchases and sales over a given period, normally one year. The layout of a profit and loss account varies but the following example demonstrates the main points.

Trading, profit and loss account for Jamie's night club

A	TRADING ACCOUNT	£
1	Value of sales	+5000.00
2	Wages	–2000.00
3	Beer, wine and spirits	–1000.00
4	**Gross profit**	**+2000.00**
5	Gross profit	+2000.00
6	Income from ICI shares	+500.00
7	Depreciation of disco equipment	–25.00
8	Telephone bill	–500.00
9	**Net profit (before tax)**	**+1975.00**
B	APPROPRIATION ACCOUNT	
10	Net profit (before tax)	+1975.00
11	Taxation	–600.00
12	Drawings	–1000.00
13	**Balance: Net profit (after tax)**	**+375.00**

As you can see, the account is in two parts. The trading account (part A) shows the total value of sales for the year (line 1). Line 2 shows the total wage cost directly related to the running of the night club. Line three shows the costs of the main raw materials related to running the club. We can summarise the trading account as showing the difference between the value of sales and the costs directly related to providing the goods or services of the firm. The figure we arrive at, line 4, is the *gross profit* figure. As this is calculated before deductions for tax it is sometimes called the *pre-tax profit*. Lines 5 to 9 take the gross profit and add any income not directly related to production - line 6. It is then necessary to remove from the figure any costs not directly related to production. In this case we have a telephone bill, line 8, and *depreciation*. By depreciation we mean the amount of value lost from an item each year. In this example the disco equipment is worth less now than when it was new. It is estimated that over the year the disco equipment has lost £25 in value. In other words, if it was sold now at the end of the year, Jamie would get £25 less than at the start of the year. The money for depreciation is set aside so that when equipment wears out the firm is able to replace it.

The appropriation account (part B) shows what remains when taxes, such as VAT, have been paid and *drawings* taken into account. Drawings refers to any money taken, or drawn, out of the business by Jamie for his own use during the year. These drawings are in addition to any wage he may pay himself. Once this calculation is done we are left with the *net profit* figure (line 13). Net profit is the amount remaining after all deductions have been accounted for. It is the net profit which is kept by the owners.

Balance sheet

While the profit and loss account shows a summary of the firm's activities over a period of time, the balance sheet shows the value of the business on a particular day. While the value of some things can be calculated exactly, others have to be estimated. Despite this element of guesswork the balance sheet is an important document for showing the value of a business. The balance sheet must contain details of:

MANCHESTER AIRPORT PLC

BALANCE SHEET 31st MARCH 1988

	1988 £000	1988 £000	1987 £000	1987 £000
FIXED ASSETS				
Tangible Assets	136270		127347	
Intangible Assets	2671		3562	
Investments	20	138961	-	13090
CURRENT ASSETS				
Stocks	720		783	
Debtors	15757		12590	
Cash at bank and in hand	68205		35439	
	84682		48812	
CREDITORS – amounts falling due within one year	(39518)		(26775)	
NET CURRENT ASSETS		45164		22037
TOTAL ASSETS LESS CURRENT LIABILITIES		184125		152946
CREDITORS – amounts falling due more than one year		(53867)		(34181)
		£130258		£118765
CAPITAL AND RESERVES				
Called-up share capital		114030		114030
Profit and loss account		16228		4735
		£130258		£118765

- Share capital and reserves – the value of issued and authorised share capital, reserves and the balance from the profit and loss account.

- Current liabilities – the amount of money owed to trade creditors, interest to debenture holders, bank overdrafts and share dividend payments.

- Current assets – the value of stock, work in progress or 'in hand', cash in the bank, cash in hand and debtors. Debtors, the people who owe the firm money, are classed as assets because they will, eventually, pay money to the firm. When the firm gives up on debt repayments these are then classified as *bad debts*.

- Fixed assets – the value of land, premises, office equipment, manufacturing equipment or *plant* and investments. Notice that for some fixed assets, such as plant, there has to be an allowance for depreciation.

- Liabilities and provisions – income tax, corporation tax and the cost of repaying debentures and bank loans.

9.3. Answer the following questions with at least a full sentence, or by writing out the missing words.

1. Explain the difference between assets and liabilities.

2. What is the difference between creditors and debtors?

3. What is an audit?

4. The profit and loss account is a ____ of the total of the business's ____ and ____ over a given time.

5. What is meant by depreciation?

6. The ____ ____ shows the value of a business on a particular day.

7. Name two details that should be in a balance sheet.

Analysing accounts

Having obtained financial information it is important that it is analysed so that managers and owners can make decisions about the running of the business. Several features will be examined in order to find out how well a business is doing. These include working capital, profitability, performance and liquidity.

Working capital

Working capital is what is left when current liabilities have been deducted from current assets. This amount represents the capital

the business has to work with. It can work with this capital without
fear of being required to pay bills as current liabilities have already
been deducted in arriving at this figure. Clearly it is undesirable
for any business to have less in assets than it has in liabilities. If
this was the case it would find it hard to meet its bills. It is also
undesirable for a business to have too much cash as these funds
could be earning money through being invested. Both overstocking and understocking should be avoided. Having too little
stock may lead to delays while orders are met while too much
stock may lead to certain goods becoming unusable if left too long.

Profitability

We saw earlier that profit could be described as the difference
between costs and revenues. There are, however, several other
points to take into consideration. Factors such as how much
money has to be spent to make a certain amount of profit are
important considerations when making decisions about future investment. The amount of money received from an investment is
called the *rate of return*. Investors need to know the rate of return
on capital employed to decide if an investment is worth taking. This
rate of return will be compared to the rate of return from investing
in other firms or putting money into a bank or building society. The
rate of return on capital employed can be calculated using the following ratio:

Net Profit : capital employed (fixed assets + working capital)

If fixed assets were £100 and working capital was £300, capital
employed would be £400. If the firm made £200 net profit the ratio
could be calculated thus:

£200 : £400

0.5 : 1

If we multiply 0.5 by 100 we get a percentage figure. In this case the
figure is 50 per cent. This means that the rate of return on capital
employed is 50 per cent. Given that most businesses manage between 12 and 30 per cent, this would be a highly desirable rate of
return. If the figure had been less, say 6 per cent, it would have been
more profitable to invest in a bank or building society account
which gives rates of interest above this figure. Such an investment
would involve far less risk.

By comparing profit to the value of sales the percentage profit can
be determined. The ratio is:

Net profit : Sales

A firm with a net profit of £1200 and sales of £7200 would have net
profit to sales ratio of 0.17 : 1. If this figure of 0.17 is multiplied by
100 it gives a percentage net profit of 17 per cent. It is possible to
do the same calculation using gross profit.

Performance

Many small businesses close because they are unable to collect their debts in time to pay their creditors. *Debtor turnover* shows how long average repayment takes. It is calculated like this:

Value of Debts : Value of Sales (sometimes called turnover)

If the total value of debtors is £600 and the firm's turnover or sales is £3000, we arrive at the ratio:

£600 : £3000

1 : 5

Another important measure of performance is *stock turnover*. This indicates the number of times stock is sold during a year. The greater the figure the more profit will be earned. This figure is arrived at by dividing the value of sales (turnover) by the value of stock. For example

$$\frac{£20\ 000}{£1200}$$

The answer of 16.67 is the number of times the stock has been sold. The higher the number the better.

Liquidity

We saw earlier that it is important for a business to be able to convert its assets into cash if the need arises. In order to judge if a business can do this several tests can be applied:

Current ratio

This ratio is one way of measuring liquidity. It is arrived at using this equation:

Current assets : Current liabilities

For example this could be

£4100 : £4500

0.91

The answer is an unacceptable result. This is because the time taken to sell stock means that a ratio of at least 2:1 is needed for the firm to be safely liquid.

Acid test ratio.

The acid test ratio is calculated as follows:

Current assets – stock : Current liabilities

Although stock is assumed to be a current asset it is excluded from this calculation to focus attention on the firm's other current assets.

A firm has stock worth £1300, the rest of its current assets are valued at £2800 and there are liabilities of £4500. Its acid test ratio would be calculated as follows:

$$£2800 - £1300 : £4500$$

$$£1500 : £4500$$

$$0.33 : 1$$

This means that for each £1 of debt the firm would have 33p if it sold its most liquid assets. This is an undesirable situation as the ratio should be 1 : 1 if the business is to be secure. In other words, each £1 of debt should be matched with £1 of assets.

Ratios have an important part to play in analysing business activity and are best used to compare similar businesses or to look at the performance of a firm over time.

9.4. Answer the following questions with at least a full sentence, or by writing out the missing words.

3. The amount of money received from an investment is called the _____ ___ _____ .

4. Name two ratios that could be used to measure the performance of a business.

1. What is meant by 'working capital'?

5. How is the acid test ratio calculated?

2. What is best described as the difference between cost and revenues?

6. How do the acid test ratio and the current ratio differ?

6. What is the difference between a profit and loss account and a balance sheet?

1. Why might a cash flow forecast be used?

7. In accounts, what is meant by the term drawings?

2. How do direct and indirect costs differ?

3. Give another name for unit cost and explain how it is calculated.

8. Name two current assets and two current liabilities.

4. What is meant by diseconomies of scale?

9. Give two examples of a fixed asset.

5. Explain why breakeven analysis might be used.

10. Describe two uses of ratios in understanding financial records.

1. The accounts of Gibbies Home Made Biscuits show fixed assets of £200, working capital of £600 and £300 net profit. Its current assets are £600 and its current liabilities are £300. The value of its stock is £300.

a) Is the rate of return satisfactory? Give reasons. *(4 marks)*

b) Comment on this firm's ability to liquidate its assets and say if you think it is satisfactory. *(8 marks)*

c) Assuming you had access to other information, what other ratios would you use to assess the performance of this business? *(8 marks)*

2. Mohammed Salim reckons that he can sell vegi-burgers in his new vegetarian burger bar for £2.00 each. His fixed costs are £100 per week and burgers, rolls and relish etc. cost 80p per burger. He sells only vegi-burgers.

a) How many burgers will Mohammed have to sell each week in order to break even? *(4 marks)*

b) Name two fixed assets a business like this might have. *(4 marks)*

c) If the landlord adds £10 per week to the rent, what is the lowest number of burgers Mohammed can sell each week before making a loss? *(6 marks)*

d) Assuming 80 burgers are sold each week, what is the average cost? *(6 marks)*

Newspapers such as *The Financial Times*, *The Guardian* and *The Times* sometimes carry extracts from company reports. Find three examples of these and compare them. Find out which firm had the highest pre-tax profits, what the earnings per share of each of them was and which had the largest number of employees.

Choose a business you would like to set up and run yourself. Using the techniques explained in this chapter, calculate what costs you would have and what you would have to charge for your products or services in order to make a profit. Describe how you would raise the finance for the business. What arguments would you use to persuade a bank manager to lend you the money you would need?

CASE STUDY

Your friend, George Sharma, has asked you to look at the balance sheet of a business he is thinking of buying and advise him on whether or not he should buy it for £20,000. In his letter to you he lets you know that the value of the firm's sales last year was £40,000.

Prepare a letter to George giving your opinion of the state of the business and asking for the other items of information you would need to help you make a better decision about the value of the business.

Balance sheet of Sprigott Enterprises Ltd as April 5 19--

FIXED ASSETS	£	£
Premises		10,000
Equipment		5,000
Depreciation	2,000	
		13,000
CURRENT ASSETS		
Stock in hand		16,000
Debtors		8,000
Bank current account		5,000
		29,000
CURRENT LIABILITIES		
Creditors	20,000	
Assets less liabilities		**22,000**
REPRESENTED BY		
Mr Sprigott's investment		15,000
Net profit		7,000

SECTION FOUR

Marketing

CHAPTER 10

INTODUCTION TO MARKETING

Unless a business sells its goods or services in sufficient quantities to meet its costs it will not survive. Marketing is the process of getting the goods (or services) the customer wants, to the place they want it, at a price they will pay and which is profitable for the firm. These factors make up the firm's *marketing mix*. The marketing mix will result from the decisions the firm takes about:

- Product – what to produce, what to call it, what design, colours and packaging are required.
- Price – how much to charge, whether to have an introductory low price, whether the price should be the same in different countries.
- Promotion – how will potential customers be told about the product, how will they be encouraged to buy it, will there be special offers, money off, competitions etc?
- Place – how will the goods be transported to the shops which will sell them, which shops will sell them?

The marketing mix for each product a firm sells will vary according to the *market* it is aiming at. By the word market we mean any way in which buyers and sellers make contact. This might be in a shop, street market or by telephone. The firm will have to decide if it is aiming for the capital goods market or the consumer goods market (see page 2). Computers, for example, could fit into either market. The consumer goods market can be broken down into the *consumer durables* market – which covers long-lasting domestic items such as freezers and televisions – and the *single use* market which covers things like food. Each of these markets can be further broken down into the type of consumer the firm is aiming to sell its goods to, for example young middle class people or older working class people. We will look at this again when we consider market research.

Most firms will have a marketing department responsible for co-ordinating the marketing activities of the organisation. It is not unusual for the marketing department to employ agencies to carry out certain tasks, for example organising an advertising campaign or market research. It is important that the marketing department has good links with the production department to make sure that goods are being produced which meet the customer's needs and that sufficient quantities are being produced. For example, production will have to be increased before an advertising campaign is launched so that there will be goods in the shops to meet the (hopefully) increased demand. Links with Research and Development will be needed to keep up to date with new product ideas, materials and developments so that these can be translated into goods which meet the customer's needs.

10.1. Answer the following questions with at least a full sentence, or by writing out the missing words.

2. Describe the difference between a single use market and a consumer durables market.

3. Name two other departments of the firm which the marketing section should work with.

1. Name the four parts of the marketing mix.

Product life cycle

The business will have to make decisions about which new products or services to offer as existing products or services reach the end of their *life cycle*. The *product life cycle* refers to how long it is profitable for a firm to produce a particular product. The length of the life cycle of each product varies but several stages are common as the following graph shows:

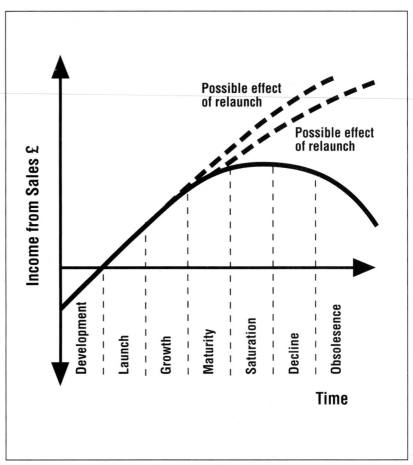

The product life cycle

Once a decision has been taken to make a product, it goes through these stages:

1 Development. At this stage the product is being researched and developed. As there are no sales there is no income from the product to cover the costs of development. These costs will include the wages of extra staff to make the new product (or the cost of training existing staff), the cost of new machines and equipment. This is why the graph starts in the negative area.

2 Launch. Once a firm is satisfied that its product is ready for sale it will be *launched* or introduced to the market. It is normal for a firm to have high advertising costs at this stage. This may be due partly to the use of special offers to interest consumers in the product. Sales will also be low while consumers discover the product.

3 Growth. As the advertising reaches more consumers, sales increase. If the product is good enough, people who bought the product when it first appeared will make repeat purchases. The growth may be due to the fact that the firm has a head start over its rivals.

4 Maturity. At this point the product is at its most profitable stage for the firm. Sales will be at their highest level but will not increase by very much. Rival firms will have introduced similar products which will account for sales not increasing as rapidly as before.

5 Saturation. By this point the increase in sales will have stopped. Rival products will have become established and the thrust of the firm's advertising will be to hold sales steady. It is likely that the firm will have started work on a replacement product which will be at the development stage.

6 Decline. Competition and changes in consumer tastes will cause demand for the product to drop.

7 Obsolescence. This is the point at which the firm decides to halt production. It may be because the product is no longer profitable or that it is no longer in keeping with the company's image or that the firm thinks a new product may be more profitable. At this stage price cuts and special offers may be used to get rid of existing stock to make way for the introduction of a new product.

It is clearly in a firm's interest to have as long a product life cycle as possible so that it earns as much as it can from the investment in equipment and staff. In order to do this a firm might 'relaunch' a product at the maturity or saturation stage. This is done by making some change to the product and advertising the change, for example 'new, improved' soap powder or a 'new look' car. It is not uncommon for the packaging or the image of the product to be changed. For example, Lucozade was a drink sold in large bottles and linked to helping the ill recover. Today it is sold in small, convenient bottles and its energy-giving powers are linked to well-known athletes and young healthy people exercising. Such a change is designed to find a new market and so extend the life cycle of the product. Another way of extending a product's life is to sell it overseas, in a different market.

A relaunch can lengthen the life of a product

10.2. Answer the following questions with at least a full sentence, or by writing out the missing words.

1. The ___ ___ ___ refers to how long it is profitable for a firm to produce a product.

2. The stages of the product life cycle are ___, ___, ___, ___, ___, ___ and ___ .

3. How will the firm try to extend a product's life cycle?

Market research

Before a firm will produce a new product it needs to know what its customers would prefer and what its rivals are offering. The way in which a firm finds out about the behaviour of its customers and its rivals is called market research. Only the largest of organisations will employ their own market researchers. This very specialised activity is done by market research agencies for example MORI or Gallup or advertising agencies such as J. Walter Thompson or Saatchi and Saatchi. These firms receive a fee for their work. By researching the market thoroughly firms try to reduce the risk of an unprofitable investment. Market research tries to find answers to questions like:

- What does the customer prefer?

- How many people will buy our new product?

- How can we reach the customer?

- What are customers prepared to pay?

- What packaging is best?

- How might customer tastes change?

- What do our rivals produce?

- What are their prices?

- What are our rivals likely to do in future?

Market research examines the likely behaviour of other firms and potential customers. The information used in market research is either *primary data* or *secondary data*. Primary data is new information directly related to the product the firm hopes to introduce. Primary data is obtained through interviews, questionnaires, observation or experiment (see Appendix One). Some firms use *consumer panels* which are groups of consumers who agree to taste or test new products and complete questionnaires giving their opinion. Before getting involved in the expense of national advertising and distribution of a new product, firms will often *test market* the product. This is done by selling and advertising the product in only one region of the country. This would probably include advertising on the local commercial television network, for example Tyne-Tees or TVS. Sales figures will be analysed and a judgement made about the suitability of the product for national launch. The research to get primary data is called *field research* because it happens away from the firm.

Field research provides important marketing information

Secondary data comes from information that has already been collected, which is interpreted to find answers to the firm's questions. Sources of secondary data include reference books, magazines and government statistics (Social Trends, for example). Information the firm already has such as past sales figures, the number of faulty goods returned or letters from satisfied customers is also secondary data. Secondary data is gathered through *desk research*, so called because it can be carried out by analysing existing information at a desk inside the organisation. Primary data is usually more useful than secondary data as it is aimed at answering particular questions to which the firm needs answers. The disadvantage is that it is the most expensive sort of research and often slow to produce results.

10.3. **Answer the following questions with at least a full sentence, or by writing out the missing words.**

1. What is market research?

2. _____ and _____ are two market research agencies.

3. How do primary and secondary data differ?

4. Explain what is meant by test marketing.

5. In which ways do desk and field research differ?

Supply and demand

One important outcome of market research is to find out if there is a *demand* for a product. Demand means the willingness and ability to purchase a particular product. We may all want a Rolls Royce car but without the ability to pay there is little point in the firm taking account of our wishes. Demand can be recorded in two ways:

a) A demand schedule, which is a type of list.

Demand schedule for chocolate bars (per week)

Price	Quantity sold per week
10p	500
15p	250
20p	150
25p	50
30p	25

b) A demand curve.

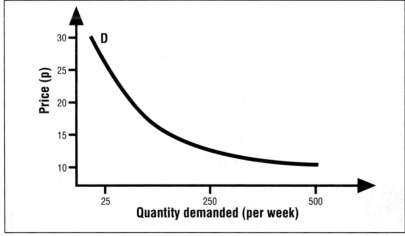

Demand curve for chocolate bars

These figures show how, usually, the lower the price the greater the demand. By establishing what the demand is for, in this case chocolate bars, the firm can begin to decide if production is worthwhile. What the firm will also need to find out is what the level of *supply* is in each particular market it hopes to enter. Supply means the amount of a product offered for sale at a given price. Again this can be recorded in two ways:

c) A supply schedule.

Supply schedule for chocolate bars (per week)

Price	Quantity supplied per week
10p	25
15p	50
20p	150
25p	250
30p	500

d) A supply curve.

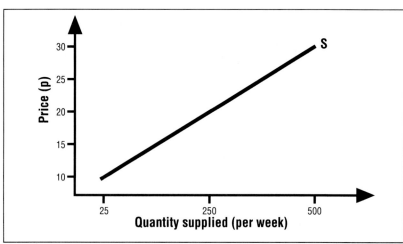

Supply curve for chocolate bars

The supply curve shows what quantity of chocolate bars will be supplied by the various firms in the market at particular prices. As the price rises firms find it more profitable to produce chocolate and so supply increases. You will notice from the two graphs that when demand is high supply will be low. This is because the price that is attractive to consumers is not attractive to suppliers. This becomes even more obvious when we put supply and demand together in one graph as shown on the next page.

The point where the two lines meet is called the point of *equilibrium*. This means that supply and demand are in balance as both are equal. In other words, at that particular price there is sufficient being supplied to meet demand. To the right of the curve is a position of *excess supply* or a *glut*. At all prices above the point of equilibrium more is being supplied than is being demanded. Some firms

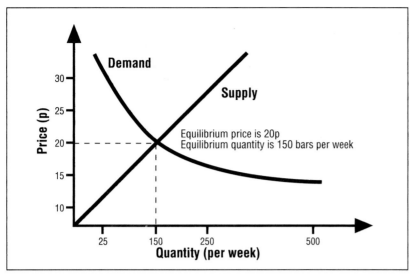

Equilibrium position for choclate bars
At 15p there is excess demand of 250 bars. This is because at this price,
suppliers wish to supply 50 bars while there is demand for 300 bars. If we
take 50 from 300 we have an excess demand, or shortage, of 250.
At 30p there is excess supply or a glut of 275. At this price only 25 bars are
demanded, while 300 are supplied. This leaves 275 bars supplied which are
not demanded i.e. 300 minus 25

will be unable to sell their chocolate and will eventually close unless demand increases. At prices below the equilibrium price demand will increase but it will not be worthwhile for some firms to supply, therefore supply will drop, creating *excess demand*. In other words, there is a *shortage*. The effect of excess demand is to force prices up as consumers become willing to pay more for the scarce product. As price rises more firms will produce chocolate and so supply will increase. Eventually supply will increase to an equilibrium point and if supply continues to rise a glut will occur. In situations of a glut firms will drop their price, hoping to sell something and at least cover fixed costs. Some firms will go out of production or move into other, more profitable activities. Eventually the amount being supplied will equal the amount demanded and a new equilibrium will be reached. This continuing shift of supply and demand is a feature of a market or capitalist economy.

10.4. Answer the following questions with at least a full sentence, or by writing out the missing words.

2. Explain what is meant by supply in marketing.

3. What happens if supply and demand are in equilibrium?

1. The willingness and ability to purchase a product is known as _____.

4. What is a glut and what is another term for it?

What has just been described is a theoretical view of how supply and demand works. It does not, for instance, account for consumer tastes. The theory assumes that consumers know about all the possible products available and that they will buy the cheapest goods. It may be the case that some firms' chocolate has a better reputation than others, or that some people are in the habit of buying a particular brand. People may also be ignorant of a firm's product. However, the theory of supply and demand does at least give a starting point for a firm trying to understand how the market works. Primary research will be much more useful, particularly surveys and questionnaires (see Appendix One).

We will now look at three factors which might influence demand for a firm's product, apart from the price of its rivals. These factors are *branding, pricing* and *packaging*.

Branding

Branding is where a firm tries to create an identity or image for its product which consumers will easily recall. An important part of branding is the development of *brand names*. Parker is a well-known brand name for pens. Some branding is so successful that it becomes the name for a particular product, for example Biro started as a brand name for pens made by the Biro company and Hoover is one brand of vacuum cleaner and yet most people refer to a Hoover rather than a vacuum cleaner. Names like Hoover and Biro which cover all products of a particular type are called *generic brand names*.

Hoover has become a generic brandname

The packaging and labelling of goods is aimed to make a product stand out from its rivals. The shape of Pepsi Cola bottles and the way the name is written is an example of this process of developing *trademarks*. Trademarks are part of the process of branding goods and cannot be copied by other firms.

Branding makes a product much easier to identify and so makes advertising it easier. This should bring about improved sales. Once customers get into the habit of using a particular brand they become less likely to change. This is called *brand loyalty* and benefits the firm as price rises have less effect on demand. Another benefit is that when the firm introduces new products under the same brand name customers may be more willing to try them. The range of Heinz soups and the different types of baked bean products they sell is an example of how the Heinz brand name works. What makes an effective brand name? This really depends on the consumers' attitude, but to stand a chance the brand name should be:

- Distinctive – It should stand out from others and be easy to recognise.

- Descriptive – The brand name should tell the consumer something about the product, for example Rentokil suggests a service for hire which will kill things, in this case rats and mice etc.

- Simple – Short, one word brands which are easy to say are most easily remembered.

It is not just manufacturers who use brand names. Large retailers will often have products manufactured on their behalf and sold under their own name, for example St Michael is used as the Marks and Spencer brand name.

1.6. Answer the following questions with at least a full sentence, or by writing out the missing words.

2. _____ is where a firm tries to create an identity for its product which _____ will easily recall.

3. Give two examples of a brand name.

1. ___, ___ and ___ affect demand, as well as the price of rival products.

4. A good brand name should be ___, ___ and ___ .

Pricing

The price a firm charges for its product or service will depend on a number of things:

- The cost of making the product.

- The price of rival products.

- The sensitivity of demand to price changes.

This sensitivity is important as an increase in price might cause a disproportionate loss of customers. Bearing these considerations in mind the firm needs to decide if it wants to *capture* the market, *cream* the market or *penetrate* the market.

A display of drinks showing the retailer's own brand goods

Capturing the market

When a firm captures a market it supplies certain basic items at a low price, but charges a higher price for items which can only be used with the product. Cartridge pens, originally supplied with a refill, might be a bargain from one firm. The consumer might then find that only that firm supplies refills which fit. These can be sold at a price which is highly profitable.

Creaming the market

When new, unrivalled, products are launched the price will be high and certain consumers will not be put off by this. For these people the new facilities or services offered by the new product are more important. By being aware of this, firms can price high and maximise profit before rival products appear.

Penetrating the market

When there is the possibility of many repeat purchases or the firm is trying to get a brand name recognised and establish brand loyalty it may set a low price. This means that profits are low but by establishing brand loyalty regular future sales are more likely, leading to the likelihood of long term profits. In retailing a similar approach is called *loss leading*. This means that certain products in the shop are priced low in the hope that customers will be attracted into the shop. Once in the shop attempts are made by sales staff or large displays etc to persuade the customer to buy other, more profitable, goods.

Once the approach has been decided the firm has various ways in which it can calculate the price. The most common method of setting the price is called *cost plus pricing*. This means that the firm calculates its costs and adds onto the price how much it wishes to take as profit. In doing this the firm must bear in mind its needs to obtain a return on capital and to maintain its liquidity. *Price discrimination* or *differential pricing* is another approach. In this approach different prices are charged to different customers. Gas and electricity, for example, are sold at different prices to home consumers and industrial users. With differential pricing the price is usually set at what the company thinks it can charge without the consumer going elsewhere.

In setting the price the firm must always be aware of what market it is aiming at. For example, low–priced luxury goods will not be successful. If the product is promoted as being elegant and sophisticated it must have a price to match. In certain cases it is not unknown for sales to increase when the price of a product has risen!

Packaging

Packaging helps to keep goods intact, fresh and ready for use but it has other purposes as well. Well-designed packaging can increase sales. The use of bright, primary colours can make the item stand out on the shop's shelf. Packaging which shows the goods to advantage also helps sales, particularly if the packaging creates the impression that there is more inside than there actually is. Packaging can make the storing and display of the product easier for the retailer and so encourage retail outlets to handle it. The Prices Act, 1974 says that prepackaged food should have the price per unit clearly marked, usually on the packaging. This means that, for example, the price per kilo should be shown as well as the price of the actual package. The Act also states that food should be marked with a *use by date*, which is the date after which the food is no longer usable. A *sell by date*, showing when the goods should be sold by is acceptable. The 1970 Labelling of Food Order said that ingredients of food should be shown on a packet in descending order of weight of ingredients. The item at the bottom of the list is in the smallest amounts in the food. Small print which made things unreadable is outlawed and the manufacturer's name and address should be marked on prepackaged food.

Food packaging should be very informative

10.6. Answer the following questions with at least a full sentence, or by writing out the missing words.

1. Describe three factors which will affect the price a firm will charge for its products.

2. In setting a price a firm should decide if it wants to ___, ___ or ___ the market.

3. What is cost plus pricing?

4. Describe three reasons for packaging goods.

5. What information should be shown on packets of food?

SHORT QUESTIONS

1. Why is a good marketing mix important?

2. At which stage of the product life cycle is a product normally most profitable?

3. What reasons might a firm have for not continuing to produce a particular product?

4. Why do firms carry out market research?

5. Explain what is meant by supply.

6. Explain what is meant by demand.

7. Why do firms use branding?

8. Explain the phrase 'loss leading'.

9. Explain what is meant by price discrimination.

10. Describe the requirements of the Prices Act, 1974 and the 1970 Labelling of Food Order.

STIMULUS RESPONSE QUESTIONS

1. *Modern Miss school note pads and pen sets show the following sales figures from the year of launch.*

Year	Annual sales
1985	6 000
1986	8 000
1987	12 000
1988	9 000
1989	7 000
1990	6 000

a) What stage in its life cycle had this product reached in 1990? *(2 marks)*

b) What stage of the life cycle did 1987 represent? *(2 marks)*

c) What options do the firm have now? *(2 marks)*

d) Why might sales have declined? *(6 marks)*

e) Suggest ways in which this product might be relaunched. *(8 marks)*

2.

Price (£)	Weekly demand	Weekly supply
3.00	100 000	1 000 000
2.80	150 000	800 000
2.60	375 000	600 000
2.40	600 000	400 000
2.20	800 000	300 000
2.00	1 000 000	200 000

a) Draw a supply and demand graph from the information in this schedule. *(8 marks)*

b) What is the equilibrium price? *(2 marks)*

c) What quantity will be demanded if the price is £2.30? *(2 marks)*

d) If consumer taste goes against this product so that 200 000 less are demanded at each price, what will the new equilibrium price be? *(3 marks)*

e) How might some manufacturers of this product react to the drop in price? *(8 marks)*

1. Buy three different but similarly-priced bars of chocolate. Before opening them measure the length, height and width of each one. Unwrap them and measure the same dimensions again. Compare your findings in each case. What does this tell you about the effects of packaging?

2. Obtain wrappers and newspaper or magazine advertisements for four different well-known products. Describe what image each product is trying to convey. What colours are used on the packaging? Is use made of brand names? How could the wrapper or advertisement be improved?

3. Choose brand names for the following products.

   a) A new shock-proof and waterproof watch, with a stopwatch function, aimed at people who play sports.

   b) A new low fat/low sugar/high fibre range of frozen foods which can be cooked in a microwave oven.

   c) Animal-shaped chocolate bars for young children.

   Explain why you have chosen these names and what image you are hoping to present.

Carry out market research in the area you live in to find out what facilities there are for young people in the 14–18 year age group. You should also find out what facilities young people would like but which are not provided. Find out the good and bad points of existing facilities. Write a report, with recommendations, showing how you carried out your research. You should carry out both field and desk research. Appendix One (on page 231) should help you to design a questionnaire.

Filofax, the company which took a glorified address book and turned it into a status symbol, has fallen into the red.

After six years of growth in which sales multiplied 20-fold, sales have fallen in 1989, undercut by cheaper lookalikes and rivalled by pocket-sized, computerised personal organisers.

As a result, Mr David Collischon, Filofax chairman, yesterday saw the value of his family stake in the company slump to £3.25 million, after he revealed a first-half loss of £554 000. When the company was floated on the stock market, the holding was worth nearly £11 million.

But Mr Collischon was unabashed: "Electronic products like the Psion have their place, but the pen and paper are still the best input tools. There is still an enormous market to be had. There are lots of people who just don't understand what a Filofax is about or what it can do".

About five million Britons are thought to have a personal organiser. Two years ago, Filofax had nearly 90 per cent of the market; now, that is down to little over half, as rival manufacturers have caught on and retailing chains have launched own-brand products.

Only last week, the head of one of Britain's largest stationers told branch managers to change the layout of stores to give less space to Filofax displays and more to cheaper imitations. "People are still buying personal organisers, but not Filofaxes by name," he said. "People like students are now buying them and if they can buy something for less than a tenner, they will. Filofaxes start at £14.50. They are becoming a utility item rather than a yuppie item."

The head of another retailing chain said: "One of the problems for Filofax . . . is that the binder lasts an awful long time."

However, Mr Collischon insists Filofaxes "are not just for yuppies". "When I took over the company in 1980, two-thirds of our sales were to the clergy and people in the army," he said.

"We always position our products as serious, practical aids to personal efficiency."

THE GUARDIAN, 23 SEPTEMBER 1989

After you have read the article discuss the following points in small groups. You should aim to arrive at an agreed group opinion.

a) Why Filofax have fallen into the red.

b) What Mr Collischon's business could do to improve its position.

Choose one person from your group to report the views of the group to the rest of the class.

DISTRIBUTION

Having decided what to produce and which market to aim at, the manufacturer has to decide the best way to get the goods to the consumer. This involves making decisions about which *channel of distribution* to use and the best method of transport in the circumstances.

It is vital to choose the right channel of distribution

When we talk of the channel or *chain of distribution* we mean the way in which goods reach the consumer after being produced by the manufacturer.

There are three parts in the chain of distribution:

- *Manufacturer* – This is the person or organisation which uses the factors of production to make a product, such as cars, clothes or industrial equipment.

- *Wholesaler* – This is the person or organisation who buys in bulk from several manufacturers and acts as a link between manufacturer and retailer. The wholesaler stores goods until they are needed and will regularly deliver them to retailers. By keeping a stock of items from different manufacturers the wholesaler makes sure retailers have a choice of goods in the quantities they require. In breaking down the large quantities bought from the manufacturer into the smaller quantities required by the retailer we say that the wholesaler *breaks bulk*. As a result the manufacturer and retailer avoid having to store large amounts at their own expense. The manufacturer is spared the inconvenience and expense of dealing in small quantities with lots of retailers. The retailer is spared the trouble and expense of contacting and ordering from many different manufacturers around the country. Wholesalers will often pack and 'brand' goods for manufacturers or large retailers (see page 140).

■ *Retailer* – This is the part of the distribution process where goods are sold in small quantities to the public. As well as providing advice and *after-sales service* to the public some retailers provide credit. An example of after-sales service is free repairs to a washing machine if it breaks down after the sale, or purchase, has taken place. As the retailer orders from the wide choice provided by the wholesaler and is situated near to where people live it is true to say that retailers bring a wide range of choice to the area they serve. Retailers often advertise the goods they sell, which benefits the wholesaler and the manufacturer if it increases sales. Wholesalers and manufacturers can find out how the public are reacting to, for example, new goods or price changes by looking at the changing orders from retailers. Retailers may pass on customer opinions to the sales representatives of the manufacturer or wholesaler. This information may lead to changes in the price, design or quality of the product.

As we can see there are several possible chains of distribution.

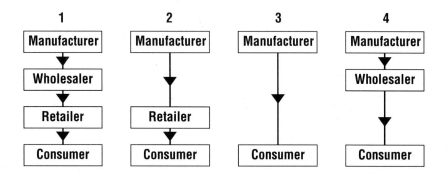

We will begin by looking at how goods can be distributed in this country. Chain one is often used for things like newspapers or clothes. Chain two will be used for branded goods sold by retailers, such as the St Michael brand sold by Marks and Spencer, or items which need to be kept fresh, such as bread. Building materials or consumer durables like furniture may be distributed by chain four. Chain three will be used for some items like double glazing, but more often for services such as hairdressing or banking. The chain of distribution used depends on the product, the market and the firm itself.

The product

A firm will normally try to sell low value items through wholesalers and large retailers who will buy the goods in large quantities. This is cheaper for the firm than having to deal in lots of low-value transactions with small shops. This would increase administrative costs and force prices upwards. Perishable goods such as fresh fruit need a short chain of distribution and may go straight to the retailer. This can also apply to goods with a short life cycle such as fashion items.

The market

Firms selling in an industrial market will often deal directly with the customer. The consumer or domestic market is more likely to involve wholesalers or distributors. Large, spread-out markets have high transport costs. In order to avoid these a manufacturer may prefer to sell to wholesalers or distributors. A manufacturer supplying large quantities to a few wholesalers, retailers or distributors will often be able to distribute the goods profitably. This is not true if the firm's customers buy small quantities.

The firm

A firm will normally seek the services of wholesalers or distributors as these carry the cost of storing goods and transporting them to the final customer. A firm which wants direct control of the distribution of the goods in order to help its image might only use selected distributors or undertake the distribution of the product itself. This is particularly true of luxury items or items aimed at a specialist market.

Wholesalers bear some of the risk of non-payment which a manufacturer might otherwise run. The wholesaler has to pay the manufacturer of the goods and then try to get the money back when the goods are re-sold. The wholesaler may make a loss if the goods involved go out of fashion or if demand drops for some other reason. As well as advising retailers about new products the wholesaler will inform the manufacturer of changes in taste and demand by adjusting his/her own purchases. Despite these advantages the wholesaler will not be used if the manufacturers believe it is possible to perform these functions more cheaply themselves.

As we have seen, goods which perish quickly such as fruit or vegetables will not usually be sold through a wholesaler. Instead wholesale markets exist, for example,

Meat – Smithfield Market, London

Fish – North Quay, Isle of Dogs, London

Fruit – Nine Elms, London

Similar markets exist throughout the country where perishable products are bought and sold, often early in the morning, and then put into the shops and market stalls on the same day.

3. How will low-value items normally be distributed?

4. Firms selling to the ____ market will often deal ____ with the ____ .

5. ____ ____ will be used by a firm wishing to keep as much control of distribution as possible.

1. What is meant by the chain of distribution?

2. The chain of distribution used depends on the ____, the ____ and the ____ itself.

The retailer is clearly important in the chain of distribution. It is the retailer who makes the goods available, on demand, in the area where people live, even though the goods may have been produced many miles away or even overseas. In this respect the retailer completes the distribution of the goods. The retailer saves the manufacturer or wholesaler having to deal with many orders for small quantities of goods. By buying from several manufacturers and wholesalers the retailer brings a wide choice to the people in the local area. Retailers will often provide credit, advice and/or after sales services which help not only the customer but also the manufacturer as they increase sales of the product. Because the retailer buys the goods he/she shares the risk of them not selling with the wholesaler. Retailing takes many forms, of which the use of shops is important.

Shops

Independent shops

These are the 'corner shop' retailers, often found on housing estates. Usually a small family business, they offer a personal, friendly service, late opening hours and, very often, credit. The choice is usually limited and prices tend to be higher than some larger stores. As the number of these shops has been declining in recent years many have formed voluntary groups such as Mace or Spar. These groups make joint purchases and share advertising costs through a common identity. The joint purchasing of large quantities of goods entitles the group to a discount, which allows for lower prices to the customer. It has been argued that the decline in the independent shops is due to the growth of supermarkets and hypermarkets.

Supermarkets

A self-service shop with a selling space of more than 186 square metres dealing in food and household goods is a description of a supermarket. Supermarkets are normally part of a chain such as Asda, Tesco or Sainsbury's. Supermarkets have the advantage of being conveniently placed in town centres, and selling at prices which are lower than in independent shops. However, they have the disadvantage of not offering the same sort of personal service as they cannot meet individual requests. Credit is not usually available. Because it is self-service, the supermarket can operate with a minimum of staff and so is cheaper to run than a traditional shop of a similar size. The large-scale supermarkets buy in bulk, which entitles them to discounts and leads to lower prices for the consumer.

Hypermarkets

A hypermarket is a store of over 4650 square metres which deals in food and household goods as well as clothes, furniture and electrical goods. The large size of these stores means that they are usually built outside town centres. This has led to claims that they damage the environment as well as attracting custom away from town centres, leading to the decline of other sorts of retail outlets. Late opening hours, low prices and a wide choice are advantages of the hypermarket. Apart from the disadvantages already mentioned, hypermarkets are difficult for non car-owners to reach and tend to be impersonal.

Variety chain stores

Littlewoods, British Home Stores and Marks and Spencer are examples of variety chain stores. This sort of retailer is part of a chain of town centre shops dealing in a range of household goods. A limited range of goods is offered in stores across the country. Prices are low and standards of service consistent. Convenience and reliability are important features of the variety chain store but with the drawback of being rather impersonal and offering a limited choice.

A hypermarket

Multiple stores

Multiple stores are very similar in their operation to variety chain stores. The main difference is that they concentrate on one range of goods, for example Dolcis sells shoes, Mothercare sells baby products and Victoria Wines sells drinks. A standard range of goods is offered in stores across the country with low prices and consistent standards of service. The multiple is convenient and reliable but rather impersonal and with limited choice.

Department stores

These large city-centre stores are made up of departments which deal with a range of goods, such as clothes, electrical, furniture etc. Often a range of services is available to customers, for example banking, travel agencies, restaurants and hairdressers. The high standards of decor and service contribute to the luxury image and high prices which are features of many department stores. Customers are attracted by the convenience and wide range of goods and services on offer. Sometimes space in department stores will be rented out to *concessionaires* who may deal in specialised items, such as musical instruments or cosmetics. Concessionaires are a separate business within the store.

11.2. Answer the following questions with at least a full sentence, or by writing out the missing words.

1. Describe a supermarket.

2. Two advantages of the independent retailer are ____ ____ and late ____ ____ .

3. Give two criticisms of hypermarkets.

4. How do multiple stores and variety chain stores differ?

5. What is a concessionaire?

6. Customers are attracted to department stores by the _____ and ____ range of ____ and _____ on offer.

Retail co-operatives

Retail co-operatives such as the North East Co-op and North West Pioneers operate a wide range of shops such as supermarkets, hypermarkets and department stores. As well as dealing with the large manufacturers, retail co-ops operate with their own wholesaler, CWS, which stands for Co-operative Wholesale Society. (See Chapter 1 for more details of co-operative ownership).

Other forms of retailing

Street traders

People selling newspapers or flowers are examples of street traders. Usually a license from the local council is required before a person can trade in this way. Street trading is a convenient way of getting goods to the customer.

Direct selling

Newspaper advertisements or letters to potential purchasers are ways in which a manufacturer can sell direct to a customer. This avoids the expense of running a shop and provides a convenient way to shop. A disadvantage is that the goods cannot be inspected before purchase and payment is usually required in advance.

Mail order catalogues

Unlike direct selling, mail order catalogues offer a range of goods on credit. The customer deals with the agent, often a friend, neighbour or workmate, who operates on a part-time basis. The goods can be inspected in a colour catalogue and may be returned if the customer is not satisfied. Disadvantages are that the time taken for delivery may be inconvenient and that colours and styles may not be quite as they appear in the photograph. Kay's and Littlewoods are well-known mail order firms.

Mobile shops

These are particularly important in country areas or for people in towns who find it difficult to get out and about. They bring a narrow choice of goods to where people live. Prices tend to be higher than in many shops because of the transport costs but convenience is a major advantage.

Automatic vending

A wide range of goods can be bought from vending machines, including hot and cold drinks, food and cigarettes. The use of microchips (see Chapter 2) has made these machines more reliable than in the past. They have the advantage of being available 24 hours a day, and can be found in many places such as public houses and leisure centres.

GEOFF WARD

Vending machine

11.3. Answer the following questions with at least a full sentence, or by writing out the missing words.

1. Street traders need a _____ from the local _____ .

2. Direct selling avoids the _____ of running a shop.

3. Name one disadvantage of mail order selling.

4. Why are mobile shop prices higher than in some other shops?

5. _____ _____ _____ have the advantage of being available 24 hours a day.

Trends in distribution

Major changes have occurred in retailing and wholesaling since the 1960s. Here is a summary of the main ones:

1. Decline of the independent retailer. Independent retailers had fifty-nine per cent of all trade in 1961 but by 1984 this was 29 per cent.

2. Fall in the number of shops. In 1971 there were 510 000 shops. This number had dropped to 340 000 by 1984. The main explanation for this is the decline of the independent trader. The average size of shop has increased as sales per full-time employee tend to be higher in large shops.

3. Growth of superstores/hypermarkets. This occurred during the 1980s and was similar to the growth of supermarkets in the 1960s.

4. Series of mergers. A number of retail groups have merged and this has produced larger retail groups, for example the Sears group.

5. Change of vending sites. Machines have tended to move from outside sites, such as shop walls, to inside sites like leisure centres.

6. Growth of franchising. This has been done by firms such as McDonalds and Kentucky Fried Chicken. (See page 188 for details of franchising).

7. Increased use of technology. This is most noticeable in stock control and *electronic point of sale* (EPOS). An example of EPOS is the supermarket checkout where goods are passed over a beam and a machine records what the items are and their cost.

8. Rise of mail order. In 1961 2.5 per cent of all retail sales were by mail order and this reached a 3.9 per cent peak in 1971. There has been a drop to 3.3 per cent since then.

9. Decline of co-operative retailing. Co-op retailers now have less than half of their market share in 1961. There are now fewer outlets due to rationalisation and amalgamations. There were 1400 societies at the turn of the century, there are now just over 100.

10. Abolition of *resale price maintenance* (RPM) in 1964. RPM allowed manufacturers to set the price at which retailers could sell goods. Its abolition led to a greater degree of competition. This partly accounts for the changing pattern of retailing since then as price competition has developed.

11. Increased pedestrianisation and development of town centre shopping areas has been followed by growth in out-of-town shopping, for example the Metro Centre at Gateshead in the North East.

As you can see there are a number of conflicting pressures on a firm when it comes to choosing a method of distribution. Final decisions will be based on cost and efficiency, as well as how well a particular chain of distribution matches the product's image and target market. A further consideration in the distribution process is which method of transport to use. In choosing which method of transport to use a firm must consider the following:

- **Cost.** If rival methods of transport offer similar facilities the question of cost will determine which is chosen, as high costs lower profit.

- **Urgency.** Some methods of transport are faster than others. If urgency is an important consideration then faster methods of transport will be chosen.

- **Distance.** Road transport tends to be faster for short journeys while other methods, such as by rail or air are better over longer distances.

- **The product.** Cheap, bulky goods will require different transport from expensive small goods if the firm is to transport them both profitably. Perishable goods need faster transport than longer-lasting items.

- **Safety and Security.** Dangerous items, such as certain chemicals, will need a method of transport which reduces risk. Valuable items have to be securely transported to avoid theft.

Once again the firm is faced with a range of conflicting pressures when making its choice. The safest method of transport, for example, might be too slow or too expensive. The firm has to decide what consideration is the most important and choose its transport accordingly. In firms operating for profit the main consideration will usually be to keep costs as low as possible.

Road transport

The road and motorway network is provided by the Department of Transport working with local councils. Firms need to decide whether to use the services of *road haulage operators*, which are private firms offering to move goods on behalf of manufacturers, or to purchase their own *fleet* or collection of vehicles. While the cost of purchasing and operating a fleet of lorries is high it does give the advantages of full control over the transport process, direct contact with customers and more flexibility in meeting customer needs. Free advertising on the side of the lorries is another advantage. Because of the high costs involved, firms can only operate their own fleets profitably if they have sufficient deliveries to ensure that the lorries or vans are fully used. The cost of fuel, insurance and the salaries of drivers under the control of a transport manager have to be considered.

Road transport is faster and cheaper than rail over short distances and can provide a door-to-door delivery. Pick-up and delivery times are more flexible with road transport than with air or rail transport where timetables have to be kept to. However, large bulky loads, for example coal, can be expensive to move by road. Trains can carry far more in one trip than lorries. Road transport can be delayed by traffic jams and bad weather, trains are less likely to be affected. The noise and pollution of road transport is another consideration to be borne in mind.

A supermarket delivery lorry being unloaded

11.4. Answer the following questions with at least a full sentence, or by writing out the missing words.

1. Name four things which have to be considered when choosing a chain of distribution.

2. In selecting which type of transport to use a firm will consider ____, ____, ____, __ ____, ____ and ____ .

3. When using road transport firms may use their own fleet of vehicles or ____ ____ ____ .

4. Describe two advantages and two disadvantages of road transport.

Rail transport

Railways are operated by British Rail, a public corporation controlled by the government. British Rail offers a range of services for moving goods. The main services are Red Star parcel delivery which provides same day delivery, Night Star parcel delivery , which provides overnight delivery and Freightliner, a streamlined delivery service for business.

As we have seen, rail is suitable for moving large quantities of goods long distances. As well as being less harmful to the environment rail transport avoids traffic jams but is still able to get to the centre of cities and towns. On the other hand, railways cannot provide a door-to-door service. The transfer to road transport for final delivery increases the cost and the risk of theft or damage. Rail transport is also rather inflexible because of the need to follow timetables.

Sea transport

The sea has long been used as a way of transporting goods to other countries. It is also used to move goods to different parts of Britain. For example coal might be moved from Hull to London by sea as both cities have access to ports. Ships which operate close to land and deliver to parts of the same country like this are called *coasters*. *Ocean vessels* are ships used to move goods to other countries across the oceans of the world.

Sea transport can move a variety of goods. *Tankers* can be used for moving oil, gas or other liquid goods. *Bulk carriers* move bulk quantities of one item, for example tons of clay. *Container ships* carry large metal containers of the same size. These containers are packed by the sender on shore. Containers can also be used by road and rail to move different items swiftly and securely. Special cranes and handling facilities are needed. The advantage of being able to move large quantities of goods cheaply is offset by certain disadvantages. These include the fact that sea transport can be badly affected by the weather and, even in fine weather, is slower than other methods of transport. Door-to-door delivery cannot be provided but the benefits of containers can speed up the delivery process.

11.5. Answer the following questions with at least a full sentence, or by writing out the missing words.

1. Name three services provided by British Rail for moving goods.

2. Give one advantage and one disadvantage of railway transport.

3. What are the advantages of using containers?

4. _____ can be used to carry oil by sea.

Inland waterways

The canals and rivers which make up Britain's inland waterways carry very little freight today. Specially-built longboats or barges are used for carrying non-urgent and non-perishable items such as timber or coal. Fragile items, such as china, can be carried safely by canal boat. Apart from being slow and only connecting certain areas of the country, the inland waterway network has the advantage of being cheap and safe. Inland waterways are best suited to carrying bulk goods long distances at regular intervals, rather than for transporting urgent items over short distances.

Air transport

Air transport provides a fast but expensive method of transport over long distances. It is an ideal way of moving urgent items such as medicines. Perishable items like flowers may also be moved this way. The ability to fly over sea and land reduces handling and speeds up the process, as well as increasing security. The main disadvantages of air transport are the cost and the limitation on the quantity of goods that can be carried. For these reasons it is mainly used for low-weight, high-value items such as diamonds or electronic goods. Further disadvantages include the facts that airports are situated outside towns or cities and that aeroplanes can be affected by bad weather.

Air freight being loaded

Pipelines

Gas and oil are commonly moved by pipelines. Whilst being very expensive to build, especially if landscaping is needed to restore the environment, pipelines are cheap to run. This is because little maintenance is needed and labour costs are low. Unlike other forms of transport, there is little pollution associated with the use of pipelines. Pipelines are not affected by the weather, delays or labour disputes in the way that other methods of transport are. The high cost of building a pipeline means that they are not used unless their future use is assured.

11.6. Answer the following questions with at least a full sentence, or by writing out the missing words.

1. Inland waterways are best suited to carrying ___ ___ long distances at ___ intervals.

2. Air transport is ___ but expensive.

3. What are the advantages of using pipelines?

Documents

Before goods can be sold a firm needs to make sure it has a system to record its various *transactions* or dealings with its customers. Each firm will design and use its own forms and documents. This section looks at the most commonly used business documents. The following diagram shows how they are sent between buyer and seller:

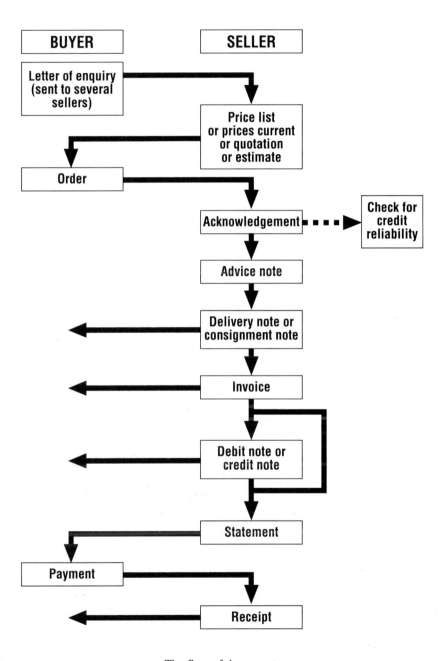

The flow of documents

Large firms may have thousands of customers. For this reason computers will be used to produce business documents, and may even send some documents automatically to save labour time and so reduce costs.

An enquiry

This document is a request from a potential customer who wants to know details of the firm's prices and *terms* – under what circumstances credit will be given, cost of delivery etc. Most potential customers will contact several suppliers and make comparisons before placing an order.

A supplier might reply to a letter of enquiry by sending a price list, a quotation or an estimate.

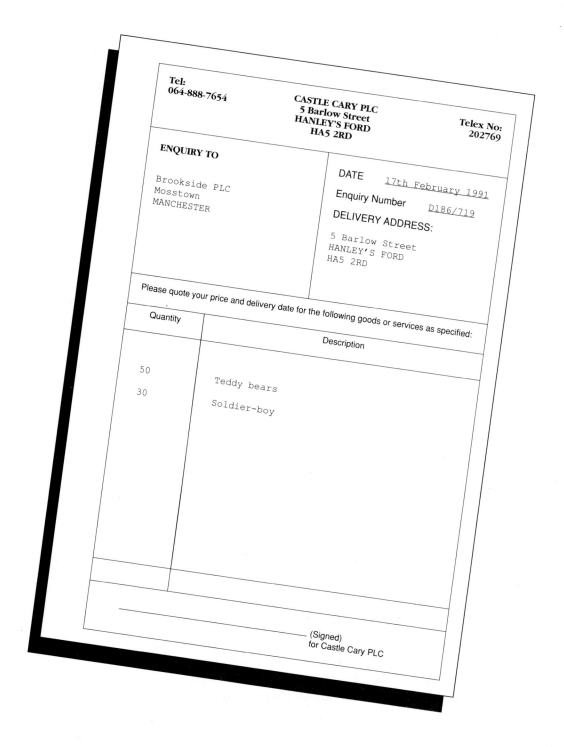

Tel:
064-888-7654

CASTLE CARY PLC
5 Barlow Street
HANLEY'S FORD
HA5 2RD

Telex No:
202769

ENQUIRY TO

Brookside PLC
Mosstown
MANCHESTER

DATE   17th February 1991

Enquiry Number   D186/719

DELIVERY ADDRESS:

5 Barlow Street
HANLEY'S FORD
HA5 2RD

Please quote your price and delivery date for the following goods or services as specified:

Quantity	Description
50	Teddy bears
30	Soldier-boy

(Signed)
for Castle Cary PLC

A price list

This gives details of the range of goods and services provided by the supplier. Information about prices and terms will be supplied. A price list will be sent when a customer has made a general enquiry to the firm about the goods and services on offer. In the case of products whose prices change quickly a *prices current* list will be sent. This will indicate that prices are liable to change. A prices current list would be used in the case of fruit or vegetables, for example.

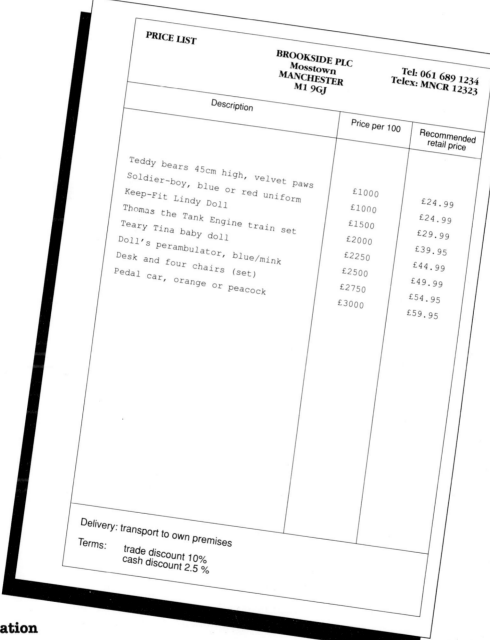

PRICE LIST

BROOKSIDE PLC
Mosstown
MANCHESTER
M1 9GJ

Tel: 061 689 1234
Telex: MNCR 12323

Description	Price per 100	Recommended retail price
Teddy bears 45cm high, velvet paws	£1000	£24.99
Soldier-boy, blue or red uniform	£1000	£24.99
Keep-Fit Lindy Doll	£1500	£29.99
Thomas the Tank Engine train set	£2000	£39.95
Teary Tina baby doll	£2250	£44.99
Doll's perambulator, blue/mink	£2500	£49.99
Desk and four chairs (set)	£2750	£54.95
Pedal car, orange or peacock	£3000	£59.95

Delivery: transport to own premises
Terms: trade discount 10%
           cash discount 2.5 %

A quotation

If the customer has asked for prices of particular items a quotation is sent. This document only gives details of the goods or services the customer is interested in. The quotation will also give details of the terms of trading.

QUOTATION

BROOKSIDE PLC
Mosstown
MANCHESTER
M1 9GJ

Tel: 061 689 1234
Telex: MNCR 12323

To: Castle Cary PLC
        5 Barlow Street
        HANLEY'S Ford   Date: 20 February 1991
        HA5 2RD

                                                               £10.00 ea

50 Teddy Bears; 45cm High with Velvet paws
Recommended retail price £24.99 ea

                                                               £10.00 ea
25 Soldier Boy; Available in Red or Blue uniform
Recommended retail price £24.99 ea

Trade discount   10%
Cash discount   2.5% one month
                   5% seven days

Valid for 30 days from date of issue

All prices are ex works

An estimate

In situations where something is being made to order, rather than purchased from stock, an estimate is given. The cost of labour, materials, overheads and profit is taken into account to produce this estimate of what the cost will be to the customer. While the price list gives details of exactly what is to be paid, the estimate is only an approximate indication of the likely cost. Unforeseen delays or changes may alter the price. Estimates are commonly used in the building industry.

The price list, quotation or estimate will give details of the terms and conditions which apply. The terms will show if the price includes the cost of delivery ('carriage paid'). If the cost of delivery is not included the phrase 'ex-works' or 'carriage forward' will be used. Terms will include any discounts given. The two common discounts are *cash discount* and *trade discount*. Cash discount is the amount that will be deducted from the price if payment is made within a certain period, for example 5 per cent/28 days means the price will be reduced by five per cent if the goods are paid for within 28 days. Trade discount is the amount deducted because the purchaser is buying in large quantities, usually to resell the goods. This discount is normally given by wholesalers to retailers. Cash and trade discounts are intended to encourage the purchase of large quantities and prompt payment.

An order

This is sent by a purchaser to the firm they wish to trade with. The order shows the quantity, type, size, amount, etc. they wish to purchase. Firms have their own printed order forms which include their name, address and telephone number. Each order is numbered to tell it apart from others and copies are kept. In some firms orders will be sent automatically by computer once stocks drop below a certain level.

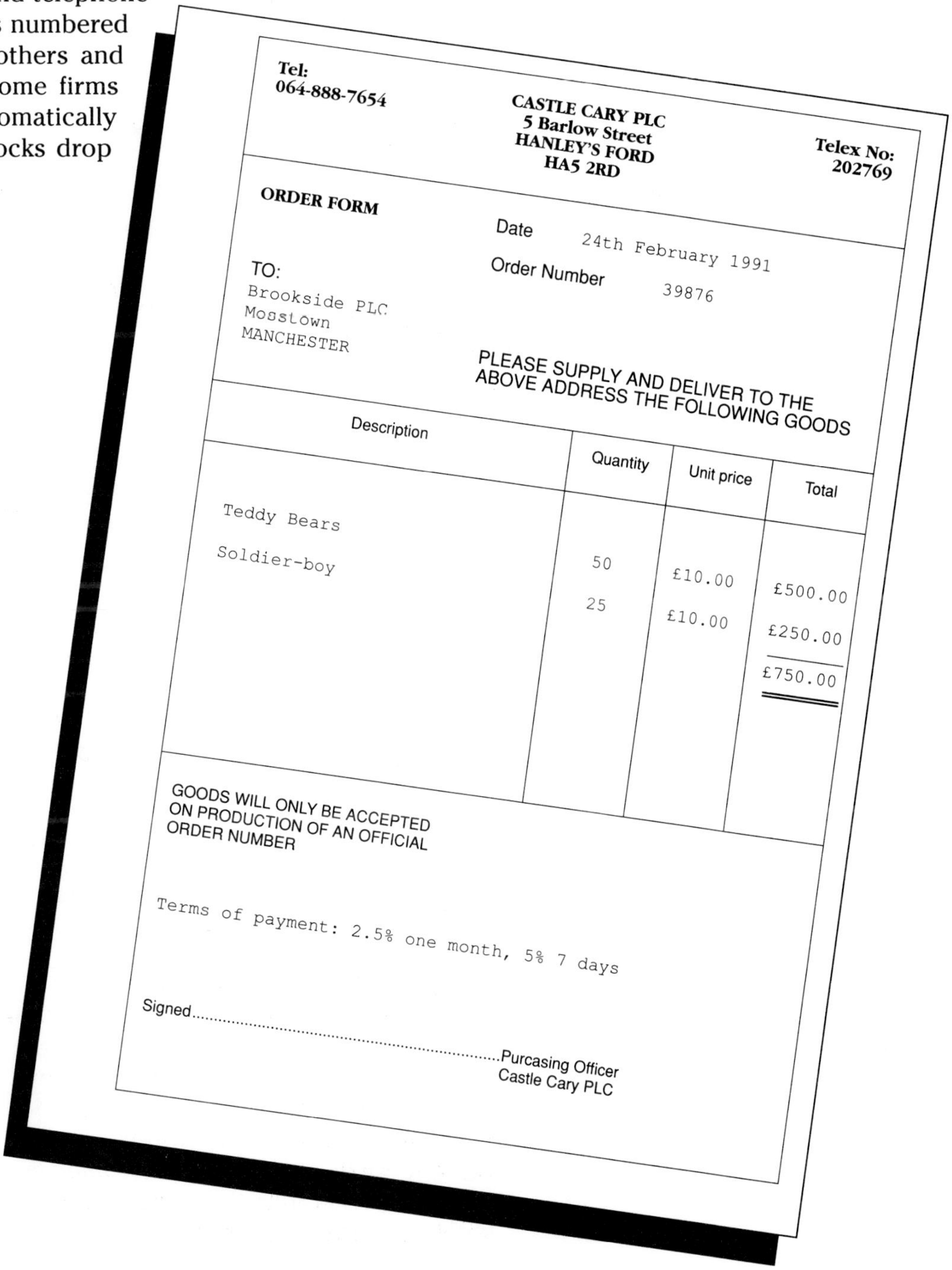

Tel:
064-888-7654

CASTLE CARY PLC
5 Barlow Street
HANLEY'S FORD
HA5 2RD

Telex No:
202769

ORDER FORM

Date   24th February 1991

TO:
Brookside PLC
Mosstown
MANCHESTER

Order Number   39876

PLEASE SUPPLY AND DELIVER TO THE
ABOVE ADDRESS THE FOLLOWING GOODS

Description	Quantity	Unit price	Total
Teddy Bears			
Soldier-boy	50	£10.00	£500.00
	25	£10.00	£250.00
			£750.00

GOODS WILL ONLY BE ACCEPTED
ON PRODUCTION OF AN OFFICIAL
ORDER NUMBER

Terms of payment: 2.5% one month, 5% 7 days

Signed...
Purcasing Officer
Castle Cary PLC

An acknowledgement

An acknowledgement is sent by the seller to indicate that an order has been received. The time between receiving the order and sending the goods is often used by the seller to check that the buyer is reliable enough to receive goods on credit.

An advice note

This is sent by the seller to advise the purchaser that the goods are being sent. This gives the purchaser an opportunity to clear the necessary space in a warehouse or shop to store or display the goods. The advice note will alert the purchaser to any mistakes in the order. This prevents the wrong goods being delivered.

11.7. Answer the following questions with at least a full sentence, or by writing out the missing words.

1. _____ are often used to produce business documents to save time and reduce ___ .

2. What is meant by 'terms'?

3. How does price list differ from a prices current list?

4. How does a quotation differ from an estimate?

5. How do cash discounts and trade discounts differ?

6. Name four items of information found on an order form.

7. An _____ is sent by the seller to show the order has been received.

8. Give two reasons for sending an advice note.

When the seller sends the order, proof will be needed that the goods have been received by the purchaser. This can be provided by a delivery note or a consignment note.

A delivery note

A delivery note is sent with goods if they are delivered by the seller's own transport. Details of the goods such as quantity, type and size are given so that the goods delivered can be checked to see that they are as ordered. This is important as sometimes orders will be delivered in parts. If the goods are as ordered the buyer signs for them. This provides the seller with proof of delivery. The delivery note is sometimes called the despatch note as it proves the goods have been despatched or sent.

A consignment note

This document does the same job as the delivery note by showing the same information. It is used when the seller uses another firm to deliver the goods e.g. British Rail or Securicor. The purchaser signs to show that the goods have been received.

An invoice

The invoice may be sent in advance of the goods, as an advice note, with the goods, as a delivery note, or after the goods have been received.The invoice is not a request for payment. It shows the details of what items have been purchased. These details include quantity, size and price. Terms are shown on the invoice. The invoice shows the total price, after discounts have been deducted and then VAT added. This can be checked against the order in case any errors have been made. The phrase 'E and O E' means Errors and Omissions Excepted. This phrase gives the seller the legal right to claim in future if they find evidence of undercharging.

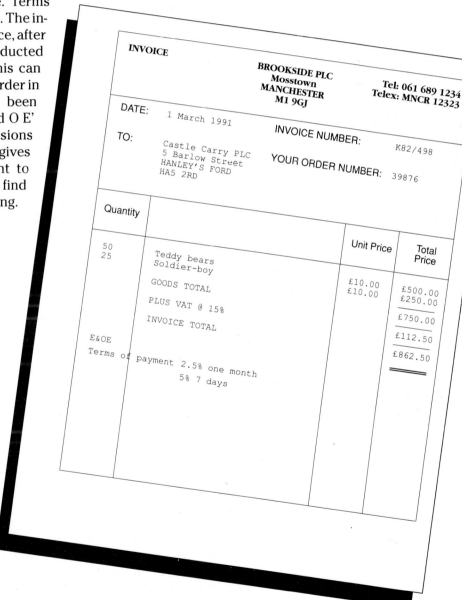

It may be that the seller overcharges or undercharges the buyer. In each circumstance a particular document is used to correct the error.

A credit note

If some of the goods are faulty, damaged, of a smaller quantity or inferior quality to those ordered a credit note will be sent by the seller to the buyer. The credit note makes up the difference between what was paid for and what was actually received and used. The credit note can be used by the purchaser as payment in future transactions with the seller. It may often be printed in red.

A debit note

If larger quantities or better quality goods are received and kept by the purchaser a debit note will be sent by the seller. This tells the purchaser that an extra amount is owed which is greater than that shown on the invoice. Rather than issue a special document most firms will issue an additional invoice showing details of the extra goods and amount to be paid. The debit note is, in effect, the opposite to the credit note.

A statement

A statement is usually sent monthly from the seller. It shows the value of each invoice sent in the month. In other words, the statement is a summary of all transactions since the last statement was sent. Credit notes will be shown on the statement and reduce the amount that has to be paid. In addition debit notes will appear and increase the amount to be paid. By deducting any payments the statement shows how much the buyer owes the seller as a result of the month's transactions. The statement does not show details of each invoice, merely its value. Terms are shown on the statement. Any amount not paid is carried over and shown on the following month's statement. The statement is a request for payment.

STATEMENT

BROOKSIDE PLC
Mosstown
MANCHESTER
M! 9GJ

Tel: 061 689 1234
Telex: MNCR 12323

TO:
Castle Cary PLC
5 Barlow Street
HANLEY'S FORD
HA5 2RD

ACCOUNT NUMBER: 12323

DATE: 30 April 1991

Date	Goods	Debit	Credit	Balance
1991				
1 March	Goods supplied on Invoice No K82/498			
6 March	Returns 3 items Credit Note CN82/498	£862.50		£862.50
	VAT (CN 82/498)		£30.00	£832.50
	E & OE		£4.50	£828.00

The amount now due is the last figure in the column headed 'Balance'

A payment

Having been informed of how much is owing the buyer is expected to pay the amount shown on the statement. As we saw in Chapter 8 there may be reasons why the buyer will delay payment. Normally payment will be made promptly to take advantage of a cash discount. Payment is usually made by cheque, sent through the post. The amount paid shows up on the following month's statement.

A receipt

Having received payment, the seller will sometimes send a receipt. This shows how much has been received. Receipts are rarely used when payment is by cheque. This is because when the bank transfers the money from the buyer's to the seller's account proof is provided through the buyer's bank statement. Cash transactions usually involve the seller issuing a receipt to the buyer.

11.8. Answer the following questions with at least a full sentence, or by writing out the missing words.

1. The delivery note provides _____ of delivery.

2. When would a consignment note be used?

3. What information is shown on an invoice?

4. E and O E means __ and __ __ .

5. What is the difference between a debit note and a credit note?

6. The _____ is a summary of all transactions since the last statement was sent.

7. A receipt would not normally be issued if payment was by __ .

1. Describe the chain of distribution that would normally be used for consumer durables.

2. When might a producer deal direct with the customer?

3. What factors will a firm consider when choosing a method of transport?

4. In what circumstances would rail be better than road transport?

5. What advantages do inland waterways have over air transport?

6. How would you justify the high costs of setting up a pipeline to distribute oil?

7. How are a quotation and a price list different?

8. Why do firms provide discount?

9. In what ways are an advice note and a delivery note different?

10. How is an invoice different from a statement?

STIMULUS RESPONSE QUESTIONS

1. a) Fill in the gaps in this statement. *(4 marks)*

   b) How is the statement different from an invoice? *(2 marks)*

   c) Why is a statement sent?
   (6 marks)

STATEMENT

BROOKSIDE PLC
Mosstown
MANCHESTER
M1 9GJ

Tel: 061 689 1234
Telex: MNCR 12323

ACCOUNT NUMBER: 123349

TO: Castle Cary PLC
      5 Barlow Street
      HANLEY'S FORD   DATE: 29 June 1991
      HA5 2RD

Date	Goods	Debit	Credit	Balance
				£350
		£350		£650
3 April	Invoice MH/7332	£300		
7 April	Invoice MH/2134		£600	
14 April	Payment	£200		
21 May	Invoice M/9337		£700	
3 June	Credit Note BP/137			£100
6 June	Payment			

The amount now due is the last figure in the column headed 'Balance'

2. *Fieldings Furnishings manufacture a wide range of expensive, luxury furniture. Having been successful in selling to firms in the area around their Birmingham factory they wish to sell their goods nationwide.*

   a) Describe the distribution options open to Fieldings and which one is likely to be best. *(10 marks)*

   b) Which method of transporting the goods should Fieldings choose and why? *(10 marks)*

LEARN IT YOURSELF

1. Collect as many different business documents as possible. Say what sort of document they are and what features they have in common. Present your findings as a wall display.

2. In groups contact the transport managers of several local firms and ask them to describe the arrangements they make for distributing their products. Give a talk to the group on your findings.

3. Design a set of business documents for the firm of your choice. Make up the name, address and other details.

Prepare a project entitled 'How transport is vital to business'. Contact British Rail and a major road haulage operator and ask about the delivery services they provide to business. Obtain as many details as possible and present your findings as a project folder.

Your firm, a timber merchant based in Glasgow, Scotland, supplies Fieldings Furnishings of Birmingham with 15 tons of timber per week to make its products. As the new transport manager you have been asked to review the transport arrangements and pay particular attention to road, rail and inland waterways.

Using maps in your college, school or local library, say which of the three methods of transport is likely to be

a) The least suitable, and why?

b) The most suitable, and why?

c) Choose one other major Scottish town and describe the methods of transport that would be necessary to move the timber to Birmingham.

CHAPTER 12

ADVERTISING AND PROMOTION

Having decided what to produce and arranged to distribute it, the business then needs to inform and persuade the public to buy its goods or service. This is the purpose of advertising. Persuasion and information may not be enough. Some encouragement may be needed such as free samples or the chance to win prizes in a competition. This process of giving a reward for purchasing the product is called *promotion*. Most large businesses employ an

An advertising hoarding – just one of many advertising media

advertising agency to organise the advertising and promotion of their goods and services. Well known advertising agencies include Saatchi and Saatchi, and J. Walter Thompson. The agency employs a number of specialist staff to help mount the advertising and promotion. *Copywriters* are used to write the text of the advertisement and to come up with slogans or phrases. Artists will be employed to design the advertisement. Scriptwriters write the words which actors will say in the radio or television advertisements the firm uses. In other words the advertising agency deals with the how and what of advertising and promotion:

What method of advertising will be used? Which advertising media will be used – for example newspapers or television? What is the most effective time of day or of the year to advertise?

How will the public be persuaded? How will they attract the attention of their target audience?

The answers to these sort of questions will be found partly through the experience and expertise of the agency and partly through the market research which led to the product or service being developed. One of the first decisions to be taken concerns the image of the product and the way it is to be made to appeal. Some ways in which products can appeal to potential purchasers include:

- *Famous people*. Someone famous can be shown using or praising the product. The impression created is that by using the product you can become talented or famous. Sports goods are often advertised this way.

- *Animals*. Certain types of animals have certain images. Puppies suggest gentleness, monkeys humour, tigers strength and power. All of these have been used in the past - what products do you link them to?

- *Sex appeal*. This is often used in advertising cosmetics. The suggestion is that by using certain perfumes or aftershave you can appear attractive to others.

- *Babies*. Like puppies, babies are used to suggest softness or gentleness. Babies are thought to have an automatic appeal to certain types of people.

A petrol advert which uses concern for children's safety

- *Health*. Certain products are promoted as being 'fat free' or containing no additives. Other goods are said to help slimming.

- *Convenience*. Some goods are sold on the basis of making life easier. This approach is used with electrical appliances but can also be used with pre-cooked meals.

An advertising agency cannot make false claims about a product. Advertising is controlled by several Acts of Parliament as well as the following two organisations.

The Advertising Standards Authority (ASA)

The ASA is an organisation set up by the advertising agencies themselves to regulate the standards of advertising. It issues the *British Code of Advertising Practice* which is a guide for advertising agencies. There is no legal requirement to follow the code as it is a voluntary form of control. The code lays down that all advertisements must be legal, honest, decent and truthful. If a consumer feels that an advertisement fails to meet these requirements they can complain to the ASA who will investigate the complaint. If the complaint is valid the firm who issued the advertisement will be asked to change it. The ASA and its code covers newspapers, magazines, leaflets, cinema, and poster advertising. It does not cover radio or television advertising.

The Independent Broadcasting Authority (IBA)

The IBA is the organisation which deals with standards of advertising on radio and television. Like the ASA it issues its own code of practice and investigates complaints about standards of advertising.

12.1. Answer the following questions with at least a full sentence, or by writing out the missing words.

1. Advertising trys to ____ and ____ .

2. In marketing what is meant by promotion?

3. What is a copywriter?

4. An advertising agency deals with the ____ and ____ of advertising and promotion.

5. Describe two ways products can be made to appeal to the public.

6. What does the Advertising Standards Authority do?

7. The ____ ____ ____ is the organisation which deals with standards of advertising on radio and television.

As well as these organisations advertisers must bear in mind the legal requirements of advertising. Several Acts of Parliament provide legal control of advertising.

The Sale of Goods Act, 1979

This law makes it illegal to sell goods which are not *fit for the purpose sold*. This means that goods which are advertised with particular claims should meet these claims, for example hiking boots should stand hard wear and tear. The Act requires that goods are *of merchantable quality*. In other words, the goods must be of the standard expected of similar goods purchased in the same way. For example a new car could not be sold legally with known defects. The goods must *meet the description*. It is illegal to make a false description of the goods.

The Consumer Credit Act, 1974

It is a requirement of this act that any advertisements which offer goods on credit should show the Annual Percentage Rate (APR) of interest as well as the flat rate. The flat rate of interest is usually about half of the APR. As the APR shows the real amount it is important for the customer that the two are not confused.

Trade Descriptions Act, 1972

This Act made it illegal to describe goods in a misleading way. A table made of pine cannot be advertised as being made out of oak, for example. Prices must also be accurately advertised.

Consumer Protection Act, 1987

Under this law it is illegal to give a misleading price indication for goods, services or accommodation. When claiming that a price is reduced the previous, higher, price should be stated. In comparing a previous price for the item it should be the last price which was charged for the product in that shop and it should have been available at the last price for 28 days in the previous six months. The act does allow price comparisons to be made which do not meet this requirement provided they are 'fair and meaningful'. It should be indicated for how long and when the previous price did apply. This is a change to the Trade Descriptions Act 1972 which did not allow any exceptions to the requirement. Under the Consumer Protection Act (1987) 'reduced to £3' should not be advertised unless the previous price is given e.g. 'reduced to £3, previously £5'. Additional charges for a product such as postage and packing, VAT or delivery charges must be clearly communicated to the consumer in advance of a purchase.

Choosing the advertising media

The *advertising media* are the methods of advertising that the firm will use. If the firm only uses one method of advertising, for example newspapers, it will be using an *advertising medium*. The advertiser will aim to reach as many people as possible at the lowest cost. In choosing methods of advertising the advertising agency will consider several key points:

- *Target audience*. Is the intended audience likely to see the advert? Toys for young children, for example, are advertised in between early morning cartoons because research shows lots of young children are awake early and will see them.
- *Cost*. The agency's budget will determine whether it can afford to use television, (which could cost £20 000 for ten seconds) or a newspaper (a local evening paper might cost £500 for a full page advertisement).
- *Product*. Specialist goods will be advertised in specialist magazines. Mass goods, such as television sets, will be widely advertised where most people can see the advertisement.

■ *Quantity.* Firms based in one area with a limited output will require a local advertising campaign. Large multi-national organisations will benefit from a far larger advertising effort in order to sell a greater quantity.

CHECK THIS OUT

12.2. Answer the following questions with at least a full sentence, or by writing out the missing words.

2. How does the Consumer Credit Act 1974 affect advertisements offering credit?

3. Which Act makes it illegal to describe goods in a misleading way?

4. Which four points should be considered when choosing an advertising medium?

1. What is meant by merchantable quality?

ARTICLES FOR SALE

HYGENA UNITS from extremely large kitchen & room. White-/dark brown in excellent conition includes 2 double sinks taps, large fridge, dishwasher ceramic hob. Bargain £1200 ono 061 225 3425 evgs 0625 6123 day

BEAUTIFUL white silk wedding dress, 1 mth old, complete with accessories, must be seen, size 10-1 £300 ovno. Cotact 406 3921 anytim

BEDS! BEDS! BEDS! New deep base divans, sgle £35, dble £60. Pine bunks £65. Free del 561 2491T

EXQUISITELY BEADED Ivory Wedding gown, with 5ft train, also matching veil & head dress £350, cost £750 Tel 561 7923 after 6.30 pm

KNITMASTER ZIPPY deluxe knittig machine. only 7 mths old. £200 ono. Tel 0606 951271

INGER ELEC Sewing mach, zig zags, holes, zips hems, gathers; fully g/teed. 24. Can be deliver. 061 572 9321

CTORIAN FIREPLACES er 150 in stock at realistic prices. Tel 25754602 or 061 526 3121 **TUBE** Bellarium S sunbeds. Good d. £100 each. Tel 0925 423151 **ALOR GAS** wall convector heaters, will separate. Tel 763 4293 **DRAWER** Divan with headboard, w £75 ono Tel 561 4232 **COND** hand radiators from £5 each various sizes

Advertising media

Newspapers

Local or national newspapers have their sales figures recorded by the Audit Bureau of Circulation (ABC). These figures allow advertisers to estimate the number of potential customers their advertisement will reach. National papers particularly have their own different type of reader. *Sun* readers generally have different tastes and incomes from *Financial Times* readers. The advertiser will choose to advertise in the paper which has a readership which matches the target audience.

Magazines

There are a range of magazines covering a large number of interests from computers to fishing or camping. Women's magazines are another distinct group. Advertisers can choose a magazine which they believe will reach most of their target audience.

Television

As we have seen, television advertising is controlled by the Independent Broadcasting Authority (IBA). Advertising is only allowed on Independent Television (ITV), not on the BBC (British Broadcasting Corporation). Independent Television is made up of Channel Four and the regional companies such as Granada, TVS, Tyne-Tees, Anglia and Thames. Television reaches millions of people but the cost of television time can be several thousand pounds. The advertiser has the additional cost of making the advertisement.

The cost of TV time will vary according to the time of day. For example, a slot before *News At Ten* will cost far more than a slot before an early morning programme. This is because 6.00 p.m. to 10.00 p.m. is the time most people watch television – *peak time* – and the time advertisers are prepared to pay most for.

Commercial radio

Radio Luxembourg and Piccadilly Radio (in Manchester) are examples of commercial radio stations. Most areas have a commercial radio station. Just like television, BBC Radio does not carry advertisements. Commercial radio can be a cheap way for local business to reach a large number of people.

Cinema

It is usual to find advertisements between films in the cinema. Cinema advertising is used as part of national advertising campaigns by both large and small businesses. Smaller firms can arrange for a standard advertisement to be shown and have their name and address announced and shown at the end of the advertisement, just as if it had been made for them. The bulk of cinema audiences are under 30 years of age. This means that the cinema is a good way of reaching this age group.

Neon signs

Colourful flashing lights are eye-catching and can be used to convey simple messages, such as the name of a shop or product. They are cheap to install and visible night and day.

Leaflets

These are cheap to produce. They are often delivered with free newspapers or posted to the homes of potential customers. When customers are contacted through the post like this, it is called *direct mailing*. This method is relatively cheap but as less than five in every hundred people approached actually respond, a large number of people have to be contacted for it to be worthwhile.

Hoardings

These large roadside posters are sometimes called *billboards*. They are eye - catching and reach the public at all hours of the day as people walk or drive past them.

Sponsorship

Businesses may pay the cost of major concerts or sporting events, for example The Littlewoods Cup in football. This gives them the right to display their name and emblem on literature, uniforms and buildings used in the event. The firm's name is included in the name of the event which also gets public attention. By choosing the sort of event which potential customers might be interested in the firm is able to present itself in a positive, helpful way. This improves its image and helps make it more of a 'household name'. It will often make sure its product is widely used in the event if possible. Several firms may sponsor an event by providing free products in return for publicity.

Other methods of advertising include beermats, paper bags, carrier bags or key rings with the firm's name or symbol. Firms may also advertise on the Oracle and Prestel teletext services.

12.3. Answer the following questions with at least a full sentence, or by writing out the missing words.

1. National newspapers have their own ___ of reader.

2. What is peak time television?

3. Name one commercial radio station and one commercial television station.

4. What is direct mailing?

5. If a business pays the cost of a sporting or some other event this is called _____ .

Sales promotion

Promotion and advertising are often confused. Advertising is about persuading or informing the public, while promotion is about giving the consumer 'something for nothing' in the hope that it will encourage future sales. An important part of selling is to persuade customers to try a product for the first time. The main aim of sales promotion is to break down this reluctance. There are various sales promotion techniques:

Free samples

Small packages of the product may be given away free. The idea is that once the customer has tried the new product they will wish to use it again and so, next time, buy it. The product may be given away in shops or on the street or delivered to houses. Arrangements can sometimes be made to have it distributed free with magazines. This situation is common with cosmetics which may be given away with women's magazines.

Coupons

Coupons are often printed in press advertisements or leaflets. They allow the customer a price reduction on the next purchase of a particular item. Customers reluctant to buy at the full price may be willing to buy at a reduced price. Once the customer has tried the new product and liked it, the next time they will be willing to buy it.

Once a customer has tried a product for the first time they may carry on buying it

Competitions

The chance to win a holiday, car, house, stereo or some other luxury item can attract a lot of attention. Often a condition of entry is to prove that you have used the manufacturer's product. This is done by sending a number of labels or bottle tops with the entry. The manufacturer aims to make the prize attractive enough so that the public will buy the product in order to enter the competition.

Free gifts

Free gifts, such as tee-shirts or sports bags, can be obtained by sending proof of purchase to the manufacturer. This type of promotion operates on the same principle as competitions as it aims to increase sales through attractive gifts. The free gift will often have the manufacturer's name on it. This provides free advertising in future. People will be encouraged to take a mail order catalogue or credit card, for example with a free gift, such as a camera or set of pans. The aim here is to encourage the customer to join something where future purchases will be easy and so, more likely.

12.3. Answer the following questions with at least a full sentence, or by writing out the missing words.

1. Describe two methods of sales promotion.

2. The main aim of sales promotion is to break down customers' ＿＿＿ to try a product.

SHORT QUESTIONS

1. Name two advertising agencies.

2. What four things are necessary for an advertisement to satisfy the ASA Code of Practice?

3. What advertising media is not covered by the Advertising Standards Authority, and who is responsible?

4. If goods are not ' fit for the purpose sold' what does this mean?

5. What is a target audience?

6. How does the product and size of output affect the choice of advertising media?

7. What does the Audit Bureau of Circulation do?

8. How can small firms use cinema advertising?

9. What are the advantages of using hoardings to advertise?

10. Why do firms give free samples?

STIMULUS RESPONSE QUESTIONS

1. *Having seen the 'Super mower' advertised on television Leroy McShane had rushed out to buy one. When he got it home he found it couldn't do half the things the advertisement said it could and the colour of the machine was different from what it said on the box. The so called half price offer they'd pointed out in the shop was the price they had been sold at for months, according to his friend Tania.*

   a) Which Act of Parliament seems to have been broken? *(2 marks)*

   b) In what ways has this Act been broken? *(6 marks)*

   c) Who should Leroy complain to about the television advertisement? *(2 marks)*

   d) Write a letter to the shop for Leroy to sign. The letter should explain the legal situation and what action Leroy thinks should be taken. *(10 marks)*

2. *'Advertising and promotion are the same'*

   a) Say why you believe this statement to be true or false. *(4 marks)*

   b) As an advertiser of baby food, describe two images you might want to present, and say why these images have been chosen. *(8 marks)*

   c) Choose two ways of promoting the baby food and say why you have chosen them. *(8 marks)*

1. Find the percentage space of a national and local newspaper taken up by classified and display advertising. If the newspapers had less advertising how do you think it would affect the price?

2. Choose two television advertisements and two newspaper advertisements. Describe the images they are trying to put over to the audience. Present your findings to the group.

3. See if you can find any articles in your local newspaper about traders who have broken the law on advertising.

4. Collect details such as leaflets, competition entry forms or free samples etc. connected to any sales promotion in your area. Explain each one to the group saying what is being promoted, how it is being promoted and why promotion rather than advertising has, in your view, been chosen.

5. Note down the television advertisements shown between nine and ten o'clock on a Saturday morning and those shown between nine and ten o'clock at night. Compare what has been advertised and say why you think different times were chosen for those products.

ON ASSIGNMENT

Write to the marketing or public relations department of a large organisation from whom you have recently bought something eg sweets, clothes etc. The address will be in *Yellow Pages* or on the packaging. Explain that you are collecting information for a project entitled 'Marketing in the Business World' and want to investigate how they advertise and promote their products. They might supply sample advertisements or other literature if you request it. See if you can prepare any questions relating to the product you purchased from them. Present your findings as a project folder.

CASE STUDY

Peter Bloom was delighted. His boss had told him that he was in charge of the Pet Foods Incorporated account that the advertising agency had just been awarded. This meant that Peter had to plan the national advertising campaign for the new dog food Pet Foods Inc. wanted to produce. Market research showed that customers wanted something that was healthy and natural for their dogs. All Peter had to do now was to plan the campaign.

a) What image and name should the new dog food have?

b) What advertising media should Peter use and why?

c) How might the new product be promoted?

d) Write a 15 second radio script advertising the new product. If possible, record it and play it to the group.

CHAPTER 13

INTERNATIONAL TRADE

We mentioned earlier that firms will also wish to trade overseas in order to increase sales. The people of the countries involved benefit as international trade overcomes problems of climate, different natural resources and different skills. If each country concentrates on those products it is better at producing there will be more goods created worldwide. By concentrating on the goods and services in which they have a *comparative advantage* countries help to raise the standard of living world wide. There may, however, be political or military reasons why governments wish to continue to produce certain goods at which they are not very efficient, for example food. In addition to the problems we have examined in *home trade*, that is, trade within Great Britain, there are several problems facing firms which wish to trade overseas.

Language

The firms will need to produce material in the language of the countries it wishes to trade with. This will apply to advertising material, instruction manuals, labels and documents. In order to be effective, staff dealing with overseas trade may need to learn the language of the country. This will require links with personnel to develop the right sort of training.

Currency

Payment for an overseas deal will normally be made in the currency of the firm selling the goods. Not only is there the complication of converting pounds sterling (£) into dollars (USA), francs (France), yen (China) or whatever the other country's currency may be; there is the problem that the values of the currencies may change between agreeing the price and making payment. If £1.00 can be changed for $2.50 in July when the price of a transaction between a British and American firm is agreed, it could change to £1.00 for $2.00 by September when payment is due. In the case of the British firm making payment it will clearly get fewer dollars per pound. To get the amount of dollars agreed it will have to give up more pounds. In effect, because of an altered *exchange rate*, the price has gone up! In addition to this sort of problem some countries restrict the availability of their currency. This *currency control* makes overseas trade difficult.

Measurement

Despite efforts by the government metric measurements, for example litres, kilos and metres, etc. are not as widely used as pints, ounces and feet. As most other countries use metric measurements there is often a need for conversion or recalculation. This complicates the trading process.

Documents

As we will see later (page 189), different documents are used in overseas trade. The documents used depend on the rules and regulations of the country in question. Special staff training and experience will be needed if the firm is to cope efficiently.

Distance

The extra distance involved can increase transportation and packaging costs. Other countries may have different times from Britain which makes personal communication difficult.

The conversion of measurements complicates trading

Cultural

The religion, history and politics of a country will cause it to have different laws and customs. Rules about alcohol in certain Muslim countries, for example, make it unlikely that efforts to sell beer or spirits will be successful. Countries may have their own rules about safety or environmental protection which firms will have to observe when selling affected products. USA rules about exhaust gases on cars are stricter than those in Britain, for example.

Restrictions on trade

Some countries will try to protect their own industries by limiting *imports*. Imports are the goods or services coming into a country - *exports* are the goods or services the country sells abroad. Trade can be restricted through a *duty* or *tariff*. This means that before the item can enter the country a payment has to be made to the government. The effect of this charge is to force the price up, sometimes to a level which is unattractive to customers. *Quotas* are another way of limiting trade. A quota is a limit on the number of certain types of goods one country will accept from another. Once the quota for a certain item is reached no more will be permitted to enter the country. Governments can also help firms in their country by providing payments which help keep the firms' costs lower than their competitors. Lower costs result in lower prices which helps the firm receiving the payments. Payments by government to firms are called *subsidies*. Subsidies are sometimes given to firms which locate in areas of high unemployment to encourage them to provide jobs. Subsidies are also used to protect firms from overseas competition if what they make is particularly important to the government. A situation where no trade restrictions are imposed is called *free trade*.

13.1. Answer the following questions with at least a full sentence, or by writing out the missing words.

1. What problems does international trade help to overcome?

2. ___ ___ is trade within Great Britain, ___ ___ is trade with other countries.

3. Name seven problems facing firms wishing to trade overseas.

4. The ___, ___ and ___ of a country will cause it to have different laws and ___ .

5. What is a quota and how is it different from a tariff?

6. Explain what is meant by a subsidy.

7. A situation where no trade restrictions are imposed is called ___ ___ .

These problems are tackled by three types of approach:

- Government help to British industry
- Government links with other governments
- British industry's joint approach

DEPARTMENT OF TRADE AND INDUSTRY

Logo of the Department of Trade and Industry

Government help to British industry

The bulk of government help to exporters is provided through the Department of Trade and Industry (DTI). The British Overseas Trade Board is the export promotion arm of the DTI.

British Overseas Trade Board (BOTB)

This organisation provides information and advice. Advice covers trade regulations, tariffs, marketing information. This organisation will help mount exhibitions and promotions overseas which British firms are encouraged to participate in.

Export Credit Guarantee Department (ECGD)

As well as providing advice and information the ECGD offers an insurance service against the non-payment of debts by overseas customers. By removing the risk of loss through non-payment the government hopes to encourage British firms to trade overseas.

Other services include publicity and information for DTI sponsored events. Trade fairs, promotion and displays are organised by the Fairs and Promotions Branch. This branch helps British firms to display their goods and services to potential overseas customers.

Government links with other governments

One way in which the government can help British firms abroad is through *trade agreements* with another country. A trade agreement is an arrangement between two countries which increases the amount of trade between them. This can be done by signing an agreement with another country to, for example, limit quotas or tariffs. An agreement between two countries like this is a *bi-lateral* or two-way agreement. A more important type of agreement is the *multi-lateral agreement*. This is an agreement involving many countries. Multi-lateral agreements have led to the establishment of several international organisations dealing with foreign trade. We shall look at the main ones which affect British overseas trade.

The European Community (EC)

The Common Market as it is called is made up of 12 countries who have signed an agreement known as *The Treaty of Rome*. Although others may join, the current membership is: Italy, France, Belgium, Germany, Luxembourg, Netherlands, Denmark, Southern Ireland, Greece, Spain, Great Britain and Portugal.

The EC is an arrangement which aims to remove trade restrictions between member countries. At the same time the EC tries to limit goods and services from outside the community. Other aims are to help the movement of workers and capital between countries. In the long term the aim of the EC is to achieve greater unity between its member countries.

Several bodies have been established to co-ordinate the work of the EC. The main ones are:

- *The Council of Ministers*. Each member country sends government ministers to the EC Council of Ministers. The government Minister puts forward the views of her or his country. The council puts forward its agreed proposals to the European Parliament.

- *European Parliament*. Each member country elects MEPs (Members of the European Parliament). The MEPs discuss the proposals from the Council of Ministers but it is the Council that has the power to make decisions. As well as being influenced by the Parliament, the Council considers suggestions from the EC Commission.

- *EC Commission*. The Commission is made up of members chosen by, but not belonging to, governments of member countries. It is this body which is responsible for the main decisions concerning how EC agreements should be put into practice.

The European Parliament at Strasbourg

- *European Court of Justice*. The laws which are passed by the MEPs in parliament are overseen by the European Court of Justice which settles any legal disputes. Citizens of member countries who feel their own country's laws break EC laws can appeal to the European Court of Justice.

Help to member countries, which affects businesses, is available from the EC. The European Social Fund (ESF), for example, provides funds to deal with the problems of unemployment. The Common Agricultural Policy (CAP) fixes the price of agricultural products and how they are distributed. This clearly has an effect on farmers and related businesses.

In 1992 most of the remaining restrictions which limit the movement of goods, services and workers between members of the EC will be abolished. There will be so few differences between the trading regulations of member countries that after 1992 Europe will be a *single market*, as opposed to 12 different markets in each of the member countries. This will mean that firms within EC countries will have even greater opportunities to sell to other EC countries. Businesses will have the opportunity to sell to the 320 million people who make up the EC. This increase in trading links with other European countries will mean that skills in European languages such as French or German will become increasingly important. The British Government has mounted an advice and publicity campaign to help firms prepare for the changes of 1992. This campaign is being organised by the Department of Trade and Industry.

As a result of growing links with the EC, work has started on a tunnel under the Channel which will link Britain to Europe. This tunnel will be used by high speed trains which will move people and goods between Britain and France. From France goods can be moved by rail or other forms of transport to anywhere on the Continent. One advantage of the *Chunnel*, as it is sometimes called, is that the bad weather which is known to prevent ships, hovercraft and planes crossing the Channel will not prevent trains passing underneath

The channel tunnel under construction

it. As a result of using rail transport the Channel Tunnel brings many of the advantages of the railways to international trade. It also brings several of the disadvantages (see page 156).

CHECK THIS OUT

13.2. Answer the following questions with at least a full sentence, or by writing out the missing words.

1. What does the Export Credit Guarantee Department do?

2. Describe the work of the British Overseas Trade Board.

3. How are bi-lateral and multi-lateral treaties different?

4. Give another name for the Common Market.

5. Six members of the Common Market include ____, ____, ____, ____, ____ and ____.

6. The ___ ___ ___ is an arrangement which aims to remove the restrictions to ____ between member countries.

7. Name four important organisations within the EC.

8. In ___ most of the remaining restrictions which limit the movement of goods, services and ____ between members of the EC will be _____.

9. What is the Chunnel?

European Free Trade Association (EFTA)

EFTA is made up of European countries who have chosen not to join the EC. Like the EC, EFTA tries to protect its members by limiting imports from non-members and promoting trade between member countries. Unlike the EC, EFTA does not aim to eventually integrate the member countries. Although there are some talks and other links between the EC and the smaller EFTA they are separate organisations. EFTA members include Finland and Sweden.

General Agreement on Tariffs and Trade (GATT)

GATT is a large organisation of over 50 countries who aim to promote trade between themselves by reducing trade restrictions. Britain was a member of GATT before joining the EC in 1973. Many GATT countries were previously controlled by Britain before becoming independent. Although no longer a GATT member, relations between Britain and GATT members are generally good.

Organisation of Petroleum Exporting Countries (OPEC)

The other organisations we have looked at so far try to reach agreement about a wide range of goods and services. OPEC is different in that its main concern is with oil and petrol. This organisation is not involved in major trade agreements between members for any other products. Members of OPEC (such as Saudi Arabia) are all important petroleum producers. OPEC is an organisation which tries to set the price and output levels of petroleum world wide. By doing so not only can supply be maintained but member countries can enjoy high levels of earnings from their production of petrol and oil. Britain is not an OPEC member but fixes the price of its oil in relation to OPEC prices. As oil and petroleum are important in all aspects of business OPEC clearly can be seen as an important organisation.

International Monetary Fund (IMF)

Most European and North American governments, including Britain, are members of this important organisation. The IMF tries to help countries with trade problems to overcome them. Loans, grants and advice are provided by the highly qualified staff at IMF. The Fund tries to influence exchange rates so that they do not change unpredictably and cause payment problems for countries engaged in international trade. By providing financial assistance the IMF aims to promote international trade.

Other help to British industry

Banks

The major British banks provide help, loans and advice to firms seeking to trade overseas. It is possible to move foreign currency through local banks so that payments can be made and overseas cheques paid into the firm's bank account.

Employers' organisations

Organisations like the Confederation of British Industry (CBI) and local Chambers of Trade or Chambers of Commerce can provide help and advice to firms about the legal requirements of overseas trade. Advice can be obtained about government grants aiming to promote overseas trade as well as to how to complete overseas trade documentation.

Colleges

As the Single Market of 1992 draws nearer an increasing number of colleges, polytechnics and universities are offering their experienced and highly qualified staff to run courses and provide advice for firms wishing to move into overseas trade.

13.3. Answer the following questions with at least a full sentence, or by writing out the missing words.

1. What does EFTA try to do?

2. GATT stands for ____ ____ on ____ and____.

3. OPEC's main concern is with ____ and ____ .

4. The IMF provides _____ assistance.

5. How can banks help firms wishing to trade overseas?

6. Name two other organisations which can help firms wishing to trade overseas.

Selling overseas

After having taken advice about trading overseas the firm needs to decide how to organise its overseas trade. There are several options.

Subsidiary

The firm can buy an overseas business or establish its own company in the country it wishes to export to. As the new business is controlled by the original firm it is called a *subsidiary*. This arrangement can provide direct control and minimise expense on transport and packaging. Locally employed specialists reduce the expense of training the firm's own staff and come with a useful range of local contacts.

Franchise

A franchise is an agreement allowing a business to copy the processes and organisation of another. While the original business (the franchiser) may lay down strict standards of service and conditions, support is often given to the *franchisee* through loans and training. The franchisee is the firm which buys the right to use the franchiser's methods. McDonald's is an international franchise operation. The advantage of a franchise is that the firm does not have the expense or risk of buying premises and equipment. It receives a fee from the franchiser who bears the cost and the risk of the enterprise.

Sell direct

ICI is a company which sells direct from Britain to overseas countries. Selling directly overseas requires specialist knowledge and training which may be expensive to acquire through training or new staff. The business has control of the process but has to overcome many problems, for example language, currency, distance etc.

Licensing

The firm allows its product to be made by an overseas company but sold under its own name. Profits are kept by the overseas firm who pays a license fee to the original manufacturer of the product. Certain 'German' lager sold in this country is made here under license. The advantage of licensing is that the firm does not have the expense or risk of buying premises and equipment. It receives a license fee from the overseas company - the *licensee*. The licensee bears the cost and the risk of the enterprise in the overseas country.

Agents

It is possible to employ agents who undertake to promote and sell the product overseas. These firms will have specialist knowledge and contacts which can work to the firm's advantage. A *commission* or percentage value of sales is paid in return for their services. This fee may be cheaper than training or employing new staff. A problem with this arrangement is that some control of the distribution passes to the agent.

Merchants

Export merchants or *export houses* agree to buy a certain quantity of the firm's product and sell them overseas. Once they have bought the goods, they have control of the advertising and distribution overseas. Some firms may see this as a disadvantage. These firms will have specialist knowledge and contacts and bear the cost and risk of selling in the overseas country. The home producer has the profit from the sale and no worry or risk about having to sell the goods overseas.

1. What is a subsidiary?

2. A _____ is an agreement to allow a business to copy the processes and _____ of another.

3. How might a firm benefit by licensing the right to produce its product to a firm overseas.

4. How are agents and merchants different?

Documents used in international trade

The bill of lading

This is used when sending goods by sea. Goods sent by air are accompanied by a similar document called an airways bill. The bill of lading gives the holder of the original bill legal ownership of the goods mentioned on it. Several copies are made: one is given to the ship's captain, one to the consignee (the person sending the goods) and one to the consignor (the person receiving the goods). The bill of lading gives a full description of the goods and says where they have to go. To take possession of the goods, the consignor must show his or her copy of the bill to the captain of the vessel or his representative.

If the goods are damaged in transit, a note has to be made on the bill. This is sometimes called *endorsing the bill*. If the goods are not damaged, the bill is said to be *clean*, but if an endorsement has been made, it is a *fouled* or a *claused* bill.

The export invoice

This is prepared in the same way as an invoice for internal use, with the addition of the marks and numbers of the packages and also the name of the ship which is transporting them. One copy of this invoice is attached to the bill of lading. Copies of other invoices which may have been received from various suppliers of the goods are attached to the export invoice, which saves having to enter details.

Certificate of origin

Countries may charge a levy or tariff on goods which they import, unless the country from which the goods are being imported belongs to a cartel like EC or GATT, in order to force up their price and thus make home-produced goods more attractive to the buyer. Customs authorities need to know from which country the goods have originated. In order to know this, Customs and Excise require a certificate of origin which states the country from which the goods first came.

Consular invoice

As well as charging import duties, countries often restrict the numbers of certain types of goods coming in so that their home products are protected. These *quotas*, as they are called, are sometimes made compulsory by the countries receiving the goods. Alternatively the importing and exporting countries may come to voluntary agreements about the amount of imports which come into a country. The advantage of voluntary agreements is that countries are not as inclined to respond with harsher quotas. The consular invoice authorises the imports to take place. The invoice contains a declaration, sworn before the consul of the importing country, that the particulars in the invoice are correct. The consul then certifies the invoice and charges a fee for doing so.

Customs specification

Everything imported into or exported out of the United Kingdom must, by law, be declared to the Customs and Excise Department. This information is used by the Department of Trade in preparing statistical information on imports and exports. When goods are exported, a *specification* on the prescribed customs form giving particulars about the goods exported is given by the exporter.

Making payments overseas

There are two problems to contend with when making payments to foreign countries. One is that countries have their own currencies and money has to be converted, and the other is that of avoiding bad debts: that is, not receiving money for goods which have been forwarded, or not receiving goods which have been paid for. Various payment methods in foreign trade have been devised to help to overcome these problems.

Bills of exchange

When a sale of goods has been agreed, the seller draws up and signs a bill of exchange, which is then passed to the buyer for acceptance by signing across it. This means that the buyer has agreed to pay the sum involved by the date (which is some time in the future) shown on the bill. The most common date is three months' time. This is legally binding, provided that the goods are delivered. The goods should arrive at their overseas destination before the bill *matures* (that is, becomes due for payment.) The buyer has the goods and the seller gets paid, so that both are satisfied.

There is still a problem if the seller wishes to receive his money earlier. One way is for the seller to *endorse* the bill, by signing on the reverse, and then to use it to pay another business for goods bought from them. The seller has then received goods to the value of the bill, and the second business waits until the bill matures and receives money, or perhaps passes it on in payment for goods from a third business.

Another way is to *discount* the bill with a bank or discount house. This means that the bill is sold for an amount slightly less than its face value. The bank holds the bill until it is mature, and claims the full value. The difference between the amount the bank paid for the bill and the amount received when it matures is the reward for waiting for payment and for taking the risk of non-payment. Bills may be discounted several times before they mature, for instance moving from one bank or discount house to another.

There is still a risk, with such bills, that the debtor may fail to *honour* the bill (that is, to pay when it falls due). A way round this is to have the bill *accepted* by an acceptance house, for example a merchant bank, which agrees – for a small charge – to take responsibility if the debtor fails to pay. This makes the bill *first-class*, and it can be discounted easily at a favourable rate.

Another risk is that of foreign currency becoming worth less to the exporter or the bank in terms of home currency, during the period until the bill matures. One solution is to have the bill payable only in sterling (for a United Kingdom exporter), while another is to have an agreed exchange rate on the bill. A third possibility is for the expected foreign currency to be sold 'forward' on the foreign exchange market. This means that the current agreed price will be paid when the bill matures. These methods help the person receiving payment to know precisely how much of his *own* currency he will receive on the agreed date.

Documentary bills

These are also bills of exchange, but there are various foreign trade documents 'attached'. These documents vary according to the requirements of the importing country, but include the bill of lading, export invoice and insurance certificate. The most important is the bill of lading which proves ownership. When the importer has paid or 'accepted' the related bill of exchange, he can receive the bill of lading and present it to claim the imported goods. The procedure is usually handled between the banks of the exporter and the importer.

While this arrangement makes sure that the bill is accepted before the goods are handed over, there is still the risk that the bill could be 'dishonoured' – that is, not paid in due course by the importer. For this reason, a more secure method of payment, called a letter of credit, may be used.

Letters of credit

These are sometimes referred to as documentary credits or bankers' commercial credits. The importer requests his own bank to send a letter of credit to an *advising* or *corresponding* bank in the exporter's country. When the exporter provides the necessary documents, including the bill of lading and other shipping documents, showing that the goods have been sent, he is paid direct by the bank. The documents are then sent to the importer's bank, which hands them to the importer when payment is made, so that the goods can then be claimed. Where a period of credit is required, this can still be arranged through the use of a first-class 'accepted' bill of exchange (see above).

By this method, the importer's bank accepting responsibility for payment, but to be safe, the letter of credit should be made *irrevocable*, so that the bank still has responsibility even if anything goes wrong. As a further safeguard, the advising bank can also be asked to give a *confirmed* credit, which means that in the case of default by the importer's bank, the advising bank will not claim against the exporter but only against the importer's bank.

Direct payment

- Bank drafts. These are used in overseas trade as well as in the UK. (See page 113).

- Cable transfers. These involve the transfer of funds electronically between banks. No money is physically transferred, so that there must be complete trust between the banks concerned, or they may be branches of the same international bank or a subsidiary. Settlement between the banks occurs later when a number of such payments are 'set off' against each other, when these payments occur in both directions. This method is extremely quick and is especially useful where urgent payments need to be made.

13.5. Answer the following questions with at least a full sentence, or by writing out the missing words.

2. Why is a Certificate of Origin needed?

3. What is a Bill of Exchange?

4. Cable transfers move money _____ between banks.

1. What is a fouled bill?

The effect of international trade on the economy

As we have seen countries need to bring goods and services in (import) and sell goods and services overseas (export). These imports and exports may be visible or invisible. *Visible* imports or exports are things that can be seen, for example machinery, food,

Invisible and visible exports

clothes, coal etc. *Invisible* imports or exports are fees for services. If a British designer designs a car for an overseas manufacturer this represents an invisible export as the service has been sold to an overseas firm. Foreign tourists in Britain pay for hotels, food, clothes, etc. This represents an invisible export as it is money earned by providing a service for someone who does not live in this country. British tourists overseas are, by the same definition, buying invisible imports. The country's total value of imports from the total value of exports gives the *balance of payments* for the nation. If more is spent on imports than received from exports the balance will be negative, for example –£23m. This is said to be an *adverse balance of payments*. If more is being received from exports than spent on imports the figure will be positive, for example +£24m. This is a *favourable balance of payments*. A favourable balance is the most desirable because it shows the country is meeting the cost of its imports and has money to spend on other goods and services. An adverse balance of payments means that overseas borrowing is needed to meet the outstanding debts. The repayments represent a drain on the resources of the country. The balance of payments shows the value of all payments received and made by a country.

These payments are divided into the three main types:

- visible items
- invisible items
- capital items

The visible items refer to the foreign trade in goods. When, in a given period (usually a year), the value of visibles exported by a country is compared with the value of visibles imported by that country, the result is called the *visible balance* or *balance of trade*.

For example:

1986	*£ million*
Value of goods exported	*1900*
Value of goods imported	*2000*
Visible balance of trade	**−100**

These figures show that the visible balance is adverse because the cost of goods imported is higher than those exported. This loss is called a *deficit*. The United Kingdom often has an adverse balance of trade.

The invisible items refer to foreign trade in services – that is invisible exports and imports. When the value of invisible exports by a country is compared with the value of invisible imports in the same period the result is called the *invisible balance*.

For example:

1986	*£ million*
Value of services exported	*1000*
Value of services imported	*800*
Invisible balance	**+200**

The figures above show that more has been earned than paid out. The invisible balance is therefore said to be favourable. This is known as a *surplus*. The United Kingdom normally has a surplus on its invisible balance.

When the visible balance is compared with the invisible balance for a country in a given period, this is called the *current balance* or *balance of payments on current account*.

Using the previous figures:

1986	*£ million*
Visible balance	*−100*
Invisible balance	*+200*
Current balance	**+100**

This produces a favourable current balance of £100 million, which is a surplus.

The third group of payments, the *capital items*, shows the amounts of money which have been lent abroad in a given period and the amounts which have been borrowed from abroad in the same period. For example, British businesses invest abroad, and foreign businesses invest in the United Kingdom, by setting up factories, buying shares in companies or depositing money in banks. The interest, profits and dividends which result from these investments appear in the invisible balance (see page 194).

When money is lent abroad, the capital sum is a transfer of money out of the country and is regarded as an import, in the same way as payment for imported goods. When money is brought into the country, it is regarded as an export in the same way as payment received for exported goods. It must be remembered that some time in the future, whether it is weeks or years, money lent or borrowed will have to be repaid.

When these capital items are considered and set against the current balance, then the *total currency flow* for the year can be calculated. Suppose that capital items produce a deficit (that is, a loss) of £300 million in the year concerned, which means that more has been lent than borrowed. Using the previous figures, we find:

1986	£ million
Current balance	+100
Capital items	–300
Total currency flow (net)	**–200**

This means that the country has paid out to other countries £200 million more than it has received in the year concerned. How is this loss going to be paid for?

Balancing the books

The central bank in the United Kingdom is called the Bank of England. A country's central bank holds the State's reserves of gold and foreign currencies. The loss of £200 million could be paid out of these reserves but, if they are not sufficient, the Bank of England for example, could temporarily borrow funds from the central banks of other countries, such as the Federal Reserve Bank of the USA, or from the International Monetary Fund (IMF) which was specially set up to help in this way. If the total currency flow had been positive, then the central bank could build up its reserves of foreign currency in order to pay any future deficits, or it could repay funds previously borrowed from other central banks or from the IMF. In this way, a country balances its books in its dealings with other countries.

13.6. Answer the following questions with at least a full sentence, or by writing out the missing words.

2. The country's total value of imports from the total value of exports gives the _____ of _____ .

3. What is an adverse balance of payments?

1. How do visible and invisible imports and exports differ?

4. What are capital items?

4. What is the Treaty of Rome?

5. Name the members of the EC.

6. Explain what is meant by the European Single Market.

1. How can a change in exchange rates make goods more expensive if the price has already been agreed?

7. What are the advantages and disadvantages of selling directly overseas?

2. Why might a government impose quotas on imported goods?

8. When would a Consular Invoice be used?

9. What does it mean if a Bill of Exchange is accepted?

3. Name a government department which helps exporters.

10. Name an invisible export.

b) How will the channel tunnel affect international trade? *(4 marks)*

c) When will the single market be introduced and what will be its effects? *(6 marks)*

d) What help can the EC provide for businesses? *(8 marks)*

1. *Now that the firm was doing well at home Mary thought that they should try to sell their brand of blackcurrant wine overseas.*

a) What help is available from the government for firms wishing to sell overseas? *(6 marks)*.

b) What problems will Mary's firm face when it tries to sell overseas? *(14 marks)*.

1. *The channel tunnel will link all Common Market members in a single market.*

a) What is the Common Market? *(2 marks)*

3. *This month's trade figures show an increase of visible imports which have resulted in an adverse balance of payments' said the newsreader.*

a) Using an example, explain what is meant by visible import? *(2 marks)*

b) What is an adverse balance of payments and why is it undesirable? *(8 marks)*

c) How could a country pay the cost of an adverse balance of payments? *(10 marks)*

LEARN IT YOURSELF

1. Collect any newspaper articles or notes of news broadcasts about the Single Market of 1992. Present them as a wall display and say, in your own words whether or not the changes are good or bad. Support your arguments.

2. Towards the end of the month look out for newspaper reports of the monthly trade figures. Give a presentation to your group about the reasons why the figures are good or bad and what the government might do to improve the situation.

3. Using a local bank or national newspaper follow the exchange rate of the Pound against the Franc and the Deutschmark. At the end of two weeks say if the changes have been good or bad for British exporters and why this is so.

ON ASSIGNMENT

Collect information from banks, the Department of Trade and Industry, the local Chamber of Commerce and local libraries about help available to firms wishing to export. Either give a talk on your findings or prepare a wall display

CASE STUDY

'Given the fact that the amount of competition in the UK market has grown 50 per cent in the last two years it is vital that Bettabikes Ltd seeks overseas markets if it is to remain profitable.' It was that phrase of the marketing consultant's report that caught Mike James' eye. Given the mood the Managing Director was in these days he knew he had better get a report ready for the Management meeting on Monday morning so they could take a decision about what to do.'

a) Write a memo on behalf of Mike James to the Managing Director explaining what problems there are for firms wishing to trade overseas, how they might overcome them and what help is available. You will need to point out the ways in which the company can sell its products overseas and advise which method, in your view, is best.

SECTION FIVE

Purchasing

CHAPTER 14

THE PURCHASING FUNCTION

In order to produce its goods or services a business will need to buy the raw materials and equipment it needs. Many firms will need to order components or equipment to their own specifications which will be used to produce a finished product. Car manufacturers will, for example, have headlights made by a specialist firm and then fit them to their own cars. If the business is to be efficient it needs to buy what it needs at the lowest price and on time, while getting the highest quality. Effective purchasing can increase profits. A one per cent reduction in purchasing costs can have the same effect as a ten per cent increase in sales for the average manufacturing company. Small firms will combine purchasing with other responsibilities but larger firms may employ specialists. The purchasing department needs to link to the personnel department to ensure its staff are well qualified and capable of meeting the firm's requirements. Suitable specialist qualifications would be those from the Institute of Purchasing and Supply (IPS). Once appointed, purchasing staff should be kept aware of new products, processes or techniques which may affect what they need to purchase. It goes without saying that such staff should be well-informed about the prices of the supplies the firm needs. Training in negotiation skills may also be needed.

Links with the manufacturing or production section of the business are important. The purchasing department needs to be informed of planned production levels so that supplies can be ordered in plenty of time and production not interrupted. Delays or changes in delivery dates may mean that production plans have to be changed.

The finance or accounts section of the firm will need to have a close working relationship with the purchasing section. This is so that invoices can be met and debtors paid the amount owing to them. Purchasing has an important role in making sure that accounts are met accurately. Before authorising payments the purchasing section may need to check that goods delivered have met the requirements of quality and reliability they laid down for their suppliers.

Choosing suppliers

The firm needs reliable suppliers. It is up to the purchasing department to make sure that the suppliers it chooses to deal with are:

- *Stable.* A firm that goes out of business part way through making your order may mean delays and hold-ups for your customers. The purchasing section should check the financial background of its suppliers.

- *Able.* The purchasing department must investigate whether potential suppliers are able to make the goods required. This may mean looking at the firm's equipment and staff expertise if a large or important order is being considered. Some purchasing departments may ask for evidence of the firm having done similar work for other organisations before placing an order. Trade directories and specialist magazines are a useful starting point in this research. A purchasing department will also want to establish that a potential supplier is helpful in business dealings. An offhand approach with delays in returning phone calls or replying to letters will be a nuisance.

- *Clear.* What is required will usually be made clear in a *specification*. The specification or 'spec' will give the exact technical details of what is needed in terms of size, shape, colour and performance etc. of the items to be purchased. The supplying firm must then meet this specification exactly.

A buyer must be sure that suppliers are stable, able and clear

An important problem all purchasing departments have to deal with is whether to use one or two suppliers or several. By using several suppliers it is argued that competition between them will force prices down. Delays or disruption at one supplier will not disrupt production too much. Arguments against this are that researching various suppliers is time-consuming and expensive, low prices might mean reduced quality, and competition may lead to claims being made which the supplier cannot meet. Using fewer suppliers for larger orders can mean that the purchaser receives greater attention and discount for bulk purchases. The suppliers used will be more involved in the firm's business and more positive in their approach, perhaps by giving technical advice helpful to the manufacturing process. The disadvantage of being affected by delays or disruption at a large supplier remains.

1. How can effective purchasing increase profits?

2. Good purchasing involves buying at the lowest ____, on ___ with the highest _____ .

3. With which departments should the purchasing department link up?

4. The purchasing department should make sure that its suppliers are ___, ___ and ___ .

5. What is a specification or 'spec'?

6. What are the arguments in favour of using one supplier instead of many?

Stock control

We know that stock represents part of the capital of a business. The purchasing department needs to ensure that not too much capital is tied up as stock. This is called *overstocking*. If too little stock is held this may lead to costly delays in manufacturing or delivering the goods to customers. Carrying too little stock is called *understocking*. As well as tying up capital, overstocking leads to unnecessary storage costs and the risk that delays might cause goods to become unusable or unfashionable. Clearly, stock needs to be ordered in advance of when it is needed, but not too far in advance. A new development in stock control is a process called Just In Time (JIT). With this system production is planned well in advance and suppliers are made aware of the firm's needs. The suppliers hold the stock, which they deliver on demand, often at an agreed time. The firm benefits by having regular supplies and low storage costs, the supplier benefits by having regular orders, satisfying the customer and being able to plan in advance.

In order to prevent stock being wasted firms may have a FIFO system of stock control. This stands for First In First Out. Under this system the goods which are received first and have been in stock longest are the first to be sent to customers. The firm will use a *stock control card* or *stock record card* to record the amount of goods issued and received.

The card will contain a description of the item with any reference number the firm uses to refer to it. Details of location are important as this tells staff where in a large warehouse items can be found. Separate columns show stock coming in and going out, together with dates or reference numbers. A third column takes 'goods issued' from 'goods received' and shows the balance or amount in stock. The *max stock* indicates the maximum number of items that should be held in stock at any one time to avoid tying up capital unnecessarily. The *minimum stock* shows the lowest amount of stock that should be kept. A

Stationery Stock Card

Item: Treasury Tags (boxes of 50) mixed colours
Ref: 727690

Max Stock: 40 boxes
Min stock: 10 boxes
Re-order level: 20 boxes

Date 1991	Receipts			Issues			Balance in Stock
	Quantity Rec'd	Invoice No.	Supplier	Quantity Issued	Requisition No.	Department	
Jan 1							
" 8							30 boxes
" 11				1 box	153	Reception	29 "
March 1				10 boxes	401	Filing dept	19 "
" 3	25 boxes	450	Office Equipment	8 boxes	477	Personnel dept	11 "
			Supplies Ltd				36 "

A stock record card for stationery

lower amount in stock may lead to delays in delivery or production. The *re-order level* shows at what point an order should be placed with a supplier to avoid the danger of running out of stock. Many firms do this automatically by computer. Once the computer record shows that the re-order level has been reached an order will automatically be printed so that stock levels can be brought up to the maximum stock figure.

Theft, damage or inaccurate records of what goods are in stock can cause a firm to lose a lot of money. For these reasons a check called an *inventory* or *stock-check* will be made. Items in stock are counted to see that the numbers actually counted agree with the figures shown in the records. Firms may use a *periodic stock-check or inventory* every month, six months or year to look at stock levels. This will usually be done when the premises are closed, causing little disruption but involving the expense of overtime payments for the necessary staff. With a *permanent inventory or stock-check* system the firm employs staff whose responsibility is to check stock the whole year round. This is usually only done in large firms.

Purchasing and stores management are two areas of business activity that are often overlooked. However, efficiency in these areas can be both profitable and productive for a business.

3. JIT stands for ___ ___ ___ which is a method of stock _____ .

4. What is a stock record card used for?

1. What is overstocking?

5. Explain the term 're-order level'.

2. Why is understocking undesirable?

6. What is a permanent inventory?

1. What qualification shows a person has some skill in purchasing?

2. Why should the purchasing department be informed of planned production levels?

3. How can the purchasing department show that potential suppliers are reliable?

4. What are the arguments against using one supplier?

5. What is FIFO and why is it used?

6. How can a firm record the amount of goods received and issued?

7. How can computers improve stock record keeping?

8. What does 'max stock' mean?

9. What are the advantages of Just In Time?

10. Why do firms carry out an inventory?

a) How should the blanks on the card be completed? *(4 marks)*

b) What should happen when the re-order level is reached? *(4 marks)*

c) In what two ways can a firm check that its stock records are accurate? *(4 marks)*

d) Why should overstocking and understocking be avoided? *(8 marks)*

JOANNE STEPHEN – HAIRDRESSING SUPPLIIES **Stock Record**

Item: __Hairbrush__   Max Stock: 30 boxes
Reference: __JB/213__   Min stock: 10 boxes
Supplier: __SJ Burnham PLC__   Re-order: 15 boxes

	Received			Issued		Balance
Date	Invoice No.	Quantity	Order Ref.		Quantity	
						10
1/9/91	YZ273	10				20
8/9/91	YZ861	—				18
10/9/91			AC/31		2	—
11/9/91			BB/17		2	—
14/9/91	DC/32	7			—	15
17/9/91			BT/71			25
23/9/91	YZ/211	10				

LEARN IT YOURSELF

1. Contact the Institute of Purchasing and Supply directly or through your careers department for details about careers in purchasing.

2. See if you can devise a system of stock control for your youth club, school or college to use.

CASE STUDY

Although he had been with the firm's purchasing department for two years, John had not dealt with or heard of Mazell Ltd. Despite the fact that they were a new business they did sound very good and their price was way below the price charged by the usual supplier John used. He was tempted to give them the whole contract for the next six months and then tell his boss what a saving he had made. That should help his promotion chances, he thought!

a) What advice would you give John about using only one firm, and using this firm in particular?

SECTION SIX

Production

THE PRODUCTION FUNCTION

Production is about transforming raw materials into a finished product or service. You should remember that even service industries such as catering or hairdressing are productive industries as they produce something which the customer wants using raw materials. Although this section will concentrate on manufacturing, much of what is said applies to service industries.

The production section of the firm will need strong links with marketing to ensure that what is being produced is what customers want; with purchasing to ensure that supplies of raw materials are available; with personnel to ensure that suitable staff are appointed to produce the goods or services the customer requires; with the research and development section to ensure that the firm is using the best materials and techniques for its purposes (see page 216).

Organising production

Production planning is about using the firm's resources to produce its products as cheaply and efficiently as possible. There are three approaches the firm can take to production: *unit production*, *flow production* and *batch production*. The choice it makes will depend on the *value of the order*, *type of product produced* and the *number to be produced*.

A skilled worker hand-painting porcelain

Unit production

This is sometimes called *job production*. It is used when the firm is making orders to the requirements of individual customers. Tailor-made suits are one example of this type of production, but it is also used to produce specialised heavy-duty equipment for industry. The individual needs of the customer can only be met by using skilled craftsmen/women. As a result the labour costs of this sort of production are high. Using large amounts of labour in this way is referred to as being *labour intensive*. Such an approach to production means that the firm must have staff who are flexible and highly-skilled so that they can adapt from one job to another. The advantage of unit production is that the finished product meets the customer's needs exactly – provided these have been properly explained in the first place!

Flow production at Ford's

Flow production

Flow production is sometimes called *mass production* as it involves producing large amounts of a product continuously. It is a technique used to produce large amounts of identical goods, for example cars, washing-up liquid or computers. To be most effective flow production uses *standardised parts*, which gives the consumer limited choices about the product. Flow production has the advantage of producing cheaper goods. One way of keeping production costs down is to have much of the production process done by machines. As the machines represent capital we say that flow production is *capital intensive*. In order to make the most efficient use of the expensive equipment involved, sales and production need to be well-planned to reduce the time machines stand idle.

Batch production

This production technique is used when the same labour and equipment can be used to produce a number of different products. Skilled machinists and industrial sewing machines can be used to make curtains, jeans or baby clothes. With a batch production system time will be spent on making one type of product and, when the required number have been produced, another product will be produced using the same equipment and labour. Although not on the same scale as flow production, batch production can be used for producing large quantities of standardised goods. Again, production planning is important. Sales forecasts need to be accurate so that products are produced in advance of increased demand. Unless sales figures are accurate capital and labour may stand idle or fail to produce sufficient quantities.

15.1. Answer the following questions with at least a full sentence, or by writing out the missing words.

1. What other departments should the production department form links with?

2. _____ _____ is about using the firm's resources to produce its products as cheaply and efficiently as possible.

3. What is unit production sometimes called?

4. ____ ____ is sometimes called mass production.

5. When is batch production used?

6. Why is production planning important?

Quality

The BSI kite mark

An important aspect of production is the need to maintain quality. This can be done by making random checks of the items produced to see that they are the right shape, size or colour etc, and without faults. Some firms employ *progress chasers* who have to see that products are being produced in accordance with the agreed plans. This is done by monitoring the product at each stage of the production process. The most effective way of ensuring quality is to have a well-planned system designed to correct errors and raise standards. The British Standards Institution (BSI) lays down standards of management and production which can help bring about good quality products. These standards are known as the British Standard 5750. Other British Standards have different numbers and these tend to deal with the quality and safety of particular products. When buying a motor bike helmet, for example, it is a good idea to check that it has been made in accordance with the relevant British Standard for that item. This will be shown by the kite mark symbol of the BSI. The manufacturing section of any firm needs to make sure its products meet the British Standard as customers find this reassuring and so are more likely to buy BSI standard products.

Computers

Computers are becoming increasingly important in manufacturing. They are capable of checking and recording many different aspects of the production process such as the size, temperature or colour of goods. These exact measurements are an important part of improving standards, increasing safety and reducing waste. *Computer aided manufacturing* (CAM) is growing in importance. Computers are being used in developing robots to help in the manufacturing process. Some car manufacturers are using robots to weld metal joints or install windscreens. These jobs were previously done by humans. As a result of using robots errors are reduced, costs are lowered and production can be increased. Computer-controlled trolleys are often used to move materials around factories automatically. This is done by programming instructions into the machines, which follow sensors to their destination. They can stop themselves if they come across an obstruction.

15.2. Answer the following questions with at least a full sentence, or by writing out the missing words.

1. What are progress chasers?

2. The British Standards Institution (BSI) lays down standards of _____ and _____ which can help bring about good quality products. These standards are known as the __ __ 5750.

3. How can computers help in manufacturing?

Location of industry

A firm must make the right decision about where to place its manufacturing section. Several factors will affect the firm's decision but as a general rule firms who use light raw materials to produce bulky finished goods will locate near the market for the product. For example, Boddington's brewery is in Manchester as it is easier to transport the light raw materials such as barley long distances to the city than to move the more bulky finished product, beer, long distances. Firms which provide a service, such as hairdressers and cafes, clearly also have to locate near potential customers. On the other hand, firms which use heavy raw materials to produce a product which is less bulky will locate near the raw materials. Having to move the less bulky finished product results in lower transport costs. Extractive or primary industries must obviously be at the point of extraction (see Chapter One). Firms producing products where transport costs are not a major consideration are able to locate more or less where they please. These sort of firms are referred to as *footloose* because of their ability to go where they choose.

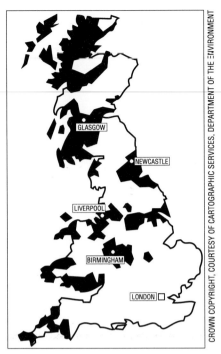

Assisted areas at July 1988 indicated by shading

CROWN COPYRIGHT, COURTESY OF CARTOGRAPHIC SERVICES, DEPARTMENT OF THE ENVIRONMENT

In deciding where to locate, a firm will consider the following four things: factors of production, transport, support services and historical influences.

Factors of production

As we saw in Chapter One, firms need the factors of production to provide their products. The availability of *land* to buy or rent at the right price is important. In certain *assisted areas* such as Glasgow, Cardiff and Newcastle upon Tyne where unemployment is high, the government provides financial help for firms building factories. The development of the Nissan car factory in Durham was partly the result of local and central government grants. *Capital* such as machines and equipment needs to be available. Once again firms in assisted areas are entitled to help from the government if they meet certain conditions in creating jobs. In these areas loans are often available at low rates of interest to qualifying firms. Tax allowances aimed at reducing tax payments, and so giving the firm more money to spend, are also provided in the assisted areas. In some places there is often an existing pool of trained *labour*. As this helps to keep the firm's training costs down it represents an *economy* or saving. As it is the result of events outside the firm it is said to be an example of an *external economy*. In the assisted areas government grants are often available to help with training costs. The area's record of strikes and industrial relations will also be a consideration when firms look at the labour of the area.

The aim of having assisted areas is to help firms develop, and provide jobs, in areas which are economically uncompetitive in terms of producing at the lowest cost.

Transport

Transport costs are an important consideration, especially if the firm deals in bulky raw materials or bulky finished products. In order to keep costs down firms require access to reliable transport systems suited to their needs. For this reason access to motorways, airports, railway stations and sea ports is considered important. (See Chapter 11 for more about transport).

Support services

In areas where there has been a tradition of producing certain products related services will have developed in the area. These save the firm money as it is usually cheaper to buy goods and services than to provide them itself. These *external economies of scale* result from there being a large enough industry in the area to make it profitable for the providers of support services to exist. For this reason external economies of scale are sometimes called *economies of concentration* – the industry is concentrated in one or two parts of the country. Examples of external economies of scale include training facilities at local colleges, such as mining courses in the Nottinghamshire area, and the production of specialised equipment to help the production process. We have already seen that the availability of trained labour is an example of an external economy. The services which support a firm's activities are sometimes called *ancillary services*.

Historical influences

As we have seen, when an area develops as a centre for making certain products it develops certain advantages. It also develops a reputation for certain products, for example Sheffield steel. However as the area develops further these advantages may disappear or other areas develop greater advantages. Firms will often stay in an area long after the advantages which first attracted it have gone. This failure to move when the advantages have gone is called *industrial inertia*.

15.3. Answer the following questions with at least a full sentence, or by writing out the missing words.

3. Certain firms are _____ because of their ability to go where they please.

4. In deciding where to locate a firm will consider ____, ____, ____ and ____ .

5. What are external economies of scale?

6. Describe what help the government gives to firms in assisted areas and explain why the help is provided.

1. Why might a firm locate near the market for its product?

2. Why might a firm locate near the raw materials for its product?

4. Explain the term 'labour intensive'.

5. Which sort of production will be used to produce large amounts of identical goods?

6. What is meant by capital intensive?

7. When can batch production be used?

8. What is British Standard 5750?

9. Why should goods meet the appropriate British Standard?

10. How can computers improve standards of manufacturing?

1. Are service industries involved in production? Explain your answer.

2. Why does production need to link up with research and development?

3. What three factors affect production planning?

STIMULUS RESPONSE QUESTIONS

Tailor-made suits, cars, teddy bears, hand-carved statues, motorbikes, jeans.

a) Which of these products would you expect to be made through batch, flow or unit production? *(6 marks)*

b) Which of these methods of production is most labour intensive? *(3 marks)*

c) Which of these methods of production is best suited to meeting individual tastes? *(3 marks)*

d) Explain two ways in which the British Standards Institute can help manufacturers satisfy the public. *(8 marks)*

LEARN IT YOURSELF

Write a group letter to a local manufacturer asking if you can visit to see their product being made. If you ask you may find out how production is organised and what sort of techniques are used.

ON ASSIGNMENT

Using the heading 'Technology at Work', research the way in which computers have affected the process of manufacturing. Your local library should be able to help, and possibly programmes like *Tomorrow's World* on BBC television. Present a project file of your findings.

CASE STUDY

Get into small groups. Each group should have plenty of plain paper, rulers, pencils and scissors. See how many paper aeroplanes each group can make in ten minutes. At the end of ten minutes stop and compare the quality and quantity that each group has made. How could the production process have been improved? Would it have been better to choose a leader at the start, or for individuals to work on their own? What skill did each member of the group contribute? What makes one plane better than another?

SECTION SEVEN

Research and Development

CHAPTER 16

THE RESEARCH AND DEVELOPMENT FUNCTION

As we have seen, unless the firm is continually improving and developing its product range it cannot succeed. It is because of this that many large firms have research and development (R and D) departments. These, usually small, departments aim to come up with new ideas to improve either the *design* of the product or the *performance* of the product. Changes in design or performance may lead to a product being relaunched (see page 135) or an existing product being withdrawn and a new one introduced to replace it. In attempting to introduce improvements and changes the R and D section must bear in mind three considerations:

- *Price.* Any new ideas they have must be for products that can be produced at a price consumers are prepared to pay.

- *Practicality.* New ideas in a laboratory or on a designers desk are one thing; making products in large quantities is something else. A new idea for a product is only useful if the product can be produced on a commercial scale. Another consideration is that the idea is only practical if the consumer is likely to buy the product.

- *Profit.* Any new idea will only be developed by the firm if it is profitable. There may often be a conflict between the consumer's need and the firm's need to make a profit.

These three considerations show that the R and D section needs to be in touch with the marketing department as well as the manufacturing section of the business. Links with personnel are obviously necessary when it comes to recruiting highly-qualified staff to work in this area. Monitoring costs of development makes links with the finance section important. Most of the work done by R and D departments is *applied research*. This is research designed to solve a particular problem or improve a particular product. *Basic* or *fundamental research* is research which is carried out without an end result in mind. The idea is that by investigating unexplored areas of science and technology discoveries which might be useful can be uncovered. This basic research sometimes comes up with the most startling and useful results. *Operational research* is sometimes undertaken through the R and D department. This type of research concentrates on the firm's methods of operating and aims to come up with ways of reducing waste and improving efficiency.

The costs of research are high. Firms will often co-operate through their employers' associations to work on areas of concern. It is not unusual to find firms paying universities or polytechnics to conduct research work for them.

216

Computers are widely used in research for recording and monitoring the results of experiments. *Computer aided design* (CAD) allows researchers to design products on computer screens. This not only saves time but also allows for the production of plans and diagrams from different angles without the need for new drawings. This is because the computer can rotate the image on the screen. Such flexibility speeds up the design and development process.

Once a plan has been arrived at a *prototype* will be built. The prototype is the first version of the new product. It will be tested to see if it works as intended, and design changes may be made as a result of practical experience. The R and D section will then work with the manufacturing section on a *test run*. The test run is an attempt to produce larger quantities of the product in the factory. Any practical problems will come to light at this stage and steps can be taken to correct them. This avoids wastage through moving straight into full scale production. Only when these various stages of testing have been completed will the firm be able to start the advertising and production of its new product.

Once new products or designs have been developed firms can stop others copying them by taking out a *patent* on the idea. This means that the firm must register the idea with the government's Patent Office. When the Patent Officer is satisfied that the idea belongs to the firm, he or she will issue a patent, which is a document stating that the new idea or design belongs to the firm which holds the patent. Each patent is numbered. Firms copying the original idea can be taken to court and the patent holder can seek compensation. Employees working for a firm which is involved in research normally have a clause in their contract of employment which forbids them using ideas developed in the firm if they leave. Written material can be protected by the use of *copyright*.

SHORT QUESTIONS

1. In what two ways can the R and D section improve a product?

2. What three things must be borne in mind when considering changing a product?

3. Name two departments which the research and development department should keep in touch with.

4. Explain what is meant by applied research.

5. Give another name for basic research.

6. What is the name of research that concentrates on a firm's methods of operating?

7. How can firms keep the cost of research low?

8. Outline the advantages of computer aided design.

9. What is a prototype?

10. Describe the benefits of a test run.

STIMULUS RESPONSE QUESTIONS

LOCAL FACTORY TO CLOSE
As a result of increased competition Blaggs Computers PLC is to close. 'Too many rival products with new features are to blame' said Harry Hawk the Managing Director. Local union leaders, angry at the sacking of their members, pointed out that Blaggs' failure to develop new products and bad management were to blame for the situation. Mark Carole, Senior Shop Steward, pointed out that the union had urged the company to develop a research and development section to improve existing products and develop

new ones. The one new development the company did introduce in their product was copied by the firm's rivals who could sell it more cheaply, he added.

a) What benefits could a research and development section have brought to Blaggs Computers? *(2 marks)*

b) How could Blaggs have stopped their rivals copying their idea? *(4 marks)*

c) In what ways could Blaggs have reduced the costs of research? *(4 marks)*

d) What sort of research could have helped overcome the problems of bad management? *(4 marks)*

e) Do you think Blaggs would have benefitted more from fundamental or applied research in the months before its closure? Explain your answer. *(6 marks)*

LEARN IT YOURSELF

1. Collect information, such as advertisements or articles, from newspapers and magazines about new products coming onto the market. To what extent are they really new –

   are they just old products being relaunched?
   Prepare a short report on your findings.

2. Look out for television or radio programmes about new inventions and developments, such as The News or Tomorrow's World. Prepare a talk for the group about how these ideas came about and what differences they will make.

ON ASSIGNMENT

Prepare a project folder on 'The Effect of the Microchip'. This should include a short account of how microchips have been developed and how they are used in business, music and at home. Explain the effects they have had in each of these areas. You should also explain what future developments might take place.

CASE STUDY

John Patternack looked at his boss Natalie Simister as she finished reading his proposal for a new lawnmower that the firm could manufacture for the coming season. Natalie smiled at him and said 'I'll let you know John, I'm a bit busy right now.' Disappointed, John walked out of the office. Natalie wasn't very happy either. The proposal was for a mower that would cost £50 more to produce than their rivals' lawnmower, and copied some of the ideas from other firms. It was, however, a slightly better machine - but she was sure they would be unable to sell it at

that price and it did look hard to manufacture and use. She would have to tell him that while it wasn't a bad idea there were several reasons why the company would be unable to use it. It was a pity really as she knew John had put a lot of hard work and some of his own time into developing the idea.

a) Write down what you would say to John if you were Natalie so that he is unlikely to make these mistakes again.

b) How could Natalie have avoided things getting to this stage?

SECTION EIGHT

Government

THE WORK OF GOVERNMENT

The purpose of this chapter is to look at government and how it can affect business activity.

Britain has, basically, two levels of government, national and local

National government

National or central government is based at the Houses of Parliament in London. Parliament is made up of two houses, the House of Lords and the House of Commons. Members of Parliament (MPs) are elected to the House of Commons from particular areas of the country called *constituencies*. Manchester Central and Newcastle East are examples of constituencies. Members of the House of Lords include Church of England bishops, some judges and those there by right of birth. Unlike the House of Commons, members of the House of Lords are not elected by the people.

The House of Commons in session

The Houses of Parliament pass laws or *legislation* which must be obeyed by everyone. These Acts of Parliament regulate much of what business can do, for example the Trade Descriptions Act (see page 173). Government is controlled by the Cabinet which is a committee of MPs from the House of Commons and some members of the House of Lords. The House of Commons is the most powerful of the two houses. The leader of the party with the most MPs is Prime Minister and he or she chooses who will be in the Cabinet.

The party with the second largest number of MPs is usually referred to as the Opposition. By relying on their MPs to vote for what they propose the Cabinet can decide what laws are needed and how the country is to be run. Members of the Cabinet include Secretaries of State and some Ministers. Each has particular responsibilities, for example Transport or the Environment. The government is assisted by civil servants. The government raises money through taxes. Taxes are used to pay for the government's activity such as road building, the army, hospitals etc. *Direct taxes* are those which we pay on our income or wealth and are collected by the Inland Revenue on behalf of the government. *Indirect taxes* are not linked to income but to the purchases we make.

Income tax

After earning above a certain level of income people pay income tax. This is a percentage of what they earn. The rate of income tax is set by the Chancellor of the Exchequer in the Budget. Once earnings reach a certain level income tax may be charged at a higher rate. For example, the government may decide that anyone earning between £3000 and £40 000 per year should pay income tax at 25 per cent (25p in the pound going to the government). If they earn over £40 000 it might be decided to charge or *levy* income tax at 40 per cent. Someone earning £44 000 would pay 25 per cent on the first £40 000 and 40 per cent on the last £4000. In this case £40,000 is the *tax threshold* because it is at this point that a person moves from one rate of taxation to another. The government allows certain things to be taken into account when calculating a person's income tax. For example, if the tax payer is a single parent raising children some of their income will not be taxed. These *allowances* are shown in the person's tax code (see page 71).

Corporation tax

Businesses over a certain size must pay tax on their profits. Like income tax, companies are allowed certain expenses or *allowances* which affect the amount of tax they pay on their profits.

Capital gains tax

If a person or business sells assets such as shares or land they may have to pay capital gains tax on any profit they make. A limited amount of gain is allowed before tax has to be paid but once this threshold is reached the rate of tax is roughly one third of the profit made.

The three taxes we have just looked at are direct taxes. The amount of these taxes paid by an individual will depend on their income or wealth. For this reason they are said to be *progressive taxes*. Indirect taxes do not alter with the level of income and are said to be *regressive taxes*. We shall now look at the different indirect taxes.

Taxation provides the government with income

Customs and excise duties

These are collected by the government's Customs and Excise department. Customs duties are collected on imported goods (see page 181) and excise duties are charged on certain home-produced goods such as alcohol.

Value added tax

VAT is also collected by the Customs and Excise Department. When value is added at each stage of the production of an item, tax has to be added. This tax is reflected in the price of the finished product. Some goods, for example children's clothes, are either excused – exempted – from VAT or have it charged at a zero rate. As the amount of VAT paid depends on the value of the product it is said to be an *ad valorum* tax.

The rate of tax a government charges affects business. If tax rates are too high firms may not find it profitable enough to invest, if tax rates are too low the government will not be able to carry out its work. Tax rates can be used by the government to *redistribute wealth* from the rich to the poor as money taken from, say, capital gains tax will pay some of the cost of benefits such as old age pensions. Firms producing goods which rely on imports or are covered by excise duty need to reflect this in their budget. If customs duties or excise rates increase this will affect their profits. If the price is increased to pass on the cost to the consumer, sales may fall.

17.1. Answer the following questions with at least a full sentence, or by writing out the missing words.

5. Explain what is meant by a tax threshold.

6. In what ways do corporation tax and capital gains tax differ?

7. How do progressive and regressive taxes differ?

8. Two indirect taxes are __ __ __ and __ and __ duties.

9. Using an example explain what is meant by an *ad valorum* tax.

1. The Houses of Parliament pass ___ or ___ which must be obeyed by everyone.

2. What is a government minister?

3. Why does the government collect taxes?

4. How do direct and indirect taxes differ?

Central Government has four main areas of concern which affect business: interest rates, exchange rates, inflation and unemployment.

Interest rates

The rate of interest is the cost of borrowing money. The higher the rate of interest the more expensive it is to borrow. As most business investment is done with borrowed money it can be seen that high interest rates might discourage investment and affect the amount of business activity. The government can affect interest rates with its *monetary policy*. Monetary policy refers to how the government influences the supply of money by controlling how much banks can lend. The Bank of England administers monetary policy on behalf of the government. Increased supply means the price of borrowing money (interest) drops. This encourages people to borrow and, hopefully, to invest. As most of the money borrowed from banks and building societies comes from the savings of others, interest rates must be high enough to encourage savings. If this were not the case there would be less money to borrow. The aim of monetary policy is to make interest rates reach a level which is attractive to borrowers and lenders and controls inflation.

Interest rates vary considerably from year to year

Exchange rates

The value of the pound in relation to overseas currencies affects the British producer's ability to sell overseas and import goods into Britain. If the value of the pound is too high overseas purchasers will not be able to afford British goods or services. On the other hand, British firms will be able to import goods cheaply from overseas. A low pound has the opposite effect. The government can influence the exchange rate by selling its stock of foreign currency or sterling or by buying foreign currency or sterling. Making more of a currency available drives its price down, while buying it raises its price. In this case the price is merely the exchange rate. The government has to strike a balance by finding an exchange rate level which is helpful to importers and exporters. However, the government is only one of several buying and selling currency and so it cannot be certain of achieving its aims in the world currency exchanges. By joining the European Monetary System (EMS) in 1990, the government hoped to reduce exchange rate fluctuations. The exchange rate affects overseas trade and so affects the Balance of Payments (see page 193).

Inflation

Inflation is the rate of increase in the general level of prices. If, as a result of exchange rate or interest rate policy, people have more money to spend without more goods being available, prices will rise. This is called inflation. High levels of inflation affect people on fixed incomes such as pensioners and the unemployed whose income does not rise in line with prices. As price levels rise demand for goods and services will drop, which can lead to unemployment. The amount of spending and borrowing the government is involved in, *fiscal policy*, will affect the level of inflation, as will its monetary policy. The government can affect inflation by trying to control demand through high interest rates, taxes or control of incomes. This is called the *demand management approach*. The *supply side* approach tries to stimulate and help business activity to meet the increases in demand.

One way in which inflation can be measured is by the Retail Price Index (RPI). This is the average price of 600 items such as different foods, clothes, rail fares etc., which are measured on a monthly basis by the government. The average is given a value of 100 so that changes can be measured easily as a percentage. The RPI was last set at 100 in January 1987, so changes are measured against the average prices of that date. By December 1988 the RPI was at 110, showing that prices had risen by 10 per cent in that period.

Unemployment

Inflation, interest rates and exchange rates all affect business activity. Interest rates affect how much firms can borrow to invest and how much the public can borrow to buy expensive goods like furniture and cars. Exchange rates affect the levels of goods sold overseas and how much British firms will import, rather than buy at home. Inflation affects prices and wage settlements. Taken together we can see that these three things – interest rates, exchange rates and inflation – will affect how many people firms will want to employ. Clearly, if the public cannot borrow money to buy cars, for example, because of high interest rates, fewer cars will be demanded. As a result there will be reduced demand for car workers. If this happens throughout the economy unemployment could develop. Similarly, if overseas goods are cheaper than home-produced goods there will be reduced demand for home produced goods and workers in those industries could become unemployed. This was the reason for unemployment in the Lancashire textile industries.

As unemployment is a major social issue the government has a role to play in solving the problem. An important economic aspect is the *opportunity cost* of unemployment. Opportunity cost is the estimated cost of a missed opportunity. For example, the opportunity cost of unemployment is what the country would have had from the unemployed in way of taxes and production had they been in employment. Unemployment arises as a result of changes in the structure of the economy and changing demand for goods and services. This structural unemployment can often be overcome through training (see page 54). The social concern over unemployment is reflected in the way people vote, which gives government another incentive for trying to deal with the problem.

The government can help with unemployment by encouraging firms to move to areas of particularly high unemployment. Firms in these areas qualify for grants, such as the Regional Development Grant, to meet the cost of buildings and equipment. Areas worst affected by unemployment tend to be in the North of England, Northern Ireland or Wales. This is partly a result of the decline of engineering, shipbuilding and coal mining – the *smoke-stack* industries. Some of the worst hit areas have been designated as *enterprise zones* by the government. This means that they do not have to pay rates or poll tax and are excluded from the requirements of the local planning system. The idea is to help the firms in these areas develop as fast as possible. Corby, Milford Haven, Salford and Tyneside are some of the 25 enterprise zones.

17.2. Answer the following questions with at least a full sentence, or by writing out the missing words.

1. Name four main areas of government concern which affect business.

2. The government's approach to matters affecting the amount of money available is called _____ policy.

3. How does the exchange rate differ from the interest rate?

4. The government approach to its spending and income is called _____ policy.

5. How can the government control demand?

6. Explain what is meant by opportunity cost.

Local government

Local town and county councils make up local government. Councillors are elected by local people to control local affairs. They are assisted by paid employees. Each councillor represents an area called a *ward*. Although they must obey national government, local councils have some freedom to decide what services to provide and how they should be run. The council receives money from the government, from charging for services and from local people paying the community charge or poll tax. Councils have sub-committees dealing with particular areas of concern, for example education or environmental health. Central or national government passes laws which must be obeyed and local government has the responsibility for seeing that they are carried out. The food hygiene regulations are, for example, carried out through environmental health officers employed by local councils. Local firms wishing to expand must meet the planning regulations laid out by the Department of the Environment but carried out by the local council's planning committee.

An important aspect of government is considering the *cost-benefit* analysis of business activity. Cost-benefit analysis looks at the social and private costs and benefits of a proposal to judge its desirability. For example, a plan to build a glue factory will result in several costs and benefits. There may be profits for the owner. This is a *private benefit*. The extra traffic and disruption is a *social cost* to the local community. They will however have the social benefit of the extra jobs created by the factory. Aspects of the channel tunnel have been looked at using cost-benefit analysis to see the likely outcome of the project. Although it is only based on estimates, such an analysis helps government to decide if the project should be prevented or supported.

As over fifteen per cent of the nation's spending is done through the government at local or national level we can see that government is a major business customer. The government can affect business activity through its purchasing and employment opportunities.

17.3. Answer the following questions with at least a full sentence, or by writing out the missing words.

1. What do we mean by local government?

2. How is local government paid for?

3. What is cost-benefit analysis?

SHORT QUESTIONS

1. What are MPs and who do they represent?

2. How is the Prime Minister chosen?

3. What are income tax allowances?

4. How do customs and excise duties differ?

5. How can tax rates affect businesses and individuals?

6. Explain what is meant by the rate of interest.

7. How do monetary and fiscal policy differ?

8. What is the exchange rate?

9. Give two reasons why governments are concerned with unemployment.

10. How is local government run and controlled?

STIMULUS RESPONSE QUESTIONS

It may be necessary to refer to the index and other chapters to answer the following questions:

1. *'Taxes are a waste of money' said the manager of the factory making hairdryers and electric drills as he looked at how much income tax he had paid on a month's earnings.*

   a) What is income tax? *(2 marks)*

   b) Describe two taxes that the owners of the factory might have to pay. *(4 marks)*

   c) Describe the ways in which national government could affect this particular business. *(12 marks)*

2. Unemployment figures, 1988

Unemployment	
January	2 519 000
June	2 324 000
October	2 158 000
December	2 039 000

   a) What do these figures show about the level of unemployment? *(2 marks)*

   b) Why is central government concerned with the level of unemployment? *(8 marks)*

   c) Describe the factors which affect the level of unemployment and explain *how* they affect unemployment. *(10 marks)*

LEARN IT YOURSELF

1. Contact your local town hall to find out how the council spends its income. Present a wall display of your findings.

2. Contact two political parties and ask them to send a speaker to talk to the group on either 'The causes and cures of unemployment' or 'How government can affect business'.

ON ASSIGNMENT

Using old copies of *The Guardian* or *The Times* find out how inflation, unemployment and exchange rates have changed in the last six months. Your local library should be able to provide these. Find out the views of the Government, The Opposition and the newspapers themselves as they explain why these figures have changed. Use graphs, tables, charts and quotations to prepare a project folder of your findings.

CASE STUDY

Andy McGee is thinking of starting a business to sell children's tricycles in Great Britain and on the continent. He knows that he has to pay various taxes to the government but, on the other hand, he thinks the government might be able to provide some help for a developing business. He is not sure whether to contact the town hall, the Prime Minister or the job centre for information.

a) Make two lists for Andy. List One should be entitled 'What the government can do for me' and List Two 'What I have to do for the government'. List One should start with 'Enterprise Allowance' and list two with 'Pay Corporation Tax'. Use the index of this book to help you complete the lists.

b) It is clear that Andy is unclear about how local and national government work. Explain this in a memo entitled 'Local and National Government – Linked but Different'.

APPENDIX 1

RESEARCHING DATA

Much of GCSE and BTEC work requires the student to conduct their own research. The aim of this appendix is to look at the approaches to research which are most useful to completing coursework.

Sources of information:

Libraries

Libraries and librarians are a vital source of information for students trying to complete coursework. In order to get the most out of your school, college or local library service you should ask your teacher, lecturer or librarian to explain the way in which the books are arranged. You should find out how the subject index is organised and the classification numbers for business studies subjects such as Accounting, Marketing and Personnel. Many libraries provide a range of information services and you should ask about these. The time spent learning to use a library is an investment for the future which will save you time in the long run. When asking a librarian for help it is best to be as exact as possible about what your needs are. For example, ask where information about redundancy laws are kept rather than 'information about sacking people'!

Atlases, telephone directories, *Yellow Pages* and past copies of newspapers are important sources of information for the business studies student and are usually available in libraries. Government publications such as *Social Trends* give useful information about consumers and business behaviour. Details about the economy, inflation and unemployment can be found in the *Economic Progress Report* and journals published by the banks such as *Lloyds Bank Economic Bulletin* or *Barclays Review*. Sunday papers such as *The Observer* or *The Sunday Times* are often good for in-depth articles on particular topical subjects.

The neighbourhood

Many local firms and organisations will be happy to help with information provided they are not swamped by the same request 25 times over from the same group. A clear, well-written group letter which gives the firm or organisation plenty of time to reply and does not cost them anything stands a better chance of a reply than several garbled telephone calls with an impossible deadline. Simple observation of what goes on around you can provide information. For example, counting the number of heavy lorries using a particular main road can provide clues about the type and level of business activity around that area. Counting the number of customers entering shops and comparing the results with those for other shops or for different times of the day can give information about people's shopping habits.

The media

Radio, television, newspapers and magazines are all sources of useful up-to-date material. Watch out for programmes that might be related to your course and record them or take notes if necessary.

National organisations

Several national organisations can help in the completion of coursework. Remember that a clear, well-written group letter which gives the organisation plenty of time to reply and does not cost them anything stands a better chance of a reply than several garbled telephone calls with an impossible deadline. Apart from the public relations department of national companies, other organisations which might be approached include:

1. The Banking Information Service, 10 Lombard Street, London EC3V 9AT. This organisation will send speakers, as well as provide free material, to explain matters related to banking.

2. Trade Union Congress (TUC), Education Department, Congress House, Great Russell Street, London WC1B 3LS. As well as providing speakers the organisation deals with a range of business-related issues that affect workers, for example industrial relations, health and safety, etc.

3. Confederation of British Industry (CBI), Education Foundation, Centre Point, 103 New Oxford Street, London WC1A 1DU. A point of contact for schools and local businesses, as well as providing employers' views on business-related matters.

4. International Stock Exchange, Wider Share Ownership Unit, London EC2N 1HP. Information about the working of the Stock Exchange and issues relating to business.

5. Post Office, Educational and Information Services, Royal Mail House, 29 Wellington Street, Leeds LS1 1AA. Information about the services and organisation of the Post Office.

6. British Telecom, Education Service, British Telecom Centre, Floor B4, 81 Newgate Street, London EC1A 7AJ. (See also Prestel 211442.) Information about the services and organisation of British Telecom.

7. The Industrial Society, Industry/Education Unit, Robert Hyde House, 48 Branston Square, London W1H 7LN. Aims to promote education and industry links through a range of activities.

8. Understanding British Industry, Sun Alliance House, New Inn Hall Street, Oxford OX1 2QE. Helps schools gain a better understanding of how industry works.

Individuals

The best course-work involves original research. Asking people is a useful way of finding out original information.

Employers, trade union members, shopkeepers, friends and relatives are just a few examples of people who can provide useful information. The most reliable research is that which is the most scientific in its approach. Before starting your research you need a questionnaire and a *sample*. A sample is a group of people representative of a wider group. For example, if you wanted to find out the views of the members of your school about advertising, the most reliable way would be to ask them all individually, but this would be too time-consuming. Instead you could ask a smaller group which you could either choose at random – a random sample – or select. A selected sample should be of similar proportions to the larger group. If your school of 1000 had 20 per cent of its pupils in each of the first five years then your sample of, say, 20 pupils should have four first years, four second years, four third years, four fourth years and four fifth years. Clearly the bigger the sample the better. Selected samples are hard to arrange and I recommend you use random samples for any research you do.

Questionnaires can be used in several ways:

1. The interviewees (the people being questioned) can fill them in in front of you.

2. You can send them by post and ask the interviewees to return them.

3. You can ask the questions and fill in the questionnaire as you go along.

I recommend the last approach as it guarantees you a return, unlike number two and it will at least be readable.

A good questionnaire has the following features:

- The person designing the questionnaire knows exactly what they want to find out, for example a questionnaire on 'wages' is not specific enough. Is it on wage levels? On women's wages? On bus drivers' wages?

- The interviewee is asked only for those details which can be recalled easily.

- The language used is simple.

- All the instructions the interviewee needs are on the questionnaire. Be clear about whether questions should be ticked, completed or filled in. If appropriate, give details of how to return the questionnaire.

- The questionnaire is short. Three well-spaced sides of A4 paper should be the absolute maximum.

- Questions are clear and deal with one topic. 'Do you buy Sudso soap because it is cheap and smells nice?' is a bad question. A person may hate the smell but buy it because it is cheap, so what do they answer? The question should be broken into two parts.

- Questions are in a logical order. Do not leap from subject to subject and then back again.

- The questionnaire is typed or word-processed if possible.

- The interviewee is thanked for taking part.

Include an example of the questionnaire in any coursework you hand in.

When compiling a questionnaire I suggest you try it out first on a small group of people to see if there are any ambiguous questions, spelling mistakes or other errors. When it is corrected and you are satisfied with it then it can be used.

Often in Business Studies information will be presented using numbers, symbols and diagrams. Imports, exports, interest rates and sales figures might be presented in this way. Many examination boards make it a requirement that students are able to analyse and use data. This appendix looks at ways of interpreting and using data so that the student can apply these techniques to the analysis of data from their own research or other sources.

Graphs

There are five simple rules to remember about presenting information in the form of a graph:

1. Be eye-catching. Use different colour pens or pencils for each part or section.

2. Always give a title. The title should explain what your graph shows.

3. Clearly label each part of your graph.

4. Show what units of measurement you are using, for example '£m' means 'expressed in millions of pounds', '000' means 'expressed in thousands'.

5. Show the amount of time the measurements were taken over, for example 'per year', 'per month', 'per week'.

Pictograms

Probably the most simple graph to draw or understand is the pictogram. In a pictogram simplified pictures are used to represent a stated quantity of what you are measuring.

Could mean 1000 lorries or

could mean 10 sailing boats.

The following pictogram shows the number of shoppers entering Brayon's department store per hour.

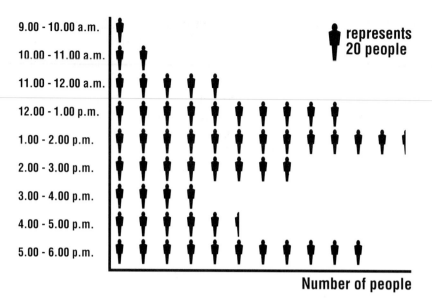

*Pictogram showing number of shoppers entering Brayon's
department store per hour*

Bar charts

The bar chart is another simple way of showing data. Each bar represents a different set of readings and a glance at the length of the bars helps you to make comparisons. The bars can be drawn bottom to top or left to right. It is important to make sure how long each bar will be and what scale you will use before you begin, otherwise you may waste much time and effort. The five rules for drawing a graph also apply here.

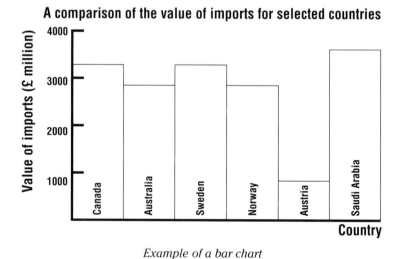

Example of a bar chart

Pie charts

Pie charts are used to show the size of each part of a total amount compared to the other parts. Each item is like a slice of the whole pie. To draw a pie chart each separate part of the total figure should be turned into a percentage of the total figure. If you are not sure how to do this look at the section below on percentages. Then, when you have found the percentage figure, find out the same percentage of 360° (the number of degrees in a circle) and that is how big the slice will be. Check your calculations by making sure that the number of degrees you intend to use add up to 360 – you have made a mistake if the figure is different.

So, if Cattygrub PLC gets 25 per cent of its profits from sales in Britain, 25 per cent from sales in France, 40 per cent from sales in Sweden and 10 per cent from sales in Zimbabwe then Britain and France would get 90° each (25 per cent of 360 being 90), Sweden would get 144° and Zimbabwe 36°. Together this gives a total of 360°.

Pie chart showing the sources of profits for Cattygrub PLC

Percentages

Percentages can be used to compare data which at first glance might appear difficult to compare. One of the most common uses of percentages in Business Studies is to calculate tax rates. If we know that £30 of Jamie Callaghan's weekly wage of £120 is paid in tax we can find out what percentage of his weekly wage this is by putting the number we wish to express as a percentage over the number it is a percentage of and multiplying by 100.

$$\frac{30}{120} \times \frac{100}{1} = \frac{3}{12} \times \frac{100}{1} = \frac{1}{4} \times \frac{100}{1} = \frac{100}{4} = \frac{25}{1} = 25\%$$

So Jamie pays 25 per cent of his weekly wage in tax. Even if the numbers we wish to measure are fractions or decimals it is easy to convert them into percentages:

Fraction to percentage. Multiply the fraction by $\frac{100}{1}$

Using this method $\frac{1}{2}$ becomes 50 per cent as:

$$\frac{1}{2} \times \frac{100}{1} = \frac{1}{1} \times \frac{50}{1} = 50\%$$

Decimal to percentage. Multiply the decimal by 100 and add the % sign. Using this method 0.987 becomes 98.7% as:

0.987 × 100 = 98.7 and 98.7% when the % sign is added on.

The calculations can also be reversed:

Percentage to a decimal. Divide the percentage by 100.

76% becomes 0.76 as $\frac{76}{100} = 0.76$

Percentage to a fraction. Ignore the percentage sign and write the percentage over 100 and divide like this:

75% as a fraction is $\frac{3}{4}$ because $\frac{75}{100} = \frac{3}{4}$ when we cancel by 25.

Be clear about the information you are looking for

Percentage changes

We may wish to compare changes in figures that are not very easy to compare. If the value of sales of two shops changes we may wish to compare them. For example, Grogan's Ltd have increased their sales from £895 per week to £1100. Salim's Ltd have gone from £990 per week to £1300. Simple subtraction of the old and new figures for each shop would give us an idea of the biggest and smallest increases but not an idea of how big the change was compared to previous sales. To find that we must use percentages in the following way.

$$\text{Grogan's Ltd} = \frac{205 \text{ (actual change)}}{895 \text{ (original figure)}} \times \frac{100}{1}$$

$$= \frac{41}{175} \times \frac{100}{1} = \frac{41}{35} \times \frac{20}{1} = \frac{41}{7} \times \frac{4}{1} = \frac{164}{7} = 23.4\%$$

So Grogan's Ltd have increased sales by 23.4%

$$\text{Salim's Ltd} = \frac{310}{990} \times \frac{100}{1} = \frac{31}{99} \times \frac{100}{1} = \frac{3100}{99} = 31.3\%$$

So Salim's Ltd have increased sales by 31.3%

Averages

To arrive at an average you should add up all the readings you are measuring and divide this answer by the number of readings you started with. If there are five firms in the same town selling car stereos and you wish to find the average profit you would first add up the various profit figures for each of the five firms:

Firm 1	£350
Firm 2	£275
Firm 3	£720
Firm 4	£550
Firm 5	£290
TOTAL	£2185

This figure of £2185 should now be divided by FIVE (the total number of firms).

$$\frac{£2185}{5} = £437$$

The answer, £437, is the average profit for the car stereo manufacturers. If three firms in the next town were selling car stereos and we wished to find the average we would add up their profits and divide by three. By comparing the answers from both towns we would know which of the two sets of firms tended to operate most profitably.

1. June Woods sells fancy cakes from her parents' house. Cakes for birthdays, anniversaries, Christmas – any type. Because her reputation is passed around by word of mouth she gets plenty of orders without having to advertise. Orders are placed by telephone or when people see her in the street, and she delivers the cakes herself.

   Since she decided to make this her living, her mother charges her £40 a month to cover lighting, heating and rent. On top of this she had to spend £50 on a complete set of icing equipment and cake moulds.

   The estimated costs of making a medium sized birthday cake are:

   Cake ingredients   £2.75

   Labour (4 hours)   £15.00

   Gas   £0.25

   a) How many cakes would June have to sell in the first year, at an average price of £25 per cake, to break even?
   (15 marks)

   b) If June sells 150 cakes in the first year, at an average price of £25 each, what would her profit be? *(8 marks)*

   c) Although June sells 150 cakes by the end of the first year of business, her profits are not as great as she expected. Suggest reasons for this. *(12 marks)*

   d) "I'm sure I could make a really good go of this but I don't know where to go from here – employ an assistant, take a partner, borrow money from the bank, start a company – it's so confusing."

   What do you think would be best for June at the moment? Give your reasons for choosing this course of action
   (20 marks)

NORTHERN EXAMINING ASSOCIATION, PAPER 1, 1989

2. Case Study

BEEBOP SHOES

Beebop Shoes Limited were set up in 1985, with 2 managers, 2 clerical staff and 1 man in the warehouse, to sell sports and leisure shoes – shoes for running, hill walking, tennis, squash, and other sports, and for casual wear.

They are owned by an Australian company which uses them as a wholesale distribution outlet. The shoes are made in Korea. Beebop's growth over the last five years has been rapid, and is shown by the information below.

Year	Sales (£ thousands)	Workforce
1985	15	5
1986	66	8
1987	307	16
1988	900	30
1989	1515	40

"Our success has been as a result of changes in the economy and in the way people live; also by careful market research, pricing and promotions"

Tom Roberts
Marketing Manager, Beebop

a) Give examples showing what Tom Roberts might mean by "changes in the economy and in the way people live". *(14 marks)*

b) Explain how market research might have helped Beebop to succeed. *(10 marks)*

c) What factors would Beebop take into account when deciding the selling price of a pair of their shoes? *(12 marks)*

d) What sort of promotions might a firm like this use to help sell their products? *(8 marks)*

NORTHERN EXAMINING ASSOCIATION, PAPER 2, 1989

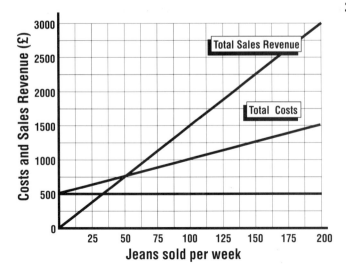

3. Study the information below carefully, and answer the questions that follow.

Ali Singh sells jeans in a local outdoor market. The graph opposite shows data on the business for a week in May.

a) Use the graph opposite to find the following:

(i)   the value of fixed costs; *(1 mark)*

(ii) the value of the variable costs when 200 pairs of jeans are sold; *(1 mark)*

(iii) the total revenue when 200 pairs of jeans are sold; *(1 mark)*

(iv) the average price of a pair of jeans. *(1 mark)*

b) How is the graph useful to Ali Singh? *(7 marks)*

c) How and why would you expect the total sales revenue on the graph to change if it showed data for a week in January? *(4 marks)*

WELSH JOINT EDUCATION COMMITTEE PAPER 1, 1989

---

4. Study the information below carefully, and answer the questions that follow.

Company	Number of Employees	
	1980	**1987**
(1) British Aerospace	79 300	75 000
(2) British Steel	166 400	54 200
(3) Courtaulds (Textiles)	93 000	68 000
(4) Imperial Chemical Industries (ICI)	143 200	121 8000

a) How many jobs, in total, were lost in the four firms named above between 1980 and 1987? Show your method of working clearly. *(3 marks)*

b) Give **two** reasons why there were far less jobs in the secondary sector in the United Kingdom in 1987 compared with 1980. *(4 marks)*

c) (i) The Chairman of Courtaulds reported that "many jobs have been lost due to imports of cheap priced clothes". Explain what he meant by this statement. *(3 marks)*

(ii) The Board of Directors believe that Courtaulds will soon be far more successful. They have introduced computer-controlled machines, and are producing a much wider range of well-designed clothes. Explain why these two changes should make more profit for Courtaulds. *(7 marks)*

WELSH JOINT EDUCATION COMMITTEE, PAPER 2, 1989

---

5. The Milchester District Council owns the Gaumont Theatre, which is in the town of Milchester. Study the organisation chart, overleaf, of the theatre and answer the questions which follow.

a) Name the sector of the economy in which the theatre is based. *(1 mark)*

b) Who is directly in control of:

(i) the resident actors and actresses;

(ii) carpenters? *(1 mark)*

c) Who is likely to be in charge of:

(i) advertising

(ii) interviewing new cleaning staff? *(1 mark)*

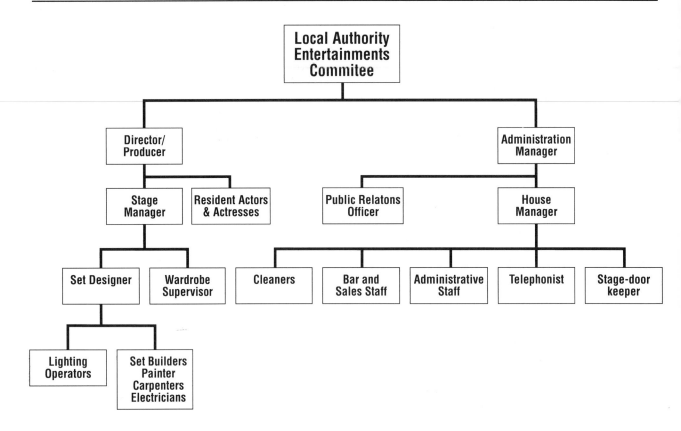

d) Explain how the work of running the theatre has been divided between the Director/Producer and the Administration Manager. *(2 marks)*

e) Explain the role of a Public Relations Officer. *(1 mark)*

f) Local authority officials have recently examined the spans of control at the theatre. They have issued job descriptions to the staff. *(1 mark)*

(i) Explain what is meant by span of control. *(1 mark)*

(ii) What is the Set Designer's span of control. *(1 mark)*

(iii) State **two** advantages to an employee from having a job description. *(2 marks)*

LONDON AND EAST ANGLIAN GROUP, PAPER 1, 1989

6. Bina and Paul completed a course in textiles and fashion at a local college last year. With the backing of their parents, who agreed to underwrite a negotiated bank loan of $100,000, they started a small business selling clothing from a local shop which they rented.

Bina manages the shop and its finances. Paul helps out in the shop and is responsible for purchasing stock. He also spends time on designing new clothes. Eventually they hope to manufacture and sell their own designs.

The final accounts showing their first year in business are shown opposite.

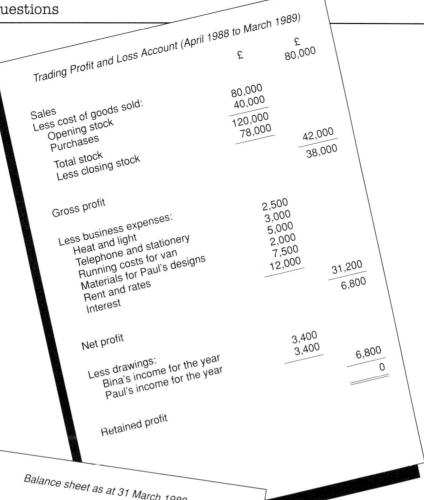

Trading Profit and Loss Account (April 1988 to March 1989)

	£	£
		80,000
Sales		80,000
Less cost of goods sold:		40,000
Opening stock		
Purchases		120,000
		78,000
Total stock		42,000
Less closing stock		38,000
Gross profit		
Less business expenses:	2,500	
Heat and light	3,000	
Telephone and stationery	5,000	
Running costs for van	2,000	
Materials for Paul's designs	7,500	
Rent and rates	12,000	31,200
Interest		6,800
Net profit		
Less drawings:	3,400	
Bina's income for the year	3,400	6,800
Paul's income for the year		0
Retained profit		

Balance sheet as at 31 March 1989

	£	£	£
Fixed assets			
Machinery (to manufacture Paul's desgns)			
Fixtures and fittings		10,000	
New van (purchased April 1988)		5,000	
		20,000	
Current assets			35,000
Stock	78,000		
Debtors	500		
Cash	1,200		
Current liabilities		79,700	
Creditors		14,700	
Net assets employed			65,000
Financed by bank loan			100,000
			100,000

Bina and Paul both found that their business did not give them a high enough income during the year. They are now thinking of closing down and applying for jobs with a large design company.

a) Making use of ratios, analyse Bina and Paul's business, suggesting answers to the following questions:

(i) What are the main problems facing the business? *(5 marks)*

(ii) Is there any evidence to suggest that the business might become successful? *(3 marks)*

b) Using the figures given:

(i) Explain how the business might have been successful if Bina and Paul had borrowed less than £100,000 to start their business. *(3 marks)*

(iii) Explain how Bina and Paul might overcome their problems and carry on in business. *(4 marks)*

LONDON AND EAST ANGLIAN GROUP, PAPER 2A, 1989

7. A manufacturer of modern household furniture plans to build a new factory. The Managing Director has to decide which method of production his firm will use to manufacture its product in the new factory.

a) (i) State how furniture would be manufactured if the Managing Director decided on job production. *(1 mark)*

(ii) Explain **one** main advantage and **one** main disadvantage of job production in this situation. *(2 marks)*

b) (i) State how furniture would be manufactured if the Managing Director decided on batch production. *(1 mark)*

(ii) Give **one** reason why the Managing Director might decide on batch production in this situation. (2 marks)

c) The Production Manager has argued that flow production should be chosen because the firm would benefit from economies of scale.

(i) State how furniture would be manufactured if the Managing Director decided on flow production. *(1 mark)*

(ii) Explain what is meant by economies of scale. Make use of a diagram in your answers. *(4 marks)*

(iii) Explain why the firm could benefit from economies of scale if flow production was the method of production used in the factory. *(3 marks)*

d) Which method of production should the Managing Director decide to use in the firm's new factory? Give a reason for your answer. *(1 mark)*

LONDON AND EAST ANGLIAN GROUP, PAPER 2B, 1989

8. Select **one** example of a business which is known to you.

a) (i) What is the business called?

(ii) What product or service does the business produce?

(iii) Who owns the business? *(1 mark)*

(iv) Is this business in the public or private sector? *(1 mark)*

b) (i) Describe **two** services offered by a bank to businesses. *(2 marks)*

(ii) Explain how **each** of thes services might be of use to the business you have chosen as an example. *(4 marks)*

c) (i) Describe two ways in which the government offers assistance to businesses. *(2 marks)*

(ii) Explain how either of these offers of assistance might or might not be helpful to the business you have chosen as an example. *(1 mark)*

d) With reference to your example, explain **two** ways in which the business could improve its performance, apart from obtaining assistance from the bank or government. *(4 marks)*

---

9. Read the information below and use it to help you answer the following questions.

"Rowntree which makes Smarties, Kit Kat, Lion Bars and Jelly Tots abandoned its 10 week battle to stay independent and agreed to be taken over by the Swiss company Nestlé, which also makes chocolate."

"Nestlé Managing Director said that the merger would benefit both companies. Nestlé plans to continue the production and marketing of Rowntree's best known brands."

a) (i) Explain what is meant by *"battle to stay independent"*. *(2 marks)*

(ii) Why might Rowntree wish to stay independent? *(3 marks)*

b) Why might a company like Nestlé wish to merge with Rowntree? *(6 marks)*

Frank Barlow is a production worker who makes Smarties. He owns 700 shares in Rowntree and has seen their price rise from 477p to 1075p, as a result of the take-over battle.

c) Give and explain **two** reasons why Frank Barlow might benefit from the take-over. *(4 marks)*

d) Explain **one** benefit to a company like Rowntree, of having workers who own shares. *(3 marks)*

e) Two types of merger, horizontal and vertical are shown in the diagram below.

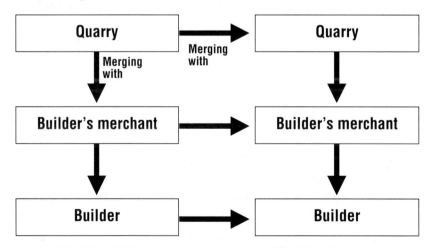

(i) Of which type of merger is the Nestlé takeover of Rowntree an example? *(1 mark)*

(ii) Explain your choice. *(2 marks)*

10. Read the information below and use it to help answer the following questions.

Wilson Ltd is a private limited company in Loughborough making slippers and "down market" shoes out of man made material. Sales of sandals last year were badly hit by the poor summer weather and by cheap imported leather sandals. The firm employs 25 workers and operates an 8 hour day. In the boom years of the early 80s the firm ran two shifts but now runs one and has spare capacity. The directors are aware of the long term downward trend in demand.

a) Explain the meaning of **three** of the followingterms taken from the information above:
  (i)   "down market"
  (ii) boom years
  (iii) shifts
  (iv) directors
  (v)   long term downward trend in demand   *(6 marks)*

b) Wilson Ltd became a private limited company 3 years ago. Why do you think it did this?   *(6 marks)*

11. Look at the following information and use it to help answer parts (a) and (b)   *(6 marks)*

a) How many pairs of sandals were sold in 1980?

b) Use the data provided to comment on the sales of shoes and sandals.

One of the directors decides to analyse the sales closely and draws up the following bar charts.

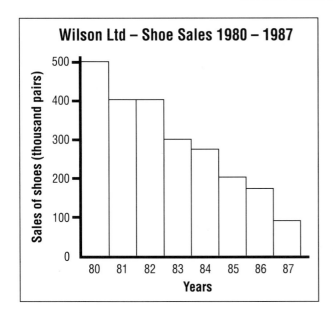

Wilson Ltd – Shoe Sales 1980 – 1987

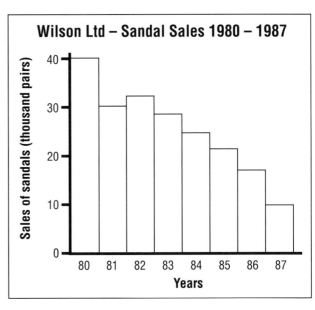

Wilson Ltd – Sandal Sales 1980 – 1987

Read the information below and use it to help answer part (c)

One idea to improve the firm's prospects is to extend the product range by making fashion bags, purses and shopping bags.

National figures for the bag market in 1986–7 show that the market divides as follows:

Fashion bags (leather)	*15%*
Fashion bags (synthetic)	*35%*
Purses/wallets	*5%*
Holdalls/shopping bags	*45%*

c) Use the figures above to complete the pie chart below.
   (2 marks)

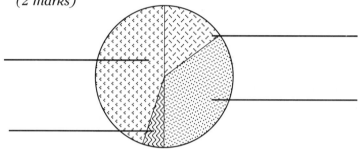

d) Figures are often presented as diagrams e.g. graphs, bar charts, pie charts in business reports.

Explain **two** advantages of persenting information in a diagram   *(4 marks)*

MIDLAND EXAMINING GROUP, PAPER 2, 1989

Wilson Ltd
Market Research Questionnaire

BAGS

Please tick where appropriate

1 Are you aged

16 – 25 ☐   26 – 35 ☐   36 – 45 ☐   46 – 55 ☐   56+ ☐

12.

Gail Fricker left college in July 1986, and started teaching drama at a school in London. She enjoyed her work but wanted to concentrate more on her skills. Gail had been thinking of setting up her own business.

Gail had been running a number of drama sessions in primary schools. These were sponsored by Lewisham Council Arts and Entertainments. This allowed her to talk to teachers in primary schools. From this it appeared that there was a need for a theatre company for primary schools. This made Gail more determined to set up her own theatre company.

In the summer of 1988 Gail established the Apple Theatre. She was to be the sole proprietor. It was to be a 'Theatre for Children and Teachers'. The children and teachers would take part in acting out different parts. This would then be followed up by work sheets in the classroom.

Apple theatre

Newly established S. London Primary T.I.E co requires:

MALE ACTOR/TEACHER

The applicant must be experienced in Primary Education and committed to expanding the role of drama in schools.

Send C.V. to:
Gail Fricker, Apple Theatre, 21 Slagrove Place, London SE13 7HT
Closing date Feb. 6th

Apple Theatre welcomes applications from all ethnic minorities

All her work would be in the South London area.

Rather than going to the bank to borrow money, Apple Theatre went to a number of firms and local councils to try to obtain sponsorship for their first tour of primary schools.

Gail decided to employ a friend from college for the first tour only. This would help her to share the work load.

The first tour of primary schools was well received and further plans were made for a future tour. Gail decided to employ her friend, Michael How, on a permanent basis.

In January 1989, Michael told Gail that he would be leaving the company in two months time. Gail needed to replace Michael because of the tours already planned.

In the middle of January the following advertisement appeared in 'The Stage' – a drama/theatre newspaper. Gail was over-whelmed by the replies. She had 60 replies to the advertisement.

Selecting the right person would be important. She would need to draw up a shortlist of people to interview.

Task 1

What were the benefits to Gail Fricker of being a sole proprietor?
(10 marks)

Task 2

a) What is meant by 'shortlisting' when recruiting an employee?
(5 marks)

b) How would Gail decide who should be called to interview?
(12 marks)

SOUTHERN EXAMINING GROUP, PAPER 2A, 1989

INDEX